THE WELSH BRAVEHEART

THE WELSH BRAVEHEART

OWAIN GLYDWR, THE LAST PRINCE OF WALES

PHIL CARRADICE

PEN & SWORD
HISTORY

AN IMPRINT OF PEN & SWORD BOOKS LTD.
YORKSHIRE - PHILADELPHIA

First published in Great Britain in 2022 by
PEN AND SWORD HISTORY
An imprint of
Pen & Sword Books Ltd
Yorkshire – Philadelphia

ISBN 978 1 39900 265 3

Typeset in Times New Roman 11.5/14 by
SJmagic DESIGN SERVICES, India.
Printed and bound by CPI Group (UK) Ltd, Croydon CR0 4YY

Pen & Sword Books Limited incorporates the imprints of Atlas, Archaeology,
Aviation, Discovery, Family History, Fiction, History, Maritime, Military,
Military Classics, Politics, Select, Transport, True Crime, Air World,
Frontline Publishing, Leo Cooper, Remember When, Seaforth Publishing,
The Praetorian Press, Wharncliffe Local History, Wharncliffe Transport,
Wharncliffe True Crime and White Owl.

For a complete list of Pen & Sword titles please contact
PEN & SWORD BOOKS LIMITED
47 Church Street, Barnsley, South Yorkshire, S70 2AS, England
E-mail: enquiries@pen-and-sword.co.uk
Website: www.pen-and-sword.co.uk

Or
PEN AND SWORD BOOKS
1950 Lawrence Rd, Havertown, PA 19083, USA
E-mail: Uspen-and-sword@casematepublishers.com
Website: www.penandswordbooks.com

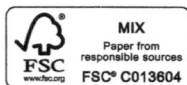

FSC
MIX
Paper from
responsible sources
FSC® C013604
www.fsc.org

Contents

Acknowledgements

Grateful thanks to so many people, not least that blithe and benign spirit who, by some incredible piece of fate, placed me in Glyndwr House back in my early days at secondary school.

Other thanks to:

My father, God bless him, who in my teenage years spent hours debating and arguing with me over my hero, Glyndwr, and, being a good Scot, his all-time idol, William Wallace. I could never convince him who was most important and I doubt if I could do so even now. But thanks anyway, Dad, great days, great boost to the imagination.

Trudy, my inspiration – hard to believe it's almost five years since you left us. You're always there, sweetheart, in my head, at my shoulder, whenever I write.

My archer neighbour, Mat Howard, for his interest in the book and his knowledge of the archer's craft – not to mention his introduction to the art of toxophily and the loan of several volumes dedicated to the subject.

Roger Mac, my rugby playing comrade and school friend from Pembroke Dock. He was in Picton House, as opposed to me in Glyndwr, which meant that we clashed many times in house matches and seven-a-side tournaments. Now his knowledge and skill with technology has yet again kept me going – bet you never thought, Rog, all those times you ground my head into the mud that you'd end up helping a Glyndwr boy out of yet another hole in the ground!

Introduction

Owain Glyndwr is symbolic of the Welsh desire for freedom and for independence, but like all great superheroes, he is also a man of mystery.

At this distance in time he can be little more than a briefly glimpsed figure who flits across the imagination and the senses like a wraith, like a wisp of autumn smoke on the hillside. Very few primary source materials from the period when he was active have survived and those that do exist are usually subjective in the extreme.

As a result of this absence the documents which might have put flesh on his bones – even down to the date of his birth and death – are few and far between. And that, of course, means that in recounting the life of a man who remains Wales's greatest hero it is hard to know where history ends and legend begins.

That does not make his story any less fascinating. For nearly twenty years this capable, cultured and educated Welshman terrified the inhabitants of the British countryside, from Pembroke in the west to London in the east, from the northern territories of Henry Percy to the southern coast of England. Children were sent to bed at night with the warning that if they did not go quickly to sleep or if they transgressed in any way the terrible and monstrous Owain Glyndwr would come to get them! He never did but the fear remained.

And yet he was not just the big, bad hero of children's imaginations. He formed an alliance with France and held court in one of the most picturesque castles in the country. He encouraged poetry and verse, sponsored musicians and artists, and was a lover of culture and tradition.

Owain Glyndwr called a Welsh Parliament, not once but twice, and cut a swathe through the forces of some of England's greatest military commanders. He forced the king of England to assemble several huge armies in a futile attempt to track him down and kill him. He did not achieve any of that through a love of literature and the arts; he did it through dogged determination, through relentless ruthlessness, through military campaigns and more than a fair share of brutality. 'Christ, Splendour of God, I beseech you destroy Glyndwr,' prayed a monk from St Albans. He was not alone in his request.

Hopefully, it will soon become clear that this book is one of 'popular' history rather than a dull academic tome. It is meant to be read and to be enjoyed.

The primary source materials that do exist, and which have been used here to substantiate the text, are the same materials that have been employed by researchers and scribes for many centuries past. The facts are the same, only the interpretations differ – maybe.

Glyndwr has been much written about. In fact and fiction his story and his deeds have regularly appeared in print, and many men and women, the present author included, have expressed their opinions on this last true Prince of Wales – opinions on him as a man and on his significance as a national figure. I offer no apologies for adding another tome to the canon and hope that it is still an accurate depiction of Owain Glyndwr, his motives and his aims.

It is not possible to look at Glyndwr in isolation. We need also to consider the times in which he lived and the physical state of the land in those years. Then there are the inevitable loyalties and discords between men, emotions which helped formulate and guide affairs of state. Above all there is the motivation of great magnates and peasants, motivations that shaped and directed the events of this turbulent and dramatic time. All of these factors and many more are important elements in the story of Owain Glyndwr.

He was always a man of contradictions. He aroused deep emotion, feelings of love or hate in everyone he met or encountered on his life journey. But even then his character was such that slivers of contrary emotion, about as far removed from peoples' original stance and feelings as the moon, still managed to find their way into their opinions and impressions of the bandit prince. The medieval chronicler Adam of Usk remains a classic example: 'As a Welshman, Adam takes special notice of events in his native country, and his account of the progress of Glyndwr's rebellion contains many details of value. Although he speaks of the national hero and his following with some contempt, at the same time he evinces a natural sympathy with the sufferings of his countrymen at the hands of the invading Englishmen.'[1]

Perhaps that dichotomy of emotion is one reason for the continued fascination with Owain Glyndwr. He is a truly three dimensional character and the opinions of one writer or reader will be as valid as the next. There is no right or wrong when you look at the career of the man.

Readers may disagree with my conclusions, as expressed here. Fine, that is their prerogative, no more than I would expect from any thinking person. Glyndwr himself was nothing if not controversial, even a little dogmatic. He could not have achieved what he did without the firm conviction that he was in the right.

The important thing for me is that you read the book, consider its contents and then come to your own conclusions. Agree or disagree, I really don't mind. Suffice to say that Owain Glyndwr deserves firm convictions, one way or another.

Much of what remains available in terms of original research material is limited. It was originally written in Welsh, Anglo-Norman English, Latin or occasionally in French. It comes from bardic poems and parliamentary reports of the time and from third- or fourth-hand accounts produced within a few hundred years of the rebellion's end.

I make no apology for, in the main, printing here the English translations. The Endnotes will tell interested readers where to find the original writings.

If there is one thing that emerges strongly from the book I hope it is the character of Owain Glyndwr. I could wax lyrical about the man striding like a colossus over the pages of history but I will restrain myself and let the reader find out for himself.

Suffice to say he was an amazing man who organised and ran one of the fiercest and most successful campaigns ever waged against the English Crown. Ultimately, his rebellion – his war, as he would have put it – failed. That only adds to his appeal.

They say tragedy and romance run close together. They is no doubt that they are inevitably and inexorably linked and the story of Owain Glyndwr is chock-full of both. Charismatic, dedicated, ruthless and yet caring, whatever you think of him his personality is such that it leaves him still as a romantic and yet ultimately doomed character.

He is, I feel, the supreme example of how to stand up to bullying powers, whether they are great or small. How would Glyndwr have reacted is not a bad question to ask of yourself when failure or disaster hover around your shoulders. There is, of course, no easy answer to that, but as a role model and an inspiration Owain Glyndwr is up there, close to the very top. He remains the national hero of Wales.

A Personal Prologue

On a personal level, I have been fascinated by Owain Glyndwr for many years. From the moment I made my first tentative appearance at Pembroke Grammar School back in the late 1950s, Glyndwr immediately established himself in a position of huge significance in my mind and imagination. More importantly, as the years went on this mystical, magisterial man managed to sustain and even develop that position in my heart and brain.

For such a powerful influence it is strange that my interest had almost nothing to do with what I was taught in the rather stultifying school history lessons. Those interminable afternoon sessions that did little more than keep me away from the rugby field seemed to concentrate solely on English history – on English kings, on the English Industrial Revolution and on English victories at battles like Agincourt, Waterloo and Trafalgar.

Wales was barely ever mentioned and only then as an afterthought. It was not until much later that I realised the significance of the Welsh nation and the vital contribution my country had made to British social, political and economic history over the years.

In school we studied Edward I's hammering of the Scots, Elizabeth's plantations in Ireland, the colonisation of the Americas and so much more. It was all important, and though I hate to admit it, fascinating stuff, but there was nothing about Wales.

Crucial pieces of information such as the fervour of the Welsh Methodist Revival in the early eighteenth century or the importance of the Welsh coalfields and iron works to the development of the Industrial Revolution were ignored in a welter of decidedly English-focused history. Nobody told us that the cannons of Nelson's Navy were forged at Merthyr Tydfil, or that the laws of Hywel Dda were 500 years before their time, or that Britain's first Labour MP represented a Welsh constituency.

What we *were* deluged with was information on things like the repeal of the Corn Laws, the dissolution of the monasteries and the six wives of Henry VIII. I wouldn't have minded but the history teacher was a Welsh-speaking North Walian with a first-class Honours Degree from Bangor!

What chance did Owain Glyndwr or any Welsh aspects of history stand in that type of Anglophile educational environment? It was, really, no surprise that Glyndwr and his significance to the Welsh nation were airbrushed out of our history lessons.

I don't necessarily blame the teachers; that was the required curriculum at the time. But it was a system which conveniently ignored the basic precepts of history teaching – start locally and move on to wider issues once you have a firm grasp of your immediate environment. Any teacher, lecturer or writer with half an ounce of common sense will tell you that is the way forward. Enough said, let me get off my soapbox and return to Owain Glyndwr.

Despite everything, I quickly discovered that within my new school there actually *was* some slight or limited nod of the head towards Owain Glyndwr. But it was, of course, outside the history curriculum.

Even before I entered its doors I was aware that my school in Pembroke – I guess like many other secondary schools at the time – ran a very well organised and significant 'house' system. It had been set up by the renowned Welsh poet, and the school's former head teacher, Roland Mathias, partly in imitation of the great public schools of England and partly in an attempt to develop inter-pupil discipline and competition.

The house system dominated school life. It involved pupils in everything from sporting events and public speaking to drama contests and the regular collection of house points. Forget academic excellence, the house to which you belonged was perhaps the most important part of the whole educational process. And it was, as long as you subscribed to the surprisingly all-embracing and wide-ranging curriculum, a truly pedagogical experience.

The highlight of the school year was the annual Eisteddfod. It was held each and every St David's Day – or as close to it as we could get – when we would write essays, sing songs and recite poems in a desperate attempt to get the better of our friends and classmates who, for the length of this one desperate day, had suddenly become our mortal enemies.

So where does Owain Glyndwr fit into this mishmash of social care and education? On entry to this grand educational establishment I found myself placed in Glyndwr House. There was nothing particularly wise about the choice of name – the school also had a house named after a wild, beer-swilling and foul-mouthed soldier who had once beaten a slave to death! So, although I could have been placed in Picton or Hywel or Tudor House it did not happen. I was a Glyndwr boy from the beginning and spent the next seven or eight years fighting hard for the honour of my house on the rugby field and on the Eisteddfod stage.

Since then very little has changed. At heart I remain a 'Glyndwr boy' although I have long moved on from school house competitions. Even so, competition remains an important factor in my life – in sport, in career moves, in the all-embracing features of life in general. I would hate to say I have grown up – because I haven't and wouldn't particularly want to – but the values and the visions I learned in those long gone days in West Wales have provided a grounding that has never left me.

The name, the character and the activities of the Welsh national hero who caught my imagination on that first day in school have remained with me ever since. They have been crucially important to my development as a writer and, I guess, as a human being.

That enthusiasm does not blind me to Glyndwr's faults and mistakes. In his campaigns against the two fifteenth-century King Henrys he displayed many of both, just as I did during my career at Pembroke Grammar School.

What Glyndwr taught me was that you can learn from mistakes and failure as easily as you can from success. The important thing is to have your heart, your mind and your ambition in the correct place. And nobody can deny that Owain Glyndwr certainly achieved that.

If nothing else I really do hope that my enthusiasm for the man and the majesty of what he achieved come through in the following text. It was a contradictory era that is still noted for its barbarity, its legends and its learning. Glyndwr and those involved with him – for and against – were contradictory characters, too. That's what makes them attractive. Enjoy the book.

Chapter One

A Prelude to it All

Contrary to public opinion, Owain Glyndwr's fifteenth-century rebellion against the English Crown was never as uniformly popular as some historians and lovers of Welsh culture would have us believe. In England, of course, he was feared both during and after his rebellion, held up as the epitome of everything that was evil and duplicitous. But even in his native Wales he was not always regarded as the saviour of the nation.

Undoubtedly he was idealised and lionised in many parts of his home country. Arguably he was even worshipped by those sections of Welsh society that he came to symbolise and represent – the *uchelwyr* or community leaders, particularly those from Mid and North Wales. But it was a sporadic and patchy approval which often changed from year to year and from region to region.

Despite this significant groundswell of support for the Glyndwr revolt, approval for his actions was far from universal and there was also a fair degree of active opposition to the man and his motives. Significant figures like Dafydd Gam of Brecon and Sir Gilbert Talbot from Goodrich opposed him to the end, more than happy to take up arms against the man who had set himself up as a Welsh saviour.

South Pembrokeshire, the 'Little England beyond Wales' of Edward Laws and Giraldus Cambrensis, even paid him money, a significant gratuity of £200 to stay away from the rolling and fertile pasture land below the Landsker boundary. Easy money for Glyndwr, a season's peace for the 'Why ayes', as they were known, of the Norman lands around Pembroke town.

These two poles – the ayes and the nays – were, however, the preserves of the committed few. There were many more, perhaps the majority of the Welsh population, who simply stood and watched. For them it was case of waiting to see the outcome of the conflict before pledging allegiance to one side or the other.

In the months after September 1400, which saw an effective and startling beginning for Glyndwr, it really did seem as if he was about to achieve what the two dominant princes of Wales, Llewelyn the Great and Llewelyn the Last, had signally failed to do. That, of course, was the recreation, the rebirth if you like, of an independent Wales. The illusion – or was it delusion? – lasted for several years and brought the Welsh nation closer to independence than it had been for centuries.

Thousands flocked to Glyndwr's banner, many coming from as far away as Oxford and Scotland. He actually had two flags, his own personal one and the more heavily symbolic banner of the Princes of Gwynedd. That particular flag, with its emblematic and iconic image of four lions rampant, seemed to draw out all that was noble in the Welsh people, with the result that warriors, labourers, even clergymen came willingly and without compunction to offer their support. How lasting that support was to be remains a moot point.

It was, of course, all something of a false dawn and from 1406 onwards Glyndwr's star was fixed to a steady downhill trajectory. Defeat followed defeat and the gains he and his armies had made in the early years of the century were relentlessly recovered by the forces of the English Crown. The 'fair weather' friends and supporters who had so willingly joined him in the early days slipped quietly away as the rebellion's feet of clay were relentlessly exposed.

Slowly but surely, after 1406 substantial inroads were made into Owain's territories. Battles were lost and the great captured castles of Aberystwyth and Harlech, symbols of the Welsh resistance, were taken back. The upper hand had been clearly seized by King Henry IV and by his son and eventual successor, Prince Henry of Monmouth.

Without wishing to overly denigrate a Welsh national hero, it was definitely a case of 'shades of grey' where the popularity of Owain Glyndwr was concerned. He was loved, he was hated, he was feared and he was revered; he was never ignored.

There is no doubt that many kept on supporting him right to the end; large numbers of Welshmen continued to risk ruin and to die for him in the years between 1406 and 1412. But many more, perhaps the majority, once the outcome of the rebellion became more or less predictable, either sought a pardon from the King or simply buried their heads and got on with their daily lives. As with so much of Glyndwr's story, the Biblical analogy is strong – in this case the people of Wales washing their hands like Pontius Pilate as Christ is convicted and condemned.

As ever with most popularist movements, the majority of the people of Wales were political and revolutionary lightweights. They liked the idea of independence but were not quite so happy to play their part in achieving it. Only in hindsight, when there was no chance of being called to arms, did many of the laggards suddenly discover that they, like Owain and his more devoted followers, were fervent nationalists at heart.

Of course, the early success of the rebellion awakened the long-dormant hopes of the more nationally conscious Welshmen. And yet in reality the revolt and the ensuing fight for independence never had much chance of coming to fruition. That was something the more pragmatic or realistic of the Welsh gentry quickly saw once the initial burst of enthusiasm had worn off.

In numbers alone, the Welsh armies were always in the minority when they took to the field. On most occasions Glyndwr's soldiers were outnumbered by perhaps as many as ten or even twelve to one. Those were significant figures in the days of medieval warfare when it was as much bulk, brutality and brawn as tactics that usually won the day.

When it came to traditional pitched encounters the Welsh simply could not put enough troops into the combat, and when allies like France and Scotland failed him, Glyndwr was always fighting a losing battle. He knew it, of course, but it did not stop him trying.

The traditionally lightweight Welsh troops were ideal for guerrilla warfare and Glyndwr quickly realised that if he really was going to continue challenging the English Crown his best chances of success lay in the hit and run tactics for which his people were famous. Unfortunately, guerrilla campaigns rarely bring total and absolute victory; there usually has to be a major reckoning, a face to face confrontation between the main participants before victory is finally decided.

*****

Arguably – and it is a hugely debatable point – the Glyndwr rebellion had little to do with Welsh nationalism. It was much more a case of people showing their dislike of Henry Bolingbroke – Henry IV as he had become after the removal of Richard II – than any fervent desire to create an independent Welsh state.

Proclaiming the popularity of Owain Glyndwr was all well and good. It was connected with people's beliefs and desires but it was not the sole motivating factor. It was almost a by-product of the moment. Such niceties were, at the time, barely noticed but Glyndwr was enough of a strategist to seize and use whatever support was liable to come his way.

Henry Bolingbroke, the son of John of Gaunt, was a usurper, a man who had seized the throne when the opportunity presented itself. He was certainly not a popular king but he was also beset with many problems in governing his domain. Chief among these was the issue of finance. Ruling the country was one thing, having the money to run it was something totally different.

The fact that his predecessor, Richard II, had been more unpopular and inefficient than him was immaterial. In the eyes of the rank and file bystanders Richard was the rightful king and Henry's claims to the throne were at best marginal. Might rather than right, many felt, was an appropriate way of describing Henry's position.

However, once Henry did finally manage to get the finances of his kingdom into shape – through heavy taxes, demands on barons, peace rather than war with France – things changed. When he was finally able to free himself from the fear of a French or Scottish invasion the economic power of England meant that the scales were always weighted in favour of Henry and his dynasty. Put simply, the longer the conflict went on the less chance there was of Welsh victory.

When looked at objectively it is clear that Glyndwr's rebellion might have been a popular uprising – for some at least – but it also caused immense damage to the Welsh economy. Arguably, it irrevocably damaged the relationship between the English and the Welsh. And for that, many people never forgave him.

As far as Glyndwr was concerned anything that was of an English origin was tainted. It meant that everything, from the newly created towns and county boroughs to isolated farms and fisheries, was fair game for Glyndwr and his rebels. Consequently, they were attacked and destroyed. The English retaliated with similar wanton destruction by putting Welsh homesteads and villages to the torch.

As the armies marched, villagers fled, with the result that fields of crops were left untended and rotting, houses and whole villages falling into disrepair. It was like Dante's *Inferno*, and though ninety-nine per cent of Welsh peasants did not have the faintest idea who Dante was, they would recognise the term from the stories and dire threats issued to them by their preachers and clergymen.

In particular, isolated manor houses, undefended villages, and corn mills – all vital components in medieval life – were easy targets for men with destruction in their hearts. That destruction was a monumental blow to the regimes and routines of the period and led to a severe setback in the growth of towns in Wales. Previously vibrant communities like the North Wales towns of Nefyn and Criccieth were sacked, and once decay set in, never fully recovered.

Inevitably, emotions ran high, with the result that the one factor which did grow, suddenly and hugely noticeable, was a wave of anti-Welsh feeling. It became endemic in the hearts and minds of English settlers and merchants who had good cause to be afraid of their neighbours. The sentiment was to be found both within the country and, in particular, along the borders or marches.

The feelings of hatred and distrust were replicated by the Welsh who, in their eyes at least, had more than enough reason to hate the English. Arguably, the friction has remained – sometimes hidden, sometimes openly on display – and if dredged deeply enough can be found even today.

The scorched-earth tactics of Glyndwr's campaigning years also led to lasting feuds between the Welsh themselves, particularly at the *uchelwyr* or gentry level. For years after the end of the rebellion those who had fought for Glyndwr and those who had not were members of bitterly divided camps. The divide between the north and south of the country also owes much to the way Glyndwr's war gave hope before finally stuttering and petering out altogether.

At the time, scorched earth tactics resulted in the imposition of draconian laws against the Welsh people. We shall look at these later; for the moment it is suffice to say that the anti-Welsh laws were something for which many blamed Glyndwr and never forgave him.

And yet, when it was all over, it was the memory and the promise of the rebel cause – both during and after the riotous years of Glyndwr's glory – that the nation remembered. For some time, memory was all that the Welsh people would have. That national memory was possibly endemic of the whole enterprise. The inevitable failure of Glyndwr's revolt was important to the Welsh persona. As someone once remarked, 'nobody does maudlin like a defeated Welshman.'

Regardless of what had created the emotion, in the years after Glyndwr's disappearance and death the memory of what had been, and, more importantly, what might have been was suddenly given shape and form in the breasts of many Welshmen. Hindsight is always the most effective science and in the years following his rebellion the Welsh were gifted with copious amounts of it.

If he had done nothing else, Owain Glyndwr had alerted and awakened the Welsh people to their heritage, albeit when it was too late to do much about it. That may not have been much consolation for Glyndwr and his more fervent supporters, but it was the reality of the situation after 1412.

It was as if the people of Wales had come alive after a long but far from dreamless sleep, and suddenly remembered that they were a proud race with a history and traditions of their own. Wales was, in heart and soul if not in actuality, an independent nation with its own language, its own culture and with hope for the future.

Perhaps, then, what Owain Glyndwr rekindled in the Welsh people was worth all of the scorched crops, the destroyed towns and the hundreds if not thousands of dead bodies scattered across the countryside. Glyndwr undoubtedly thought so, even though the conflict had seen his own residences destroyed, his lands forfeited, most of his family killed or rotting in prison, and which, in the final years of his life, left him a hunted outlaw.

It is interesting to note that throughout his period 'on the run', with a bounty on his head, no one ever attempted to turn him in, to betray their prince for the proverbial thirty pieces of silver. The people of Wales certainly had the opportunity, but they chose, whether deliberately or by default, not to exploit it.

Henry Bolingbroke, increasingly a broken and disheartened man, someone for whom the crown had become a wearisome weight upon his shoulders, feared that something like that might happen to him. He eventually died a solitary, unhappy and haunted shadow of the warrior he had once been. Owain Glyndwr, though we have no way of knowing, would probably have gone to his grave – his unmarked, unknown grave – a much happier and fulfilled individual.

*****

Even now, over 600 years since his death, there remains a huge temptation to first anoint and then, secondly, to revere Owain Glyndwr under the banner of the 'Welsh Braveheart'. It is a form of acknowledgement of his deeds, using the inflated vocabulary of the cinema screen, but ultimately the appellation is used in imitation of Scotland's William Wallace.

It is a temptation, yes, but that is where imagination should stop. It does not take a great deal of consideration to realise that while the cause of their two rebellions in Scotland and Wales, and the intentions of their leaders, were much the same, Owain Glyndwr was not an imitation of anyone. This was a man unlike any other. He was a unique figure, flawed in many respects, but perhaps more interesting because of those flaws. He was a hero, a villain, a warrior, a prince, a scholar and a far-sighted diplomat, as noble in defeat as he was in victory.

Glyndwr was also a brutal warrior who would do what he had to do in order to achieve his aims, a man for whom killing became second nature. He was a man of many parts, but more than anything, he was a man who carved out a role and a reputation that were symbolic of the Welsh desire – sometimes hidden, often simply unacknowledged – for independence.

In many respects Glyndwr was the father of the Welsh nation. His fame, his charisma, his influence and, above everything else, the cause for which he stood have all remained intact. That is his legacy and that is what has made him a legend. He remains a symbol for Welsh independence, as powerful and memorable as King Arthur, Hector of Troy or Alexander the Great – and, yes, even as remarkable as William Wallace of Scotland.

He was well aware of the legends about a 'Welsh saviour' who would restore the nation's standing and independence. He had been fed such prophesies all his life. He was equally as conscious of his own family connections with the royalty of Wales. And yet there still remains an element of doubt about his motives, at least to begin with. Did he, in the early days of his rebellion against the English Crown, really wish to eliminate the country's overlords, to revenge Llewelyn the Last? Or, on a more prosaic level, did he see himself merely as a man fighting to right a wrong that had been done, not to the nation but to him?

Certainly at first glance it seems that the whole Glyndwr uprising did not develop from patriotism or a desire to reclaim Welsh independence but from a simple personal slight inflicted on Owain by Lord Grey of Ruthin. If that is the case then Reginald Grey has to bear a very large portion of blame for what was to follow.

Grey's slight and Owain's anger may have been fuelled and enlarged by the reluctance of Henry IV and Parliament to give Glyndwr the justice and the recognition that he felt he deserved. But if we are to believe this version of events then the whole rebellion occurred simply because Owain Glyndwr felt himself wrongly treated. Or did it? Read on MacDuff, as the poet might once have said, all will be revealed!

Patriotism or personal pride, whichever it was, set Glyndwr off on a long and sometimes very slippery road. Lauded, applauded, condemned and cursed, it was a road he deliberately chose and, sensing his significance as the leader of the enterprise, kept to for the rest of his life.

At the end of what ultimately, and probably inevitably, became an unsuccessful attempt to re-establish an independent, free-standing Wales, Owain Glyndwr must have known the significance of his name and the power of his persona. Why else would he refuse the offer of pardon from the English king and slip silently away to live out the mysterious and secluded final years of his life in the Welsh Marches that he loved so much?

After 1412 Glyndwr was never seen again, at least in public. His war was not over, even though it was sliding towards atrophy. Glyndwr knew that only too well. Always a charismatic and flamboyant figure, the decision to just slip away – if indeed it was a decision he was in a position to make – was typical of the man. It was both effective and infuriating.

When looked at now it is clear that disappearance from history is as much a part of his story as the battles, the diplomatic victories and the nobility for which Owain Glyndwr is usually remembered. Glyndwr's disappearance was, arguably, the ultimate strategic move in a campaign that would go on even when he and the two Henrys who opposed him had long since left the arena. Unlike Llewelyn the Last, there would be no body, no head to sit in humiliation on the spikes of the Tower of London or on London Bridge. For the Welsh it was very simple – Owain Glyndwr had never died.

Fighting for what was always a losing cause, Glyndwr was probably a man out of his time. A thousand years before he would have stood alongside Arthur against the marauding Norsemen; in 1485 he would have ridden with Henry Tudor to the battlefield of Bosworth; in the Zulu Wars he would have waited with his comrades in the South Wales Borderers and faced annihilation at Isandlwana or Rorke's Drift.

There is an old legend that tells of Glyndwr walking before daybreak on the flanks of the Berwyn Mountains. It is a story that sums up the way he is still regarded by the Welsh. During his walk Glyndwr meets the Abbot of Valle Crucis Abbey and tells the monk that, regardless of his religious calling and duties as a man of the cloth, he is awake and out of bed too early. 'No sire,' the Abbot replies, 'it is you who has risen too soon – by a century.'[1]

The story might be apocryphal but the sentiment is more than appropriate, although three or four hundred years too early might be a more accurate analogy than a mere century.

Owain Glyndwr was far from the typical rebel or freedom fighter of the medieval period. To begin with, he was nearly 50 years old when his revolt first broke out in September 1400. That was an age when most men of the time were happily preparing themselves for the fourteenth- or fifteenth-century equivalent of the 'pipe and slippers' routine.

He came from a wealthy Marcher family, establishing himself as an Anglo-Welsh gentleman, or *uchelwyr*, who was able to move easily between Welsh and English society. He was born into privilege, certainly when compared to the farmers and peasants who battled against the land and the elements in order to make a living.

He spoke effectively and elegantly in both Welsh and English and lived in genteel affluence on his estates at Sycharth, close to Oswestry. Looked at objectively, the pre-revolt Glyndwr seems to be the last man to ever consider rebellion against the English Crown.

Conscious and proud of his Welsh background, he was not blinkered and understood the necessity of living in harmony with his powerful neighbours beyond Offa's Dyke. He was, in almost all external respects, a typical anglicised and assimilated border Welshman.

And yet, within a few months of his uprising breaking out, Owain Glyndwr had put aside his privileged lifestyle and pledged his body and soul to a cause that was the very antithesis of the *uchelwyr* concept – benign toleration and acceptance of the status quo. It was a remarkable turnaround.

Legend declares that the revolt began because of a quarrel between Glyndwr and his neighbour. It is possible, and we will return to this matter later. But regardless of what actually started it, by the end of 1400 the Glyndwr revolt had grown and developed far beyond the simple matter of a man fighting to recompense himself for an insult from a local baron and the King.

By the New Year of 1401 Owain Glyndwr was leading the strongest challenge to the English throne since Henry Bolingbroke himself had rebelled and deposed King Richard II two years before. It was a challenge that would not die for nearly fifteen years.

So what was it that made Glyndwr such a significant figure? That remains something of a rhetorical question, but the answer – if there can ever be one – goes far beyond the blood and fury of the longest Welsh war in history. It is an answer steeped in longing and legend, a romantic dream that, while ultimately bound to fail, somehow managed to impinge itself on the Welsh consciousness.

His reputation has little to do with his ability as a soldier, significant as that might be. He fought and won many battles but he also lost more than a few. His real skill as a general or commander was in conducting a guerrilla campaign, with all of the devastation that such warfare caused to both sides. The scribe Adam of Usk, a somewhat contradictory man who vacillated between contempt and admiration for Glyndwr, summed up the situation in his *Chronicles,* written at the time of the events he described: 'Wherefore the English, invading those parts with a strong power, and utterly laying them waste and ravaging them with fire, famine and sword, left them a desert, not even sparing children or churches [...] Yet the same did Owain do no small hurt to the English, slaying many of them and carrying off the arms, tents and horses of the king's eldest son.'[2]

However, Glyndwr went beyond the rigid confines of a military leader, and as we shall see, attempted to build and develop a nation – or at least a national consciousness. In this his skill more than equalled his warrior status.

Whatever the motivating factor, in the first decade of the fifteenth century Glyndwr's name alone was enough to strike terror into the hearts and minds of the English – administrators, settlers and soldiers alike.

Arguably, even the English king, Henry IV, trembled at his power, knowing that if he was going to retain his throne he could only do it by defeating Owain Glyndwr. The threat of the Welsh rebellion was that strong.

The king's fear of France and Scotland may have been as great as or even greater than his fear of the Welsh, but for almost all of Henry IV's reign Owain Glyndwr was the real thorn in his side. France and Scotland were potential threats; Glyndwr was a real, raw and very present danger.

Two hundred years later the playwright William Shakespeare was impressed enough to include him as a character in one of his early efforts, *Henry IV, Part One*. In the play, Shakespeare portrays Glyndwr as a wild, exotic and magical man, but also – albeit through the eyes of the English nobleman and Glyndwr's son-in-law, Edmund Mortimer – as one of great compassion and learning:

> At my birth
> The front of heaven was full of fiery shapes.
> The goats ran from the mountains and the herds
> Were strangely clamorous to the frighted fields.
> These signs have mark'd me extraordinary;
> And all the courses of my life do show
> I am not in the roll of common men.[3]

In Shakespeare's play Glyndwr goes on to show his tact, statesmanship and tolerance when, in the face of much goading from Henry Percy – 'O he is as tedious/ as a tired horse, a railing wife'[4] – he shoulders the abuse for the sake of the Tripartite Indenture with Lord Percy, with his son-in-law, Edmund Mortimer, and himself against King Henry.

From what we know and can judge, Owain Glyndwr was undoubtedly a man for all seasons. At a distance of over 600 years there is little that now remains in the way of objective primary source material – if there was any in the first place. The man himself left no diary, no written account of his rebellion. It is something of a shame as Glyndwr was an educated man, well able to offer an objective view of proceedings, and his view of the rebellion would have been memorable.

Writers like Adam of Usk, Iolo Goch and Gruffudd Llwyd all produced contemporary accounts, but with Adam and Iolo in particular, their motives were invariably questionable. It was understandable: Iolo Goch and Gruffudd Llwyd were house poets, family scribes, all with a vested interest in keeping the *uchelwyr* happy. Praise poetry was very much the order of the day. It is fine to look there for atmosphere, for love and honour, but it is not the place to look for objective, un-biased views of events.

Loyalties, always dubious in any sort of civil war or popular uprising, were particularly changeable in the early fifteenth century. So despite what was written at the time and has survived, we really know very little about Owain Glyndwr, the man, the warrior and the prince.

There is not even a portrait or likeness of the man himself. Coming from the *uchelwyr* class, Glyndwr and his family were undoubtedly rich enough to pay an artist to produce a likeness of the great man. They may have done so, particularly before 1400, but if that were the case the portraits have long disappeared.

Once the rebellion broke out there were practicalities to take into consideration. Very few professional artists would have risked their livelihoods and their lives by coming to Wales to paint the portrait of a rebel. If there is a portrait of Glyndwr out there somewhere it has certainly been kept well-hidden for many years.

The danger inherent in commissioning a portrait was particularly obvious in Owain's final years. With his home destroyed, his farm lands devastated and with everyone trying to scratch a living from the little that had been left by the ravages of Henry of Monmouth – and, of course in the wake of the scorched-earth tactics of Glyndwr himself – it was a hard and dangerous time. Nobody came to or travelled across Wales unless they had very good reason to do so.

Not only that. After 1400 Glyndwr was hardly in a position to take out several weeks from his nefarious activities in order to allow a painter to produce something as cerebral as a work of art. A man of mercurial temperament and energy, sitting for a portrait would have been about the last thing on his mind.

There have been suggestions that a portrait held at Kentchurch Court in Herefordshire shows Glyndwr as an old man, but this is unlikely. The wizened nature of the man in the portrait, the lack of an identifying wart on the forehead of the subject and the presence of a Cardinal's hat hanging across his back all seem to indicate that the portrait is not of Glyndwr.[5]

During most of his later life Glyndwr was too busy fighting and planning to sit for a portrait. Unlike modern photography, the process of 'being captured on canvas' was both time consuming and expensive, something that only men and women of leisure could usefully contemplate. Owain Glyndwr would have surely had other things on his mind.

The deciding factor has to be that the precautions he took to avoid detection in his final years would certainly preclude the likelihood of such a bold stroke of vanity. Portraits, in an age when everyone knew *of* him but very few of his opponents actually knew what he looked like, could most certainly lead to identification and capture.

No portrait, then, but Owain Glyndwr was much written about and lauded by the bards like Iolo Goch. There would have been many more than the few we recognise, but bardic poetry was essentially an oral art. Very little was written down and has, therefore, now been lost.

There is also the issue that most of the bardic peons of praise in his honour were written in hindsight and were largely laments for the past combined with predictions of an almost Biblical second coming. They were hardly biographical, at least not in the true sense of the word.

Inevitably, as with all of the literary efforts of these wandering poets who spent their lives travelling from one great house or hall to the next, it is hard to separate fact from fiction in their work. The poets and performers were, after all, literally singing for their supper and the myth of Owain Glyndwr was nothing if not a great place to start.

And yet, despite the lack of hard evidence he was still 'of his time', a much-needed figure in a despotic age when English opinions about the Welsh were negative and unyielding. It can be argued that what Glyndwr gave to the Welsh was quite simple – self-respect.

The Welsh were far from blameless for their poor social standing. Their attitudes and actions undoubtedly contributed to their own ill-fortune. At times it seemed as if the Welsh nation took particular joy and pleasure out of being disregarded. Looking back, there often appears to be an almost self-destructive element to the behaviour and attitudes of the Welsh people, from the death of Llewelyn the Last onwards. It is a masochistic trait that reflects not only their hopelessness but also the inevitable failure of any attempt to climb out of the slough of despond in which they appear to be grounded.

The English nation with its soldiers and lawmen, its officials and superior trade connections, always had the upper hand, especially if there was no Owain Glyndwr figure on the opposite side to knock them back. Even so, as far as so many Welshmen were concerned it was a case of 'Come on then, how far can you push me?' It became, unfortunately, a fairly typical response to any setback.

It was inevitable that at some stage the downtrodden would kick and buck at their overseers. For the lamenting bards the memory of Owain Glyndwr, what he symbolised and what he promised, was one way of doing exactly that.

Even now he remains a fascinating character, someone who goes far beyond the realms of normality, even of all humanity. He has become a symbol, so much so that it is now almost impossible to separate the man from the nature of Welsh identity and dreams.

Owain Glyndwr, the Welsh Braveheart? Yes – and no. He certainly carried the often crippling cross of freedom for Wales, leading from the front, as Wallace did against Edward I. And he certainly put his own situation to one side in the quest for that independence – again, just like William Wallace.

Wallace was also a man fuelled initially by a desire for vengeance. Dreams of freedom took over, but what made him special was the fact that he prepared the way for Robert the Bruce. Several years after Wallace's death 'The Bruce' fought for and provided Scottish independence from England – for a short while at least.

Owain Glyndwr did not consciously prepare the way for anyone. There was always a personal element to his activities, with him leading as the Prince of Wales. He was always conscious of *his* destiny, *his* position as leader. Yet his rebellion and the legend that was created around his deeds certainly set the scene for another, arguably even more significant individual.

To use a Biblical analogy, Owain Glyndwr played John the Baptist, albeit unknowingly, to a very special man, the founder of what was to become the greatest royal dynasty ever to rule in Britain. Wales had to wait almost a hundred years before his coming, but in 1485 the dreams and aspirations of Owain Glyndwr were finally realised in the shape of one man who was to change British society and effectively usher in the modern world.

That man was Henry Tudor, someone who would not fight for independence but who set his aims considerably higher. He would take and hold the English throne, the only Welshman ever to rule both Wales and England.

That is the essential difference between Wallace and Glyndwr. And that is what makes Glyndwr great.

Chapter Two

Wales Before Glyndwr

The killing of Llewellyn ap Gruffudd, ruler of all Gwynedd and the acknowledged Prince of Wales, was a seminal moment in Welsh history. It was, I believe, a killing rather than simply a death in battle. It is a semantic division or separation, perhaps, but in my opinion there does remain a clear distinction between the two styles of death.

Even in November 1282, men and women on both sides of the national and political divide were shocked by the event. They knew that with Llewellyn's death one great age had come to an end and that a new era was about to begin.

The age that was ending had not been totally idyllic for the Welsh and had certainly not been a time without its problems. But whatever the difficulties, for the previous 800 years Wales had been a largely independent country, a separate entity from the rest of Britain. It had existed and arguably had thrived, with its own laws, its own language and its own idiosyncratic customs.

The years between AD 410, when the Roman Legions abandoned Britain, and the death of the last native-born Prince of Wales in the winter of 1282, had been dynamic. They had seen the growth of a unique Welsh culture, a way of life and set of beliefs that may have been impenetrable and alien to the English but which provided the bedrock to Welsh identity and belief.

In the first 600 years after the Roman departure, power in England rested with the Anglo-Saxons, the Celtic peoples of modern-day Wales having retreated or been pushed to the fringes of the island. There they could be left in isolation, not exactly splendid but certainly remote. In reality, the process and practice might have been somewhat more complicated than that rather simplistic view, but it is exactly what happened during those years of immediate post-Roman occupation.

Wales was a poor country during those years and entirely dependent on agriculture. Its population never climbed higher than 800-900,000 and at least until the end of the ninth century there was not a single stone building anywhere in the region. There were incursions from Viking marauders and occasional forays from the Saxons themselves, but provided they remained beyond the boundary of Offa's Dyke, the Welsh were largely left alone.

Then, in the course of one October afternoon in the year 1066, Duke William the Bastard from Normandy and his mercenary French soldiers turned the world of England on its head and utterly destroyed the Anglo-Saxon heritage. Even though he had killed their king in battle, established supreme power in the country and seized their traditional holdings, Duke William inherited a land that was still riven by Saxon anger and resentment. Victory at the Battle of Hastings was only the overture: William's next and most significant task was to pacify the men and women of his new kingdom.

As a consequence, defence of the realm was more important than extending it. For the moment at least the western Celts could be left to themselves. The establishment of huge Marcher Lordships, wild frontier territories along the border between England and Wales, did exactly what it was supposed to do, create a buffer between the incoming Normans and the sitting tenants of the western lands, the Welsh.

It was a situation that was destined never to last. Initially at least, William I, as William the Bastard had now become, was disinterested in what went on in the Welsh Marches. However, the lords of these Marcher territories, by nature the most ambitious and troublesome of the army that had accompanied William to Hastings, took a rather different view.

In the Marches the lords or barons were undoubtedly masters of all they surveyed, ruling their territories with a mixture of might and main. Put simply, their word was law. The Welsh Marches were, effectively, independent kingdoms and the old cliché that in these areas the King's Writ did not run was undoubtedly an accurate statement.

Inevitably, as they became secure in their own territories, the Marcher Lords, keen to extend their fiefdoms, began to push westwards. The very nature of Welsh society, a collection of small kingdoms each with its own prince or ruler who was intent on pursuing his own objectives and his own rivalries, made them a relatively easy target for the mounted knights of the Norman lords.

As the Marcher barons became more and more powerful, the kings who followed William I naturally found themselves interested in what was going on in the western territories. Successive English kings soon realised that to allow these Marcher Lords to grow too strong would be simply storing up trouble for themselves and for those who came after them.

In a warlike age it was only too easy to remember that Duke William had become king by military force, by conquest. No English monarch was likely to allow such a thing to happen again, at least not easily, and over the course of the late twelfth and early thirteenth centuries the influence of the Crown gradually began to supersede that of the Marcher Lords.

It was a difficult, warlike age but by the middle years of the twelfth century large swathes of Welsh territory were in the hands of the powerful Marcher Lords. Significantly, several of the old Welsh kingdoms had also come into the possession of the Crown. Strong motte and bailey castles, wooden to begin with but gradually replaced by gigantic stone monoliths, were built to control and protect the coast. Equally as important, castles were soon being built to monitor strategically vital areas such as roads in and out of the country, territorial border lines and the all-important river crossings.

Around these castles grew Norman lordships and towns – places like Brecon, Criccieth and Cardiff – mirroring the boroughs of England. Here in these mediaeval 'new towns' the influence of the English was strong. The Welsh culture and language may not have died out exactly but they were certainly relegated in importance to the second or third division.

The next stage of English domination was both clever and effective, but subtle it was not. Almost before they knew what was taking place, a series of transplantations worthy of any Middle Eastern warlord hustled the Welsh out of the fertile low-lying farming areas around the coast. Modern-day Pembrokeshire, the Gower Peninsula and the flat lands along the North Wales coast are classic examples of those parts of Wales that saw successful transplantations.

The Welsh were replaced in their traditional homelands by English or, as in the case of what is now southern Pembrokeshire, by Flemish settlers and farmers who came to establish the wool trade. The native Welsh were reluctantly confined to the upland and inland areas where they continued their traditional farming methods in unproductive parcels of land. The two parts of the country, each distinctly different in purpose and typography, became known as the Englishry and the Welshry.

It was not a process that was meekly accepted by the Welsh. They fought and they fought hard against the incomers. In the south west and in the north east, where the Princes of Deheubarth and of Powys led fierce resistance movements, the incursions of the Marcher Lords and the Crown were bitterly resented and opposed. However, it was in the north west of the country that resistance was particularly strong: 'Much the most powerful and successful were the princes of Gwynedd in north-west Wales, firmly based on the mountain strongholds of Snowdonia and the fertile granary of Anglesey [...] They tried to unite lesser Welsh princes and chieftains under their own leadership.'[1]

The two great Welsh princes of Gwynedd, Llewelyn ab Iorwerth and his grandson, Llewelyn ap Gruffudd, were men of courage and determination. They provided the English with a series of significant but very different challenges. Llewelyn ab Iorwerth, Llewelyn the Great as he is now known, was a warrior and strategist of some note. He was a man who undoubtedly earned the appellation of 'Great' and was a significant figure in both England and Wales. He began his forty years of dominance in Wales by making himself sole ruler of Gwynedd before casting his eyes at the rest of the country.

Llewelyn could ill afford discord with his English neighbours and consequently formed alliances with both King John and Henry II, cleverly accepting their sovereignty and over-lordship. He even married John's daughter, Joan, before siding with the English barons in forcing Magna Carta on the reluctant monarch.

Through skilful diplomacy, clever strategy, and, when necessary, ruthless and bloody war he established himself as the premier Welsh nobleman. So great and so efficient were his diplomacy and grasp of politics that, with the blessing of the English Crown, he became the effective ruler of all Wales before his death in 1240.

It was not the first time Wales had been united under one ruler. Rhodri Mawr had more or less achieved that feat in the ninth century, only parts of South Wales remaining outside his domination. Since Rhodri's demise – killed in battle against the Vikings on Anglesey in AD 878 – the country had again fragmented into small kingdoms, each of them ruled by a petty prince or chieftain with his own agenda. It took a man of Llewelyn's character to put an end to that situation.

Llewelyn had spent his last years 'wheeling and dealing' with the other Welsh nobles to ensure that his son, Dafydd ap Llewelyn, would be accepted by the Welsh as his natural successor. Llewelyn was desperate that Dafydd would follow him as ruler of not just Gwynedd but of all Wales. Sadly for him and for Wales, the alliances and agreements that Llewelyn had forged quickly fell apart once the great leader was no longer there to enforce them.

Dafydd might have been the son of Llewelyn the Great but he did not have his father's ability or charm. The minor Welsh princes were more interested in their own positions than in a united Wales and quickly fell back on the old policies of isolationism that had previously led only to fragmentation of the country. King Henry II was not inclined to support Dafydd's claim to rule all of Wales, and with almost no support from the other Welsh princes, it was inevitable that war should break out.

Dafydd died before any sort of conclusion to the conflict could be reached. After his death in 1246 Gwynedd found itself in the hands of his sons, in particular Llewelyn and Owain ap Gruffydd. It was a complex and complicated period in Welsh history, but in what had become something of a 'tradition' with the Welsh princes, it was inevitable that the two boys would soon quarrel and fight over ownership of Gwynedd.

It was a situation that lasted until 1255 when Llewelyn eventually achieved supremacy, defeated his brother and seized control of all Gwynedd. Then, like his grandfather, he decided to deal with the rest of Wales and the troublesome native Welsh princes who had become a very prickly thorn in his side. It was civil war but it was a conflict that had to be fought if Wales was ever going to present a united front and resist the rapacious advances of England and her monarchs.

To begin with, Llewelyn was hugely successful. One by one the smaller and less powerful princes submitted to him and at one stage King Henry III of England was even forced to recognise him as Prince of Wales. It was to be the height of Llewelyn's power and he was destined to be the last native Welsh born prince, at least until the advent of Owain Glyndwr.

For a number of years there were relatively good relations between Llewelyn ap Gruffudd and the English Crown, even though the succession of Edward I in 1272 brought a new and immensely powerful king to the throne. To begin with, Edward was happy to maintain the status quo, but to everyone, apart from Llewelyn, it was obvious that the situation could not possibly last. A separate kingdom and power base on his doorstep? It was never going to last.

The weakness of Henry III had aided Llewelyn ab Iorwerth to rise to a position of strength in Gwynedd, but the power and the ambition of Edward I meant that his grandson was forced to deal with an altogether different and more difficult challenge. Edward was far more forceful, far more ruthless than Henry III had ever been, but the Prince of Gwynedd failed to see the difference, at least not until it was too late.

A brave and capable war leader, Llewelyn ap Gruffudd was somewhat lacking when it came to statesmanship. Despite being recognised by the English Crown as Prince of Wales and being granted sovereignty over the rulers of the other Welsh regions or territories, he clearly felt that his position demanded special treatment from the English king.

He antagonised Edward – deliberately or by total lack of thought, it is unclear which – deciding not to attend his coronation and refusing on no less than five occasions to swear homage to the new English monarch. Regardless of his position and his feelings, it was a foolish way for Llewelyn to behave, an approach that was almost self-destructive in its intensity. It was the excuse Edward needed and as a consequence of Llewelyn's temerity the English prepared for war.

The inevitable invasion by the forces of a now thoroughly exasperated English monarch resulted in victory for Edward. At the subsequent Treaty of Aberconway in November 1277, Llewelyn lost all of his lands apart from his holdings in the western parts of Gwynedd.

The war had been disastrous for the Welsh. English troops were now, once more, an occupying force in the country and Llewelyn had also forfeited his position as overlord of the other rulers of Wales. King Edward, already suspecting that this was not the end of the troubles, began planning for the final showdown. Slowly, carefully and inexorably he started to build new castles at places like Aberystwyth, Rhuddlan and Flint. The iron English grip on Wales tightened, but, coiled as it initially was inside a velvet glove, Llewelyn, his advisors and his family yet again failed to notice.

Llewelyn had retained the title of Prince of Wales after the Treaty of Aberconway. It was about the only thing he did manage to retain, but it was an empty honour which, ultimately, led only to a further rebellion.

Llewelyn's headstrong younger brother, Dafydd, began the conflict on Palm Sunday 1282 by attacking the castle at Hawarden. It was an attack made without Llewelyn's agreement or knowledge, but almost immediately riots in support of Dafydd broke out all over Wales.

Relations between the two brothers had never been good, something of a perpetual problem amongst all of the siblings, and Llewelyn could easily have found reasons to remain outside the conflict. However, he soon realised that he had been placed in an untenable position. He would have to join in the rebellion or lose his status and title – the only thing he now had left to him – as Prince of Wales and as the national leader or chieftain.

There were, initially, a number of successes for the Welsh. Edward's troops were defeated at Llandeilo in the south of the country, and a seaborne force from the Isle of Anglesey – Ynys Mon as the Welsh called it – was destroyed as it tried to cross the hazardous Menai Straits. It was too good to last.

In an attempt to shore up what he perceived as a weak situation in Mid Wales, Llewelyn moved south towards Brecon, accompanied by an army of nearly 7,000 foot soldiers and a small number of cavalry. Even as he set off, the Welsh prince knew that he would come up against formidable opposition. He did not know just how formidable.

Under the command of John Gifford, Edmund Mortimer and Roger l'Estrange, a force of 6,800 experienced soldiers had gathered to meet him. Llewelyn actually had superior numbers, but the Welsh force was made up of, mainly, spearmen. The English army consisted of knights, bowmen, men-at-arms and a large number of cavalry. The advantage lay most definitely with them.

Many believe that Llewelyn was deliberately lured southwards by false intelligence and by the deceptive promise of a quick and easy victory. Whether that was true or not, it was an expedition that was doomed to end in disaster, both for Llewelyn and for Wales.

However, to begin with no one in Llewelyn's retinue saw the danger. The expedition to the south, particularly now in hindsight, has long been cloaked with an air of doom and disaster. Llewelyn did not know it but he was marching out of history and into legend. There are several versions of the death of the last true Prince of Wales.

The traditional view is that on 11 December 1282 he was scouting, on foot, ahead of his army. Behind him his forces became engaged with the

English on the north bank of the River Irfon at Cilmeri, outside Builth Wells. The noise of the battle was audible to the Welsh prince, now some miles away, isolated and out of touch with the conflict.

It has always been unclear what the Welsh leader was doing some distance away from his main army with just a few protecting warriors. Scouting out the enemy was a task for others, not the Prince of Wales. That, however, is the traditional view and it was an exercise that brought Llewelyn to a cataclysmic end that affected all the country.

With the sound of the two armies clashing and ringing in his ears, Llewelyn desperately attempted to get back to his troops and in the confusion he was surprised by a squadron of English horsemen. A knight by the name of Stephen de Frankton, without recognising the Welsh leader, charged at Llewelyn and ran him through with his lance.

Versions of the story differ from this point onwards. Some say de Frankton merely wounded the prince, seriously but not enough to kill him outright. Others take the view that he was immediately despatched by the thrust of the Englishman's lance.

One perspective that has been increasingly believed is that Llewelyn, lying desperately hurt on the ground, felt that the wound was fatal. The identity of the wounded man was made known when he asked for a priest to give him last rites and so revealed his name. The ceremony over, Llewelyn was promptly finished off by the exultant English soldiers – about as close to murder as you could get in the heat of battle.

There are many who subscribe to the view that Llewelyn's death was more of an execution or assassination than it was an act of war. He was, many believe, deliberately tricked or lured into the woods beside the river, perhaps on false information or to bring to a conclusion the message that had brought him south in the first place. Once isolated, alone and unarmoured, Llewelyn was an easy target. Whichever way Llewelyn met his end, the last Welsh prince was dead. The legends, the folk tales and the foretelling of a return to glory could now begin: 'The spring wherein the head of Llewelyn ap Griffith (Gruffudd), last Prince of Wales, was washed after it was cut off, and which is in the village of Builth, throughout a livelong day did flow in an unmixed stream of blood.'[2]

Having realised exactly who it was they had killed, the English took immediate and bloody action. The Battle of Orewin Bridge did not last long, and in the wake of their prince's death the Welsh forces were quickly routed.

From a purely military perspective the defeat was a major disaster for the Welsh, but with time it could have been overcome. The death of Llewelyn effectively spelled the end of the war, and, as it turned out, of a truly independent Wales.

Llewelyn's head was severed from his body. Crowned by a wreath of ivy – in derision of a long-term prophesy that he would one day ride through Cheapside wearing a silver crown – it was sent to London where it was displayed at the Tower for many months.

*****

In the years after Llewelyn's death Wales entered a period of ignominy and humiliating oppression by the English overlords, victorious at last over the troublesome Welsh princes. In 1283 Dafydd, brother of Llewelyn and the man who had begun the Welsh slide to disaster, was cornered, caught and imprisoned at Shrewsbury. Tried and convicted of treason, he was subjected to the dreadful punishment of being hanged, then drawn and finally quartered. The spirit of rebellion died with him.

For a long while Wales was struck by atrophy, but memories of the great days remained in the hearts and minds of the Welsh people. Those memories were distant recollections, little more than evocations of a past age, like the legends of King Arthur, Merlin and the court at Camelot. No one dreamed they might ever come again.

Following his victory, Edward I immediately took ownership of Llewelyn's lands in Gwynedd. They were not to be part of an English kingdom; they were to be Edward's personal possessions. To guard them and to keep the Welsh in their place he brought in architects who were experts in castle building. Men like the famous Master James of St George and Walter of Hereford created a series of huge stone edifices at strategically crucial places like Caernarfon, Harlech and Conwy. The castles duly became the symbols of English power and control.

Llewelyn's kingdom of Gwynedd was divided into three parts, brand new shires in the English fashion being carved out of the old Welsh region – Anglesey, Caernarfon and Merioneth. Together with Cardiganshire and Carmarthenshire in south-west Wales, these new counties or shires became collectively known as the Principality.

In 1301 Edward's son, later Edward II, was proclaimed Prince of Wales. It was an important moment and a crucial event for the king and for the Welsh people.

David Powell, a clergyman in the sixteenth century, came up with the story that young Edward was offered as their prince to the Welsh chieftains when he was still a babe in arms. It was, Powell said, done in response to their request for a leader who could neither speak nor understand a word of English. The old tale remains a great legend but it has not a single shred of truth. Edward was no baby, being awarded the title in 1301 when he was 16 years old. And despite Powell's story, the proclamation was bitterly resented by the Welsh.

The next hundred years saw a mixture of peaceful co-existence on the one hand and harsh repression of the Welsh nation on the other. It all depended on the attitudes of the local sheriffs and other Crown officials and on the assimilation – or not – of the *uchelwyr* who, when allowed or encouraged, were generally happy to work with the king's men in the administration of the shires.

Where there were significant difficulties – and there were many – they tended to revolve around the issue of English law. This, instead of the old established Welsh rules and regulations, was now imposed on the people. Large numbers of the Welsh-speaking inhabitants of the country simply did not understand the new system, and as many of the rulings seemed to favour the English there was inevitably dissent and unhappiness.

In particular, all lands that became escheated – i.e. land and property forfeited because of death, rebellion or some other crime – were claimed by the Crown rather than being shared out amongst the immediate family, as would have happened under the Welsh legal system. Anyone unable to pay dues or taxes also had their land seized and given to the English monarch.

Heavy taxes were inevitably a cause for concern, as was the strict ruling that Welsh farmers and tradesmen were limited to selling their produce and goods only in the English-run boroughs. The prices Welshmen received for their produce in the weekly markets of these English boroughs were inevitably low.

In 1315 bad harvests and a severe famine hit Wales. It began a vicious cycle with famine striking again in 1316 and in 1317. Three years of starvation caused untold hardship at all levels of society in both Wales and in England. Prices of corn and other essentials shot up and there were many deaths right across the country. Even so there were no concessions or help from the English overlords.

They may not have helped with relief but the English merchants and landowners certainly noticed the appalling conditions. The more educated of the Welsh could not help noting that the interest and concern of these men was not how the famines affected the newly conquered territories in Wales but how the high prices caused subsequent hardships in England.

In the *Flores Historiarum*, compiled at Westminster Abbey just a few years after the famines, the following comments were made about the events of 1316 and 1317: '[There was] great scarcity in England because of abundance of rain [1316], so that in parts of Strigoil [Chepstow] a quarter of corn was sold for 16 shillings sterling. Scarcity of corn continued throughout the whole year [1317]. On account of this scarcity there was a great mortality of men.'[3]

The problems that were about to beset Wales went far deeper and wider than the issue of famines and dead bodies across the length and breadth of the country, however. They were far more general in their scope but ultimately just as damaging.

It was a difficult and dangerous time and to many of those watching from the safe distance of their monasteries or castles, their great houses and their banqueting halls, it seemed as if the whole fabric of society was being ripped apart. Even for the protected few, that was a troubling, disturbing prospect that everyone knew would, sooner or later, rebound on them.

The fourteenth century was an era of great schism in the church, the Avignon Papacy being established under a breakaway Pope in 1309. This eventually led to the Western or Great Schism when, from 1378 until 1417, there were two Popes, one at Avignon in southern France and the other in Rome, both issuing contradictory edicts and rulings.

Confusion in the upper echelons of the church hierarchy meant confusion in the lower ranks as well, so much so that corruption and self-indulgent practices became common. This in turn created a situation where spiritual succour for the suffering Welsh – not to mention other nations across Europe – was limited and marginal.

Read Chaucer's *Prologue to the Canterbury Tales* where the activities of the Reeve, the Pardoner and the others will give an indication of what was going on. Or perhaps you should try Adam of Usk. In his *Chronicles*, Adam quotes a verse he was given by a priest from Bohemia, two lines that summed up the corrupt nature of the church at this time. They concerned the practice of simony – selling church offices, positions and sacred objects. Simony was something that was rife across the continent. Wales, where very few of the churchmen could speak the language of the ordinary men and women, and were, in the main, not even Welsh, suffered along with many other parts of the world:

> These two evils shalt thou bear, if that thou be Simon's heir:
>   Thou shalt burn when thou art dead; living, thou shalt want thy bread.[4]

As if all that wasn't enough, in 1348 the whole of Britain was decimated by the Black Death. It is estimated that almost half of the entire population of Britain died in the three years that the bubonic plague ravaged the country, and to make matters worse, the pandemic came back every ten or fifteen years for the next few centuries.

Wales, with its more scattered population, was probably not as badly affected as England, but that did not mean that the Welsh nation escaped untouched. The plague first struck Wales in the manorial areas of the south east, migrating from the nearby port and city of Bristol. It came again by sea, through the major wool importing town of Carmarthen in the west, and by 1349 had spread throughout the country.

The plague thrived in the close-knit, unhygienic towns of the time, and, luckily for the Welsh, there were very few large communities like London or Bristol in the Principality. Even so, the towns that did exist suffered from the repeated visits. Pembroke, in the west, was badly hit: 'There was a heavy death rate and the population high of the year 1340 (over 2000) was not reached again until the late eighteenth century. Many houses were left empty as the plague had simply wiped out whole households, the east end of the town suffering badly.'[5]

Other Welsh towns were subjected to a similar fate. Dilapidated properties, empty shops and old Roman roadways that had been allowed to crumble and subside were the order of the day. In the winter the roads were coated in thick, glutinous mud; in the summer swirling dust lashed like rain into people's faces. Together, they made travelling a nightmare. Traditional fairs and markets were, in many places, abandoned or discontinued because there were just not enough people in the town to make them viable.

In the country areas whole villages were devastated, leaving fewer people to work manorial lands, with the result that field after field of valuable produce was left untended and unharvested. The crops withered, rotted and were not replanted. There were just not enough people left alive to carry out the work and farms literally closed down. Buildings went to ruin and animals were left to wail and wander across the countryside until they died from exhaustion and lack of food.

In 1337 the Hundred Years' War began. It led to more heavy taxes being levied to pay for the various campaigns and to a devaluation of the coinage that was crippling for ordinary working men and women. They did not have much in the first place, but now even the few pennies they did possess were being taken from them.

For the Welsh peasants it was a puzzling time. They could not see why they were being taxed to support the English king's desire to add France to his list of possessions. They failed to see why he wanted to fight a war that had absolutely nothing to do with them. Very few of them understood the causes of the war or even realised that Henry II, the first Plantagenet king of England, had once ruled an empire that stretched from the Scottish borders in the north to the foothills of the Pyrenees in the south. The wastrel King John had lost it all, of course, and from an English point of view the Hundred Years' War was simply an attempt to reclaim lands that the English kings felt was rightfully theirs. It was inevitable, therefore, that they would tax their subjects to pay for it. Such reasoning was beyond the understanding of most people, particularly in the more rural and isolated parts of Wales.

For those who had the ability and cared to look at the problem it was clear that it went far deeper than simply the reclamation of lost land and territories. Economics and social structures lay at the root of the problems, even if the more able of the peasants would have been hard pushed to describe them as such.

If the peasants could not understand what was going on, the nobility and the landowners *would* not. That lack of understanding between the Crown and the people was the beginning of a disassociation from the feudal systems of the past, one that left most of the population rootless and dissatisfied.

Faced by ruined landscapes and by empty and idle farms, more and more men were forced to tramp off to find work. For most of the Welsh labourers that meant crossing the border into England where they were treated as cheap labour and immediately came up against the animosity of English labourers who were themselves struggling to find enough work to live.

The itinerant labourers left behind their families and homes where they and their ancestors had lived for years. It was hard, it was cruel, but there was no alternative. They had to work in order to survive, and emigration, temporary or permanent, was the only way. It was a dilemma that has faced working men and women of many nations ever since.

To take just one Welsh example, in the commote of Mefenydd by the end of the year 1349 only seven farm workers out of a potential workforce of 104 four remained available to till and work the manor land. The situation was simply untenable.[6]

In Wales, in England and all over Europe, the old feudal systems for the holding of land – traditional ways of life that had been in existence for centuries – were beginning to collapse. To most of Europe's peasantry there was cold comfort in the greater freedoms they now inherited. The old security of the feudal system, a system that had kept them content and safe in the knowledge of understanding and accepting their place, had been smashed away.

The feudal landlords attempted to shore up the old way of life, not by compassion or care but by the use of draconian legislation and the Statute of Labourers (1351) which limited the money that could be earned by the working people. Misguided and inept, these 'cures' simply widened the gap between the labouring classes and their lords and masters. Time was that the landlords, the barons and squires – the *uchelwyr* in Wales – had cared for and cared about their workers. Not any longer.

In England the oppression was added to by the unjust and thoroughly detested poll tax that had been instigated by the advisors of the boy king, Richard II. Disgruntlement and anger were close at hand, exploding in the Peasants' Revolt of 1381. In Wales, the anger lay dormant but dangerously in wait for a man like Owain Glyndwr to create the spark of rebellion.

Even the better-off farmers of Wales were sometimes forced to sell their lands and homes in order to make ends meet. The *uchelwyr* certainly felt the pinch as English gentlemen from the border areas began to view them as potential opponents for the very limited amount of land, money and influence on offer.

Ambitious Welshmen, ranging from humble farm labourers looking for work to divinity students at Oxford, were a sudden threat. Throughout the fourteenth and fifteenth centuries their presence in England was something that was regularly denounced in Parliament and sometimes met with anti-Welsh riots and outbursts of violence.

Opportunities within the church, which had traditionally provided a good living for second or third sons of the *uchelwyr*, were no longer readily available to them. The wealthiest and best livings went to the highest bidder, which in the late fourteenth century effectively meant Englishmen. In the last quarter of the century only one out of a total of sixteen available Bishoprics in Wales was held by a Welshman.

In the face of such chaos and confusion it was hardly surprising that the widely held belief the world would end in 1400 achieved such prominence. It was a superstitious time and the church was simply not available to curb such rumours and to put people at ease.

For relatively small regions like Wales what all of this created was an unhappy and disgruntled group of individuals, both at the *uchelwyr* level and amongst the Welsh labouring classes. Relationships between the Welsh and the English had always been fragile, now they were brittle as glass.

Men who had been happy to co-exist with the English, to do their bidding in return for work, money, rank and privilege, were increasingly being marginalised, even degraded by their English counterparts. Labourers had little option but to shrug their shoulders and continue with the battle for survival. The *uchelwyr* fumed and fretted, waiting for the one leader who would end the trials and tribulations that had fallen across Wales. It did not make for a happy and contented nation. Clearly there was great trouble ahead; it was just a matter of where and when it would arrive.

*****

If there was a saving grace for the Welsh it came in the double-pronged virtue of war and culture. Both of them were almost traditional forms of employment for the Celtic peoples of Britain. Wars against countries like France, Ireland and Scotland had been a regular occurrence for years, but the coming of the Hundred Years' War provided a near-continuous and much-needed outlet for Welsh warriors. If they could stay out of the ale houses and survive the brutal campaigns, it brought much-needed money for their families.

The Welsh were rugged, doughty fighters, enormously experienced in the arts of guerrilla warfare. They were ideal foot soldiers, but despite being well paid for their work, they were also cannon fodder for the English armies in France and so their ranks were in regular need of replenishment. That suited the Welsh perfectly. As Giraldus Cambrensis had written: 'They will take up their weapons and willingly sacrifice their lives. They deem it a disgrace to die in bed.'[7]

They were, then, good foot soldiers, but the real talent of the Welsh, as everyone knew, came in the form of archery. The Welsh had long been recognised as the most skilled archers in Britain, their use of the artillery bow enhancing the reputation of British fighting forces – English fighting forces, as the king and his barons would have described it – across the whole of Europe.

The artillery bow was a stout, robust and effective weapon. It was relatively short compared to other types of bow and was much preferred to the traditional longbow, which was an altogether more delicate and recreational piece of machinery. The longbow was fine for the butts and for the castle forecourt but not for the mud and horror of the battlefield.

Archers were a crucial element in any army of the period. In the main they were ordinary low-born peasants who did not have one tenth of the riches owned by the lumbering, armour-clad knights who charged in the van of the battle, but no war could be successfully fought without them.

The other type of bow in common use during these years was the French crossbow. Like the longbow – delicate, accurate, lengthy but unwieldy – it had significant advantages but perhaps even more disadvantages. The crossbow was sturdy, usable in any weather and packed a wicked punch. It did not require the constant maintenance and attention demanded by the artillery bow and the longbow, and yet it had never been a popular choice for the English ruling classes.

To begin with it was slow to load and lacking in accuracy at anything more than thirty paces. However, unlike the Welsh artillery bow, which needed an archer of some skill and power for it to become an effective weapon, the crossbow could be used by almost any foot soldier after just a few hours' instruction. That was both its strength and its fatal weakness.

The French nobles, seeing how easy it was to train infantrymen in the techniques of the crossbow, invested heavily in the weapon, to the detriment of longbows and other forms of archery. Longbows were used by the French but only in limited numbers.

The mechanism of a crossbow was, by its nature, heavy and cumbersome. While loading his bolt the crossbowman was invariably bent over his weapon, wedging or resting its tip on the ground and at the same time winding back the drawstring. The process took several minutes, during which time the crossbow was effectively out of action.

To make matters worse, at those moments the crossbowman was vulnerable to the rapid fire of the English and Welsh archers. As he bent over his weapon to reload his bow, his back was open to attack. In contrast, the artillery bow was quick to load, aim and fire. In the hands of skilled bowmen it was also deadly.

While renowned for their speed and accuracy, the standard rate of fire for the artillery bow when used by an experienced Welsh archer was still approximately only twelve arrows a minute. That was twelve arrows aimed deliberately and accurately at a target rather than being simply loosed off in a series of terrifying but not always accurate volleys. With bowmen carrying just twenty-four arrows in their belts – missiles that were stuck into the earth in front of them for easy access whenever combat threatened – archers and their weapons were, therefore, valuable assets and were harboured or protected accordingly.

Inefficient practice, like the use of archers at the wrong moment in a battle, could easily lead an army to defeat and disaster. Shortage of ammunition was a perpetual problem. It was not always possible to pick up spent or used arrows, the traditional method of gaining extra weapons or refreshing your stock on the battlefield. The archers' average of twelve arrows each minute needed to be very carefully managed. And yet twelve arrows a minute was a great deal faster than any partly trained crossbowman could achieve. Load and shoot before the opposing crossbow man could wind in his bowstring; that was the traditional Welsh tactic.

The artillery bow might be easy to shoot, in contrast to the crossbow, but it was devilishly difficult to master. Long periods of practice and training were required to achieve anything like reasonable efficiency and accuracy. Once achieved, however, the bow was a deadly weapon in attack or defence; one of the reasons monarchs like Richard II decreed that no servant or labourer was to carry any weapon other than a bow.

Richard was the first English king to pass a statute ordaining regular archery practice for every servant, serf or peasant in the kingdom. The statute met with a mixed response.

Virtually all of the labouring classes in Britain disliked the king's edict declaring that they should practise with their bows on Sundays and holidays rather than playing their favourite games such as wrestling, or knapan, an early Celtic form of football. Not so the Welsh who took to archery with flair and enthusiasm. Giraldus Cambrensis, three parts Norman and one part Welsh, was clear about the dedication of the Welsh to the craft of archery and war in general: 'In peace they dream of war and prepare themselves for battle by practicing with their spears and arrows [...] The men of that part of Wales (Merionethshire) are very skilful with their long spears. The men of the south, especially Gwent, use the bow to great effect.'[8]

According to Giraldus, who had been born and brought up at Manorbier Castle in Pembrokeshire, the Welsh artillery bows were made from wych-elm and were capable of delivering a hugely powerful blow that would kill in the blink of an eye. In the hands of a skilled expert an arrow from an artillery bow could pierce the thickest of church doors or cut through the leg armour of a mounted knight, pinning him to his saddle.[9]

The Welsh love of archery was beautifully caught and described by the poet Iolo Goch, a man who later came to write several verses in honour of Owain Glyndwr. For Iolo, as for many archers, the arrow was a crucial element in the archer's equipment: 'a straight round shaft with a well-rounded neck, having long slender feathers of a green silk fastening, and a sharp edged steel head, heavy and thick, an inch wide, of a green-blue temper, that would draw blood out of a weathercock.'[10]

Iolo Goch, however, also loved the practice and process of archery, viewing it almost as an art form. He waxed lyrical in his description of the process of letting the arrow loose at a foe or target: 'With my foot to a hillock and my back to an oak, and the wind at my back and the sun towards my side [...] I would shoot him such a shot, so strong and far-drawn, so low and sharp, that it would be no better there were between him and me a breastplate and a Milan hauberk than a wisp of fern, a kiln rug or a herring net.'[11]

Welsh archers served in the English armies throughout the Hundred Years' War and contributed greatly to famous victories like Crecy,

Poitiers and Agincourt. The legend that the Welsh soldiers waved the first two fingers of their right hands – the fingers that drew back the bow string – at the defeated French at Agincourt has little substance, but the fact that it has been believed for so many years gives some indication of the significance of Welsh archers during the Hundred Years' War.

Their enlistment provided much-needed employment, even for men who had fought against the English Crown in the past. Henry V, for example, filled the ranks of his archery units with men who only months before had been fighting for Owain Glyndwr and against the forces of the Crown. Ability with the bow was, it seemed, more important than questionable loyalties.

*****

The second saving grace for the Welsh people was culture, something at which they soon became equally as interested and adept as they had done at fighting and archery.

Culture, at this time, meant mainly poetry. Not everyone could be a poet but everyone could listen to the words of the bards and enjoy them. The poems were mostly performed by travelling writers and actors, the famous bards of Wales, who would sing their verses in the homes of the *uchelwyr* or at dramatic competitions known as eisteddfodau.

The first eisteddfod had been held in the grounds of Cardigan Castle over the Christmas period of 1176. The event had been organised by Rhys ap Gruffydd, The Lord Rhys as he has become known. Rhys was the Welsh ruler of Deheubarth, a man who had experienced life in Norman England and bought into the culture and way of life but always remaining a proud Welshman.

As a way of celebrating his cultural and intellectual significance to Wales, but at the same time reinforcing his links to the English Crown, Rhys called the bards of Wales to the event at Cardigan Castle. Prizes were on offer and Christmas in Cardigan was eminently preferable to nights spent, cold and lonely, on the moors. Dozens of performers flocked to West Wales.

The choice of Cardigan was an important one. The Lords of Deheubarth traditionally lived and ruled from their fortress at Dinefwr in the Carmarthenshire countryside, but by choosing to hold his eisteddfod at the newly created and updated castle at Cardigan he was deliberately ushering in what he hoped would be a new spirit of cooperation with the English.

The event at Cardigan is regarded as the first eisteddfod, but to begin with the term 'eisteddfod' was not used either for this first event or for the majority of subsequent meetings. Not until 1451 was the word 'eisteddfod' formally employed, but the idea or concept had taken hold and gatherings of bards and singers did occur on several occasions.

The importance of the gatherings, their significance in the growth of Welsh cultural identity, was always more important than a title or a name and was a sure way of garnering fame for the participants. That, inevitably, would lead to a warm welcome in the coming months for the poets from the owners of the great lodges and houses around Wales.

Eisteddfodau were a French/Norman tradition rather than Welsh, but the concept had an immediate appeal for the literary minded residents of Wales. In particular, they had meaning for men and women of intelligence, people of a romantic nature who could sit back and enjoy the stories of their nation. In the hands of a skilled and capable spinner of tales, someone who could pick up the mood of his audience in an instant, such material was dynamite.

The bardic performances symbolised the Welsh love of poetry and music, and the bards who spent most of their lives travelling from one great hall to the next were quick to see the potential. There was both a practical side to their interest –the provision of food, warmth and a safe roof over their heads – and a more complex creative element. The development of a singular poetic style, a cultural revolution, soon became unique to Wales.

Despite the ravages of the Black Death and the seemingly continuous afflictions of war, during the second half of the century men like the renowned Dafydd ap Gwilym and Iolo Goch travelled the length and breadth of Europe singing and chanting their verses at the universities and at the palaces of the great noblemen.

Troubadours from France, balladeers from the warm regions around the Mediterranean, minstrels from the forests of Bavaria, all mixed easily and fruitfully with the Welsh poets. It was a cultural flowering that pre-dated the Renaissance by a hundred years but which was equally as significant to men of culture and learning.

In the main, the Welsh bards composed their odes and other verses using the alliterative Welsh metres and intricate rhyming patterns of *cywyddau* and *cynghanedd*. It was a far more complex style of poetry than that employed by their French or Germanic counterparts and experts like Dafydd ap Gwilym and Iolo Goch were admired and honoured for their talent and skill. Their subjects were, mostly, love, nature and long dead heroes from the Welsh past.

Despite – or perhaps because of – the suffering of the people, the late fourteenth century was an age of great literary experiment and achievement. It was an age of patronage, culminating in the work of men like the Italian Dante and Geoffrey Chaucer from London who were renowned at the time and who have since acquired iconic status. However, for every literary master like Chaucer there were a dozen lesser lights, all practising their art and trying to make a mark on society.

All over Wales and throughout Europe, literature – poetry in particular – flourished. It was a glorious celebration of the world in which people lived, and ran in direct contrast to the huge toll inflicted on people's lives by war and by diseases like the Black Death. The surge also coincided with the development of the printing press, although, in Wales at least, poetry remained a firmly oral form.

It was a flowering that had not been seen for hundreds of years, not since the great Greek writers of antiquity had celebrated the deeds of Ulysses, Paris and the other heroes of the Trojan War. The poets of the 1300s, however, had more on their minds than the warriors and sages of ancient times. That applied particularly with the Welsh poets.

The *uchelwyr*, the princes and the lords of Wales actively gave their support to the travelling bards, feeding, clothing and offering them shelter whenever they appeared at their door. News of their coming usually preceded the poets and the fires were built higher that night, the food increased in quantity and quality, as everyone waited expectantly for the arrival of the bard.

The presence of these men in the halls of the *uchelwyr* and other leaders on the long, cold winter nights gave comfort and entertainment to the whole household, from the prince or the *uchelwyr* himself down to his family and servants. They were as necessary as the later masques, miracle or mystery plays and pantomimes that gave entertainment and a degree of education to the people.

The poems and songs about the past greatness of Wales, and of its legendary heroes, were immensely popular. That was, perhaps, inevitable for a defeated and oppressed nation. The second coming of a great warrior prince who would lift the people out of the morass into which they had fallen was one of the bard's most powerful images. It was a subject, a theme that almost everyone knew about and believed.

The smoke-filled halls of the *uchelwyr* and the squires, dimly lit and patterned with dark mysterious corners, were the perfect environment for stories of mystery and legend. The bards knew that well enough and honed their tales accordingly.

It was widely accepted that the ghosts of King Arthur, the magician Merlin and the knights of Camelot lingered still in Wales. Arthur, the Welsh believed, was a Celt who, when he was not campaigning, lived in Wales and created his great court of Camelot at Carmarthen. Merlin was apparently born in the town. Some disagreed and said that the court sat at Caerleon where the amphitheatre of the old Roman fortress had offered a great circular auditorium. It hardly mattered; the belief that Arthur and his knights had a Welsh connection was strong at this time.

The legend went beyond locating the site of Camelot. The great warriors and the aged Merlin had not died but were asleep in the darkness of deep mountain caves, resting and waiting for the day when they would be called upon to fight once more for their people.

That myth was crucial to the bards; it was part of their staple diet and one that they used constantly in their poems and songs of the glorious past. It would return and linger even longer in the hearts and minds of the Welsh people after the eventual defeat of Owain Glyndwr.

Travelling from the house of one lord or *uchelwyr* to another, the bards kept the tradition and the legends of a returning king at the forefront of people's minds. They might, in their nightly performances, sing poems and songs of love and nature, but what everyone in the audience was really waiting for were the verses of how great and how majestic the returning warriors would be.

According to these strolling poets, the returning king would come with a mission – to restore the people and the nation of Wales to their previous greatness. When the people had little else to cheer them the old stories were a great comfort and succour.

As the son of one of the *uchelwyr*, Owain Glyndwr would have known of such prophesies and the old legends as well as anyone. He would have been reared on them, listened at his mother's breast and at his father's knee, and with wooden sword and shield would have fought many desperate battles against dragons and Viking raiders – and, of course, the English.

As a child he would have welcomed the arrival of the bards to his father's house. Their regular visitations would have provided a delightful break in the routines of daily life, perhaps in the same way as Christmas is welcomed by modern children. Glyndwr would have sat with his mother and his siblings and listened as the visitors sang their tales of glories that had gone and glories still to come. As he grew to adulthood his love of the bardic tales did not diminish or disappear.

Glyndwr's antecedence was known throughout Powys, Gwynedd and the whole of North Wales, probably even further afield. With his family links to the royal houses of the country, it is highly likely that he would have been earmarked by many as the potential or possible deliverer of the freedoms for which the Welsh were desperately waiting.

It is all too easy to minimise the raw longing for the arrival of this saviour by the Welsh people. For many of the *uchelwyr* class and for the bards there was an almost evangelical edge to a belief that had slowly but surely metamorphosed into something far more than a myth.

The saviour, when he came, would be mystical and he would be magical but above all he would be real. That expectation would have lodged itself into the brain of Owain Glyndwr. Certainly as he grew into adulthood it became more and more likely, at least to those who knew him, that this man might actually do something of note with his life – and in Wales at that time such a belief almost certainly meant doing something for the nation.

The bard Iolo Goch, keen to create a significant lineage for the returning warrior, was not the man to neglect any opportunity to 'puff' his patron, and, at the same time, advance his own reputation. After one visit to Glyndwr's house at Sycharth, Iolo was moved to write about the children of the house as 'A fine nest of chieftains'.[12] Perhaps he knew something that Glyndwr and the rest of his family did not!

All bards tailored their verses to fit their audience. They were constantly on the move between one house and the next and the heritage of the *uchelwyr* who was their host one particular night would have been well known to them. The next night and the next benevolent *uchelwyr*, wherever and whoever they were, would not expect to hear praise poems about his colleague in the next village or township.

Flattery was what the *uchelwyr* expected and that was what the roaming bards of the country provided. Iolo Goch became something of a 'house poet' for Owain Glyndwr, welcomed with open arms whenever he appeared at the door. This inevitably meant that his work was then, and remains now, somewhat subjective in its content and style. Nevertheless, his words do manage to convey something of the way in which Owain Glyndwr was regarded by the people:

A baron whose lineage I know,
there was no baron more zealous.
Any baron is a man of no account
except one of the stock that this one is descended from.[13]

Quite how much Owain took in is unknown, but as a child, an adolescent and as a young, newly married man he would have had to be rather simple not to have picked up the undertones. And while Owain Glyndwr might have been many things he was certainly not simple.

Chapter Three

Early Life

At the risk of being too circumspect, too off-hand or glib, Owain Glyndwr was born in Wales. That simple, bald statement is, sadly, about all we really know of the man's origins. The rest is a combination of myth, half-truths and speculation. Even the spelling of his name has the air of changeability or uncertainty that surrounds much of his early life.

The name Owain Glyndwr, Lord of Glyndyfrdwy and self-proclaimed Prince of Wales, is often written as Owain Glyn Dwr and the purists will happily explain that this has always been the correct way to write his name. The Anglicised spelling, commonly adopted by the English – playwright William Shakespeare amongst them – has always been Owen Glendower.

However you spell or pronounce his name it is translated into English as 'Owen of the Glen of Water', a typically Welsh descriptive title. It derives from one of the two holdings owned by his family in North Wales. The ownership was granted or allowed by the English Crown – for which the family pledged their allegiance to whichever monarch sat on the throne – and was but a small reflection of the property once held by the Lords of Glyndyfrdwy.

Glyndyfrdwy, the first of these lordships, lay along the River Dee between Corwen and Llangollen and was the one that gave Glyndwr his name. It was an area of deep woods and valleys, flanked by high hills and gorges, full of half-hidden pathways through the trees. Cynllaith, the second of the two holdings, was some miles away across the rugged Berwyn Mountains, and with its rich pastures and fertile lands was the logical location for the main family residence at Sycharth.

The exact date and location of Glyndwr's birth are still unclear: three possible dates have been given – 1349, 1354 and 1359. Although many have tried, it has not been possible to narrow down the choice and even historian John Davies in his seminal account *A History of Wales* has been forced to hedge his bets: 'Owain Glyn Dwr was born about 1354 and there were by the 1380s men in Wales who were grooming him for the role of the second Cadwaladr. "Baron, I know your lineage," sang Iolo Goch.'[1]

Where he was born is equally as undecided. The logical location is Sycharth, the family home in Cynllaith. A luxurious and beautifully positioned manor house, it was made of good quality timber and tiles. The roof was surmounted by numerous chimneys, a rare luxury which indicated properly sited fires in the rooms beneath. No smoke-filled hallways for the lords of Glyndyfrdwy. It is hard to imagine the birth taking place anywhere else.

However, there is a persistent myth or tradition stating that Glyndwr's birth occurred in South Wales. This story says that the event took place in his mother's original home at Trefgarne, close to the border of north Pembrokeshire and south Cardiganshire.

According to the myth, Glyndwr's mother, Elen, had gone to Pembrokeshire to visit her family and the baby was delivered there. It remains unlikely, however, as travelling the length of the country was difficult enough for anyone in the mid-fourteenth century; for a heavily pregnant woman in the last stages of confinement it would have been nigh on impossible.[2]

There may be several unanswerable questions about his date and place of birth, but Glyndwr's ancestry and heritage are well known and remain beyond dispute. The birth line was an important element in his rise to power and his leadership of the longest lasting Welsh rebellion.

Descended on his father's side from Madog ap Gruffudd, *Tywysog*, or prince, of Powys, Owain Glyndwr was able to trace his ancestry back to renowned Welsh heroes who had once walked and ruled in this area. These included men like Gruffudd Maelor and Bleddyn ap Cynfyn who had died as the Marcher Lords began to exert their influence in 1075.

On his mother's side his ancestry was even more renowned, conjoining the family to some of the most notable men in Welsh history. Through her, Owain could trace his ancestry to many of the princes of Deheubarth, in particular to figures like the famous Lord Rhys, founder of the first eisteddfod at Cardigan Castle.

It was a noble heritage, made even more spectacular by further links to the rulers of Gwynedd. This came through his great-grandmother Gwenllian who was descended from one of the ancient and long dead princes of Gwynedd. It was a link through a maternal relative and therefore regarded as being of little real consequence.

The Gwynedd link would have been marginal, hardly worth a nod of acknowledgement, but the death of Owain Lawgoch in 1378 – assassinated by an agent of the English Crown – changed everything. Owain Lawgoch was last in the male line of Gwynedd rulers and this now placed Glyndwr, coming from the maternal side, in a very significant position. It enabled him to claim direct lineage to the great warrior princes of the past, Llewelyn the Great and Llewelyn the Last.

Owain Glyndwr's father, Gruffudd Fychan, was one of the *uchelwyr* of Wales. Like many of his class he was a descendant of the royal princes who had ruled the country before the arrival of the Normans, and, despite the conquest, still held a position of some substance in Norman/Anglicised Wales. Due to his ownership of the two tracts of land at Glyndyfrdwy and Cynllaith, Gruffudd Fychan was also fairly wealthy with an annual income of around several hundred pounds.

Gruffudd had made an advantageous marriage to Elen ferch Tomos, daughter of Owain ap Tomos Llewelyn of Cardiganshire. As part of the traditional wedding settlement, where a wife's possessions automatically came into the ownership of the husband, he took possession of substantial holdings in the south, in what was the old region of Deheubarth.

The lands in the south west of Wales would later pass to his son and increase Owain's already substantial holdings. More importantly, it gave Owain Glyndwr territorial possessions in those parts of Wales where he was able to claim his ancient rights to leadership and so underline his potential claim to be Prince of Wales.

Gruffudd Fychan had no political desires or inclination. He wanted to do nothing more than raise a family and live out his life in the luxury of his house at Sycharth. The property was both substantial and well appointed.

According to the bard Iolo Goch – writing when the house had become Owain Glyndwr's on the death of his father – the building and its environment were nothing short of magnificent. He described the place in some detail in one of his verses. After waxing lyrical about the roof tiles and the chimneys, Iolo's poem of praise moved on to list the other refinements:

An orchard, a vineyard near the bright court,
a fair mill on the smooth water,
and his dovecote, a bright stone tower;
a fishpond, a little hollow enclosure

where nets may be thrown at need;
a place of great abundance, no doubt about it.[3]

Iolo's words are, perhaps, an idealised impression of Sycharth, written
to please and flatter Glyndwr, but there is no doubt that what Iolo was
describing was a building of some substance.

It was not all flattery. Later excavations of the site show that Iolo was
fairly accurate in his description, the actual house being made of fine
wooden stathes and standing on the summit of a small hill. It contained
many rooms, all beautifully created and furnished. A moat, crossed by
a bridge, ran around the bottom of the hillock, more of a scenic device
than protection.

The wonder is not that such a house should be available to anyone in
the final years of the fourteenth century, but that Owain Glyndwr should
be prepared to give it up or at least put his ownership of the place at risk
it for the sake of a perilous rebellion against the English Crown.

We know little about Owain's childhood. To begin with, he was
presumably tutored at home, like most children of his rank and class,
becoming fluent in speaking and writing both in Welsh and English.
He also developed skills in French and Latin.

He would have run and played with his brothers in the grounds of the
family house, fished in the trout stream and listened, wide eyed, to the
tales of visiting bards and story tellers. He would have ridden across his
father's lands, climbed trees and enjoyed the easy life of any boy coming
from a well-to-do family of the time.

It was inevitable that the ever-expressive Iolo Goch should offer some
words about Owain's childhood. It would have been expected of a bard
who enjoyed so much hospitality and comfort in the Sycharth house.

He probably saw the young man only on those occasions when he
came to Sycharth in his role as a travelling bard, and how much he truly
understood about the son of the house cannot now be known. Lack of
knowledge, however, was never going to put off this professional poet
and incessant flatterer:

He was never a bully.
He never took a toy against his will
from a boy, only what he would get willingly.
He never caused by stroke or blow

grief to him with his hands.
He never beckoned nor said
so much as "boo"; wise discretion.[4]

The lines quoted above are a part of a much longer poem that goes on to exalt Owain Glyndwr's exploits as a warrior in Scotland – a warrior for the English Crown. It was the sort of thing bards were expected to produce and Iolo was never one to fail his paymaster.

*****

Owain Glyndwr was still young when his father died. Once again the exact date of the death is unclear, some accounts saying Owain was just eleven, others taking a more circumspect route and stating simply that the event occurred at some time before the boy reached the age of sixteen.

However old he might have been, he was now technically a landowner with the responsibility of maintaining and overseeing his estates. That included the care of the men and women who lived on his lands and worked for and with him.

Glyndwr, as a property owner, would probably have employed a steward to carry out the day-to-day work on his estates, but the responsibility remained with him and with him alone. And yet, in the eyes of the world he was still a boy, in the charge of his mother and she now decided that his education needed to be taken to the next stage.

Glyndwr was not exactly 'fostered out', but Elen was anxious to provide her son with the training necessary to become an eligible and acceptable member of society – English society, it should be noted. As a result he was sent to spend time at the nearby home of the Earl of Arundel, Lord of Chirk and Oswestry. There were family connections, Glyndwr's father having been one of the earl's officers at some stage in the past, and there seems to have been genuine friendship between Arundel and the widow of Gruffudd Fychan.

The Earl of Arundel, Richard Fitzalan to give him his family name, was one of the most significant English noblemen of the day and in his house the young Glyndwr was trained in the necessary skills of jousting and combat. He was also taught the rules of knightly etiquette and the polite manners and behaviour to succeed in life.

More importantly, simply by offering Glyndwr residency in his house and with his family Arundel was providing the young man with his patronage. Patronage of this sort was something that no ambitious Welshman could do without if he wanted to get on in the English court. And at this stage Owain Glyndwr was certainly keen on doing well in the upper echelons of English society.

During his adolescence Owain also spent time at the home of Sir David Hanmer at Maelor Saesneg in the district of Bangor Is-Coed. Once again, dates are unclear, but it is more than likely that his time at the homes of Arundel and Hanmer – and back in his own domain at Sycharth – dove-tailed easily with each other.

A lawyer of considerable note, David Hanmer was to have a profound effect on the young Glyndwr. English by birth, Hanmer was an educated and intelligent border squire, a man of compassion and learning with adherence to and affection for both England and Wales. He was a landowner, an administrator and man of the law who regularly took commissions from the great lords of England.

Hanmer easily and happily encompassed English and Welsh culture, both languages being spoken in his house. He was married to a Welsh woman and was typical of the more enlightened border gentry of the age. Visiting Welsh bards such as Iolo Goch and Gruffudd Llwyd were as welcome in his house as they were at Sycharth.

Living, working and enjoying life at Hanmer's home, Glyndwr soon became friendly with his three sons, Gruffudd, John and Philip. The three boys became long-lasting comrades of Owain, men whose influence and help would follow him into adulthood and his forthcoming revolt.

Perhaps more important than his friendship with the three brothers, Glyndwr was strongly attracted to Margaret, the daughter of David Hanmer. It was no mere infatuation and as time went on it was clear that his feelings were reciprocated. Little is known about Margaret's character but she appears to have been an attractive and compassionate woman who understood the complexities of her lover's make-up and personality.

At some stage towards the end of the 1370s Owain Glyndwr was sent – possibly at the urging of David Hanmer and with the agreement of the Earl of Arundel – to the Inns of Court at Westminster. He took easily to the routine and life in London at what was, effectively, a finishing school for the upwardly mobile. At the Inns of Court young men like

Glyndwr not only learned about the law and government but also how to behave in the very best of society.

Despite claims from some writers that he was at the Inns of Court for seven years, it is likely that his stay in London was somewhat shorter than that. It probably lasted, at most, for just three or four years. Even so, it was a significant period in his life. He met important people, was called as a witness in one of the most notable lawsuits of the day between two nobles, and enjoyed the fine dining of the nation's capital.

Glyndwr was in London during the Peasants' Revolt of 1381, although he took no part in the final destruction of Wat Tyler's army. He would have felt the panic of the people, the lords and ladies in particular, and noticed the behaviour of the great and the good when the going got tough. In his description of events, the chronicler John Froissart – although violently opposed to the aims of the revolt – did quote part of a sermon from the radical priest John Ball: 'We are called slaves, and if we do not perform our service we are beaten, and we have no sovereign to whom we can complain or who would be willing to hear us. Let us go to the King, and remonstrate with him; he is young and from him we may obtain a favourable answer, and if not we must ourselves seek to amend our condition.'[5]

The threat, of course, comes in the last part of the quotation. It was a time of huge political unrest, the peasants and working men of Britain attempting to shrug off the old laws and rules of servitude which had kept them beaten down and in thrall to the nobles of the land for more years than anyone cared to remember. Unlike so many others, most of the lords and nobles cowering out of the line of fire, the ending of the Peasants' Revolt saw the 14-year-old King Richard II at his best, certainly at his most courageous.

While it remains supposition, Glyndwr's long-lasting admiration for a king who, in 1381, had not yet reached his majority might well owe something to the closing moments of the rebellion at Smithfield. There, at the climax of the revolt, while his chancellor, the Archbishop of Canterbury, was murdered in the Tower, Richard bravely faced down thousands of angry men baying for his blood.

Despite the validity of their grievances, Wat Tyler, Jack Straw and John Ball were either killed or executed and their followers put to flight. It could so easily have gone the other way and King Richard, for the moment at least, basked in the glory of his victory.

Glyndwr had no intention of becoming a lawyer like David Hanmer, but those aspects of the English law which he had studied would stand him in good stead in the future. He did, however, want to be Hanmer's son-in-law and by 1383 he was back in Wales. That is the year when, it is commonly supposed, Owain Glyndwr and Margaret Hanmer were married. They settled down to married life at Sycharth, but for Owain at least that was only a temporary sojourn.

If Owain Glyndwr had ambitions in the knightly field – and it appears from his time with the Earl of Arundel that he did – he would have known that connections alone were not enough. To be a knight he had to act like a knight. He enjoyed jousting and was apparently very good at it. According to the poet Gruffudd Llwyd, his fame as a competitor in the tilting yard was renowned:

> He will win, whenever he wishes,
> boots, fine buskins
> of speckled cordovan – bold powerful stag –
> jousting in a tournament,
> bruising bodies, overthrowing a hundred.[6]

Jousting was fun, but if he wanted to advance his career and push his claims for a knighthood nothing could substitute for the real thing. In March 1384, Owain Glyndwr entered English military service when he mustered for garrison duties at Berwick-on-Tweed under the renowned Welsh warrior Sir Gregory Sais. He was accompanied by his brother Tudur and by his friend John Hanmer.

Sir Gregory Sais was a native of Flintshire, his name 'Sais' (translated into English *as* 'English') deriving from the fact that he spoke the language, not that he actually *was* English. He was, however, one of the most notable Welsh warriors of his day, being called 'a second St George' by Gruffudd Llwyd. Owain Glyndwr, as he headed north, following Sir Gregory's fluttering pennants, must have thrilled at the prospect of serving under such a notable character.[7]

Despite Glyndwr's enthusiasm, and despite Gregory's fame as a war leader, garrison duty at Berwick appears to have been a fairly low-key period of service. But it was Owain's first time as a soldier and the experience, with its long periods of inactivity and boredom, would have given the young man a taste of what soldiering was really all about.

In 1385 he again took up arms, serving once again as a soldier in the army of King Richard II, this time campaigning north of the Scottish border. No significant battle was fought but there were skirmishes and regular patrols into enemy territory. Glyndwr impressed everyone with his courage, fighting and charging in the van even when, on one potentially lethal occasion, his lance snapped and left him virtually unarmed. Already he was beginning to earn the admiration of the men under his command.

Yet more military service came in the spring of 1387 when he was enlisted as a member of the personal retinue of the Earl of Arundel for a campaign against the French. According to historian Glanmor Williams, this was a seminal moment for Glyndwr who was clearly well thought of by Arundel, being 'numbered eighth among the earl's esquires and his brother Tudur twentieth.'[8]

The earl was in command of an army of nearly 3,000 men and a fleet of sixty warships. Glyndwr was now gaining new experiences of warfare and beginning to realise that sea power was a significant factor in most military campaigns. Arundel was opposed by a combined Franco-Castilian- Flemish fleet that was made up of between 250 and 300 ships and many thousands of soldiers.

The expedition concluded in March 1387 with the Battle of Margate, which resulted in the total defeat of the French, England's first victory at sea for nearly twenty years. It was undoubtedly a victory that prevented a potential Franco-Spanish invasion of England.

There was disappointment for Owain Glyndwr, however. In the wake of Arundel's victory many of the esquires of his retinue were knighted by a grateful King Richard. For some reason Glyndwr was not included in their number. It was an oversight, or evidence of neglect, which troubled the Welshman and began to whittle away at the core of his loyalty to both Arundel and the king.

So far Owain Glyndwr had enjoyed considerable success in his short military career. However, he was about to realise that feats of arms were only one aspect of life as a soldier. Politics was also a significant factor and in a turbulent period like the 1380s and 1390s his patron, the Earl of Arundel, was up to his neck in deceit, manipulation and political manoeuvring.

Arundel was one of many nobles who were becoming increasingly unhappy with King Richard. At this distance it is almost impossible to say whether the disgruntlement of this influential group reflected the mood of the country or if the ordinary men and women of England took their lead from the nobles. Either way, by the time he achieved his majority, King Richard II had become one of the most disliked sovereigns the country had yet seen.

There were many reasons for the discord, not least being Richard's desire for peace with France, a stance that was in direct contrast to the wishes of the country's warlike elite. There was money in war, not to mention glory, fame and the opportunity to release tensions that would have been coiled like gigantic springs inside the minds of these simplistic but deadly men.

Then there was the old complaint. Richard had a distinct inclination to gather 'favourites' to his side, men whose advice he would invariably seek and take, regardless of the views of more experienced courtiers. Jealousy invariably raised its head and the king was more than capable of playing off one group of courtiers against the other.

There were rumours of homosexual cliques in Richard's court of favourites, and the image presented by the king was of a monarch more concerned with art and culture than with the guidance of his people. Richard seemed not to be aware of his negative image, at least not to begin with, and was committed to the concept of the divinity of kings. He was king because God had decided that it would be so and, therefore, he would tolerate no opposition to his views and ideas.

While Richard was still a minor, the Earl of Arundel had been an important member of the Regency Council where he, along with his friend – and uncle of the king – the Duke of Gloucester, took great pleasure in thwarting Richard at every opportunity. When the Regency Council mutated into an advisory body Arundel and Gloucester continued with their negative and critical approach.

By the summer of 1387 the rogue pairing of Arundel and Gloucester were at the head of a growing clique of troublesome and self-seeking noblemen, the Lords Appellant as they were called. Finally the king had had enough. In a fit of pique he replaced both Arundel and Gloucester on his council, inserting men of his own choosing, a group that inevitably became known as 'the King's Favourites'.

It was a slight that neither Arundel nor Gloucester was prepared to take. Call it demotion, call it dismissal, it was not to be tolerated. Neither of them had faith in Richard and to be treated like this was one insult too many. Tension exploded into anger, insults were exchanged and both groups gathered their forces around them. There was a brief stand-off, but then in December, at the Battle of Radcot Bridge, Arundel and Gloucester defeated 'the Favourites' and forced themselves back onto the king's council. They promptly had their opponents condemned to death by what was quickly, and accurately, dubbed the Merciless Parliament.

Richard fumed, particularly when the Earl of Arundel refused clemency, even though Richard's queen, Anne of Bohemia, had gone on her knees to beg mercy for Sir Simon de Burley, one of the condemned. In the wake of the executions there appeared to be some degree of reconciliation between the two men but in reality King Richard never forgave Arundel for the humiliation he and his new wife had suffered.

It was a period that was latent with hostility, but, for the moment, the peace seemed to hold. There were exceptions, though. In 1394, when the earl turned up late for the funeral of Anne, the king struck Arundel across the face and drew blood. It was put down to Richard's grief which was intense (he even had Sheen Manor, where she died, pulled down) and for the moment at least Arundel was still in a position of power. However, for those who had Richard's ear it was clear that the earl was living on borrowed time.

Owain Glyndwr was not directly involved with the in-fighting and thrusting for power but he must have looked on with growing concern. He had always liked Richard and had been happy to serve him whenever he could. The other contender for power, the Earl of Arundel, had been his first and arguably his most important patron.

In 1388, however, there appears to have been some sort of falling out between Glyndwr and his powerful friends. Early that year Glyndwr was listed as a member of Arundel's retinue for an invasion of France, but a line through his name indicates that he did not actually take part. Whether he withdrew from the expedition or was removed by someone else is not immediately obvious. No explanation for the withdrawal was given.

Even now Glyndwr's reasons remain unclear. If he removed himself an important question has to be asked: was that withdrawal down to his unhappiness about the actions of the king, or the earl, as they struggled for control?

There were other possibilities. Maybe Owain simply wanted to spend more time with his family – simplistic but possible. Then again, he might no longer be trusted, either by the king or by the earl, and was therefore removed from the list against his wishes. Or had all of the manipulation and treachery of the previous few years finally got to him? If that were the case Owain Glyndwr would certainly have been confident enough to stand on his principles and withdraw from what was guaranteed to be a financially rewarding exercise.

During his service with the king in Scotland, Glyndwr had witnessed huge antagonism between the monarch and the Earl of Northumberland, head of the powerful and truculent local Percy family. The Percys were probably the most powerful and famous of all the barons and nobles – they were also the most ambitious. Add in the skulduggery and in-fighting of the recent past and there remains the very real possibility that Owain Glyndwr had simply grown sick and tired of it all.

The questions might now be unanswerable but what is equally unclear is the matter of his loyalty to the Crown. Just where did that loyalty now lie? And if it remained was it loyalty to the concept of monarchy or to the person of Richard II?

Whatever reasons he may have had for declining the offer of further service in the name of the king, Owain Glyndwr remained at home in Powys rather than take the opportunity to gain more military glory in France. There is a slim possibility that he was recruited to serve with King Richard during the campaign in Ireland in 1394, but there is no written record to confirm or deny this and, to all intents and purposes, Owain Glyndwr's last service to the English Crown was in the campaign of 1387.

Certainly by 1397 he was out of contact with the Earl of Arundel. And in that year King Richard II finally stepped forward to take his long-awaited revenge. In July Arundel and Gloucester were arrested and put on trial for plotting against the life of the king.

Gloucester died in the English garrison at Calais while awaiting trial, thereby very conveniently circumventing Richard's acknowledged dilemma about executing a close member of the royal family. There were rumours that he had been killed on Richard's instructions. Given Richard's festering hatred of the duke, that is more than likely, but in the eyes of the people the king's hands remained unsullied.

With Arundel there were no such reservations. He was not a member of the royal family, just a normal power-hungry nobleman. He was arraigned for treason and hauled in front of the Lords where he was duly found guilty by his peers and sentenced to death. The sentence was carried out on 21 September 1397. 'Do not tarry long,' Arundel told the executioner, 'strike off my head in one blow.'

Killing Gloucester and Arundel was the start of a period that has since become known as King Richard's Tyranny. At last, Richard felt, he could do what he had wanted to do for months, years even. It was a momentous if terrifying time, at least for the king's enemies.

Having removed his most dangerous opponents he was now free to take out any of the other noblemen who had opposed him. There were many disaffected nobles, and, as far as Richard was concerned, scores that needed to be settled. Chief among these waiting victims were the Lancastrian patriarch John of Gaunt and his children.

The son of John of Gaunt, Henry Bolingbroke, had been one of the main participants in the manoeuvrings of 1387 when so many of Richard's favourites had been removed or killed. The king suspected that the hand of John of Gaunt had been involved somewhere but John himself remained too strong to attack. His son was not, and before very long Richard decided to strike.

*****

The execution of the Earl of Arundel was a major blow for Owain Glyndwr. He had already lost his other patron, his father-in-law, David Hanmer, who had died ten years before. Now the death of Arundel left him alone, bereft of all forms of patronage and with little hope of extending either his reputation or his position in society.

He had no option but to put his ambitions on hold and retire to his home at Sycharth. He was not exactly on the poverty line; indeed, by the standards of the time he was more than well off. His house was comfortable, luxurious even, and there he would content himself with dreams of past glory and with bringing up his children.

Glyndwr and Margaret Hanmer had six sons and three daughters. The boys were Gruffudd, Madog, Maredudd, Thomas, John and David, although some accounts say that David was an illegitimate child. The daughters were Alys, Jonet (or Janet) and Margaret. There were also, not unusually for the time, a number of illegitimate offspring, children for whom Margaret Hanmer cared as if they were her own.

To some extent it was an idyllic time for Owain, attending to his estates and fulfilling his role as one of the main landowners of northern Powys. On the outside at least he seemed content.

The men and women of the Marches were happy to have him among them once more. He may not have achieved great standing in England, but along the border counties between England and Wales he was a man of position and influence, a wealthy *uchelwyr* and someone who was greatly respected, even loved.

And yet in the dark reaches of the night, when the wind howled like a fusillade of strident trumpet calls around the corners of the house, Owain Glyndwr must have twisted in regret and bitterness. He would not have been human had he not harboured at least some troubled thoughts. Turning thoughts into action took time, however, and Owain Glyndwr was not a man to be hurried.

Apart from support and comfort from Margaret, and possibly his brother Tudur, by 1397 he would have been a resentful and disturbed man, beset by dreams of what might have been. He was undoubtedly disillusioned but if there is one word to describe his state of mind at this time it has to be 'disappointed'.

When he looked back at what he had achieved over the past few years it was plain to see that it could, and perhaps should, have been so much better. Despite his fine house and respected position it was still very much 'local glory'. He had been denied the real accoutrements of success – formal recognition and a position at court – and with every passing month the snub grew greater. Slowly but surely it bit deeper into his soul.

His main gripe was that, despite his success on the battlefield, he had failed to win the knighthood that would establish his position in society and mark him out as being different, being superior to other men. So a knighthood was an honour he coveted. It was undoubtedly something that he believed was his due.

After the campaigns on the borders and in Scotland, and victory in the Battle of Margate, it is difficult to see why he had not been honoured. So many others had been singled out, but not Owain Glyndwr. In a fit of Welsh self-indulgence or self-pity he might have been excused for thinking it was because of his nationality – perhaps, after all, the country could only afford one Gregory Sais.

All of his life Glyndwr had been conscious of destiny. The bards had sung so often about a Welsh redeemer, many of them even choosing the name Owain to fix to this long-awaited character. He would have been remarkably self-effacing not to think that maybe, just maybe, he was the man the Welsh were waiting for.

He must have guessed that in the eyes of many, the gentry and *uchelwyr* in particular, he had all the virtues and attributes required in such a saviour. He was brave, fearless in battle, but caring and compassionate to those less fortunate than himself. He could be relied on to offer fair judgement and had a genuine interest in the ordinary working men and women of Wales. When it was needed he could be ruthless, even brutal, something was appreciated by those under his command and by the colleagues who fought alongside him.

Owain Glyndwr undoubtedly had the breeding. He had the heritage and he also had the experience of war that any leader in the medieval world needed to possess. But he had been overlooked for honours and for position.

Above all, he would, at times, have felt let down by the system, by the state, even by the young king whom he still respected and liked. As the months passed and there was no sign of belated recognition it was inevitable that disillusionment should begin to set in.

Betrayed would probably be too strong a word to describe Owain's feelings, at least at this stage, but in the truly introverted and defensive attitude of the thwarted Welshman he must have wondered if his time had come and passed him by. There could be no answer to that, but it did add a huge volume of regret to Glyndwr's already troubled mind.

He was not the type of man to stew in his discomfort. There was always a purpose behind his actions and beliefs. He would have analysed things, thought them through until they had been put into perspective in his mind. But that very state of mind could not have made him an easy person to live with and accept. Margaret Hanmer might fume or fret but, unlike her husband, there was nothing she could do about it. For her there were household duties to carry out, for Glyndwr there was only the emptiness of unfulfilled dreams.

Put simply, he had restlessness and a series of wishes or desires that would not let him go. And now, wherever his thoughts took him, his greatest, most significant dream was becoming increasingly centred on the Welsh people.

Once again there is a Biblical comparison, this time with the Old Testament prophet Moses, who led his people out of bondage and humiliation in Egypt. Could he, Owain Glyndwr, Lord of Glyndyfrdwy, be the man to lead the Welsh out of their state of captivity?

Since the Norman Conquest there had always been Welshmen of honour who refused to accept the oversight of England and maintained the spirit of their country's independence. After the death of Llewelyn the Last many of these had been forced to live abroad, earning their living as mercenary soldiers and warriors.

Owain Lawgoch had been a typical example. He understood the tactics and the political strategy of the times, but above all he was a fearless warrior, even defeating Gregory Sais in one campaign when he was fighting for the French. The two men were household names in Wales.

But after Lawgoch was murdered by an English agent in 1378 there seemed to be no immediate Welsh successor. The mantle of leadership may not have settled on Owain Glyndwr, not yet, but it was certainly hovering over his shoulders.

Sitting comfortably in Sycharth, surrounded by family and friends, Glyndwr was as open as anyone to the silver words and prophesies of the visiting bards. Omens and prophecies were a part of medieval life and Glyndwr had immense belief in these links to the past. Their influence over what was to happen next in Glyndwr's life should never be underestimated.

It is not difficult to make an assessment of his state of mind and his disposition in the final years of the fourteenth century. It was troubled and uncertain, and if he had been twenty or thirty years younger he would have been called, at least in today's parlance, 'a mixed-up kid'. By 1399, though, he was no 'kid'. On the threshold of medieval old age, he was experienced in war and well versed in the running of farms and estates. He was caring about the men and women in his domains and was respected by almost everyone. (The term 'almost everyone' is important, as we shall see.)

Owain Glyndwr might well have been disappointed and unhappy with the way he had been treated by the king, but he was still unable to shake off the last vestiges of loyalty to the Crown. That would only come later.

He would also have had a vivid sense of history combined with several other important factors: genuine understanding of his heritage; compassion for the working men and women of Wales; susceptibility to the images of men like Iolo Goch. Add in a strong dose of disillusionment and resentment over his treatment and you come up with a pretty potent brew, one that was gradually simmering over a period of months. He had never been one to act quickly or unexpectedly, always preferring to consider his options before finally making a move.

Whatever the move might eventually turn out to be, it had invariably been well thought through. Now, in the troubled and troublesome 1390s, the brew was bubbling its way up the stew pot. Soon it would begin to boil over, and, for a man like Owain Glyndwr, once that heady mixture reached boiling point it was inevitably going to be explosive.

He might have sat and thought for weeks, even for months on end, but when the time came his actions would be decisive. Then, as those who knew him well would testify, somebody was going to be seriously and very badly hurt.

Glyndwr has been accused of being a psychopath, and the slow burn of his emotions, rising steadily until they can be contained no longer, might be taken as proof of this. We would need to be there at his side before making any sort of accurate judgement about this.

Suffice to say that Owain Glyndwr kept his emotions in check, sitting there thinking and planning until something triggered their release. His fury was not the red-blooded anger normally associated with the Welsh. It was cold and it was calculated. From the beginning Glyndwr knew what he was going to do, maybe not then, not at that precise moment in time, but soon. If that is the behaviour of a psychopath so be it.

Sit and think he certainly did. But increasingly the poems of men such as Iolo Goch, and, in particular, Gruffudd Llwyd fuelled the idea that while he, Glyndwr, might be relatively content and secure the people of Wales were suffering more and more under the increased oppression of the English.

The message that Gruffudd Llwyd gave to the people was not the romantic and idyllic memory of the past that so many of the bards loved to offer. Far from it, his world was one of deprivation and neglect:

> A gloomy world, a transitory life,
> is this, as far as the sun shines.
> It is full – and no-one is happy –
> with a surfeit on the one side
> of goods for those who had no need.[9]

Gruffudd was perhaps the most pessimistic of all the wandering bards. He was also one of the most popular and the doors of Sycharth and other *uchelwyr* holdings were always open to a man of his skill and passion.

His words seem to catch much of the discontent of the time, discontent that simmered, hidden but waiting to be brought out, in the beating hearts of the Welsh nation. He was also not above using his talents to goad the people into anger and action:

> The Welsh, because their oppression is so great,
> are a kindred of wretches like drunken crows.
> I could – I would not beg for gain –
> call them a kettle of tripe.[10]

It was brutal stuff, shocking in its intensity, but it was a fairly accurate picture of the time. The more he listened to the words of Gruffudd Llwyd the closer Glyndwr came to making the momentous decision to do something about the unhappiness of the Welsh nation.

The anger and the hurt were there, and they feature time and time again in Gruffudd's poems. All that was needed was a spark, something to ignite the flames of rebellion. The Welsh had their 'leader in waiting' – now they simply needed something to start the war.

Chapter Four

Rebellion

The Welsh rebellion – Owain Glyndwr's war – cannot be looked at in isolation. It was part of a wider conflict, one that involved the deposing and killing of a king and the establishment of a usurper on the throne of England. It took place at a time when murder and mayhem were, if not daily occurrences then certainly regular events. It was a time when armies marched across the land, burning and pillaging as they went. In its brutality the era foreshadowed only too clearly the destruction of the later Wars of the Roses.

The tyranny of Richard II was short lived, barely two years, but it saw a seismic change in the upper echelons of English society. The arrest and execution of the Duke of Gloucester and the Earl of Arundel in 1397 had clearly unblocked some sort of dam in Richard's head, causing him to lose whatever little self-control he had possessed.

He had come to the throne early and had been fêted and lauded all through his childhood and adolescence. There was no doubt that he was brave, his performance during the Peasants' Revolt had shown that, but Richard was sadly lacking in judgement. As an absolute ruler he had no reason to be self-critical or to question either his ability or his actions. Whatever he did was right, it had to be – after all, he was the king.

Now, following the success of his coup against Arundel and Gloucester, Richard felt all-powerful. When, in 1398, his position was made even more comfortable by the sudden death of another 'enemy', Roger Mortimer, the Earl of March, his emotions began to surge and propel him forwards.

Suddenly the king's natural desire for dictatorial rule burst into the open. Unlike most mediaeval monarchs, Richard had very little in the way of guidance or assistance from older, wiser nobles. He was alone and made his mistakes alone.

One of the first things he did was to remember his antipathy towards the Duchy of Lancaster and banish his cousin Henry Bolingbroke, the son of John of Gaunt. The popular and powerful Bolingbroke, Henry of Lancaster to give him his correct title, was perceived as a major threat and exile seemed an appropriate way to deal with this potential opponent. It was mistake number one – Richard would have done better to kill him.

Perhaps luckily for John, decidedly unluckily for Richard, Bolingbroke's father, John of Gaunt, Duke of Lancaster, died in 1399, less than twelve months after his son had been exiled. Rather than allow Bolingbroke to return and claim his rightful lands, Richard took them himself and refused permission for the exiled Lancastrian to come back from France – mistake number two.

After that the situation might have dissipated, or at least eased a little, but for the thorny and seemingly interminable problem of Ireland.

The strangely named but still powerful Art MacMurrough-Kavanagh, King of Leinster, already an implacable enemy of the English Crown, now took the opportunity to rise in open rebellion. With powerful Marcher Lords like Arundel, John of Gaunt and the Earl of March out of the picture, Art seized his chance. Obviously, to him it seemed like the ideal moment to challenge the English Crown.

Richard, having disposed of the very men who would otherwise, at his command, have waged war against MacMurrough, had no choice but to deal with the problem himself. That was mistake number three. In Ireland he would be 'out of the loop' and the style of government he had recently imposed demanded that Richard be present to keep control of the situation.

The king hastily gathered together an army and in the early summer of 1399 sailed for Ireland. He had barely set foot on Irish soil when he heard the news he dreaded – Henry Bolingbroke had landed at Ravenspur in Yorkshire with a small band of well-armed supporters.

Bolingbroke marched south. His intention, at this early stage, was simply to administer a sharp slap on the wrist to his cousin and reclaim the lands that were rightfully his. Any thoughts he might have harboured about seizing the crown were lodged away at the back of his mind.

However, as he moved southwards more and more people flocked to his banner. He had landed with barely 300 followers, though, according to some reports, within a week this figure had grown to nearly 100,000. The number is probably a gross exaggeration, but as he marched more and more voices began to whisper in Bolingbroke's ear. It was clear that Richard's unpopularity had intensified during the few months Bolingbroke had been away. And no matter how he might try to push it away, a seed had been planted in Henry's mind.

Faced by growing acclaim from the public and with the unpopularity of Richard now firmly lodged in his consciousness, Henry Bolingbroke began to adapt his ideas and his aim, although for the moment he did not declare them openly. To his immediate advisors, however, he eventually made it clear – he would dislodge Richard from the kingship and take the throne himself.

For some reason Richard delayed his return from Ireland, but at last he realised that he had no option other than to confront Henry Bolingbroke. Leaving most of his army in Ireland he landed in Milford Haven on 24 July and moved north towards Conwy. He had always enjoyed a groundswell of support in North Wales and its immediate borders, and hoped to gather together enough soldiers to wipe out any challenge from a man he saw as no more than a returned Lancastrian renegade.

In fact, the opposite occurred. Once holed up in Conwy Castle, Richard found himself bereft of supporters. They did not so much leave him – as has been claimed – they simply did not turn up. Richard was dismayed and totally perplexed, not understanding the mood of the people.

Desperate now to find support, he changed location, moving to the castle at Flint. This powerful fortress was closer to the border and what he hoped would be his strongest card, the previously loyal city of Chester. The change did Richard no good at all. The few followers he had managed to hold onto simply melted away and when Bolingbroke, accompanied by thousands of supporters, appeared outside the castle walls the king decided that he had no choice but to surrender.

According to legend, Richard promised to abdicate, provided he was allowed to live. He changed his mind once he and Bolingbroke had made the long journey to London, with Richard riding in ignominy behind Bolingbroke the whole way. His change of heart made no difference. Richard was formally deposed on 1 October 1399 and Henry Bolingbroke was crowned king just two weeks later.

Bolingbroke, Henry IV as he now became, had a relatively poor claim to the throne. Richard had been deposed because, through his tyranny and misrule, he had shown himself unfit to be king. No one argued with that. There were others, however, who had a better claim to the throne than Bolingbroke, notably Edmund Mortimer, 5th Earl of March. Mortimer was the great-grandson of Edward III's second child, Henry Bolingbroke a descendent of the third.

However, Mortimer's descent was through the female line, whereas Henry's from the male. That was enough to convince Parliament and the nobles that Henry was the most appropriate candidate. Perhaps more importantly, he claimed the throne by might, having disposed of Richard by the power of the sword. At the time it did not worry Henry. Only later, as Glyndwr's rebellion grew in significance, did his right to be king begin to trouble his conscience.

At first Richard was lodged, briefly, in the Tower. That, however, was too public and he was soon taken out and carried down the Thames by barge. Coming ashore somewhere in the Essex marshes he was slowly and gradually moved northwards.

To begin with Henry was disposed to let Richard live, but news of a plot by some of the former king's favourites changed his mind. The plot was unravelled, the ringleaders executed and Richard died in Pontefract Castle in February 1400, starved to death, probably on the orders of the new king.

*****

So where does Owain Glyndwr fit into this world of chance and chicanery? In the early stages he was a mere bystander, playing no part in the momentous events that were unfolding around him. But in less than a year everything had changed. The whole of Wales seemed to be up in arms against the English Crown and Owain Glyndwr was occupying the central role in a drama of earth-shattering proportions. It was, to continue the analogy, an astronomical switch.

Richard II had always had great affection for the Welsh and maintained something of a prejudice in their favour. That had led, until at least the final moments of his reign, to something of a false position for the king. He knew that he had always enjoyed considerable support in the Principality – particularly from men like the Tudor brothers of Anglesey – and derived a degree of comfort from that fact. In 1399 there was no reason to suppose that anything had changed.

But then, fatally as it turned out, Welsh support seemed to just ebb away. Whatever the reason, Glyndwr's lack of response or reaction to the crisis was typical of the attitude of the *uchelwyr* at this time. It was to prove fatal for Richard.

Despite his undoubted disappointment at the lack of formal recognition for his previous service to the Crown, Owain Glyndwr does seem to have retained something of his affection for Richard. Given those feelings, in 1399 he might have been expected to weigh in on Richard's behalf, but obviously the hurt and neglect he had suffered had cut deep. He made no move to help the king and issued no statement in support or in his defence.

The other option, of course, would have been for Glyndwr to throw in his lot with Bolingbroke. There is no reason to suppose they did not know each other, and they had possibly even campaigned together in the past. If Glyndwr had been disgruntled and angry at Richard then support for the opposition at this crucial moment might have been one way to proceed. He chose not to take that option, but instead kept a low profile during the events that were taking place in the summer and autumn of 1399.

When the new dynasty was established, Glyndwr seems, at first, to have accepted it. He had no great love for the new monarch, although some historians claim that he had served as an esquire for Henry Bolingbroke during the campaign that culminated with the Battle of Radcot Bridge in 1397. There is no proof of that, but such an enlistment might well have been expected of him, demanded even, by his patron Arundel who was then intent on re-establishing his position as one of the first lords in the land. Even if Glyndwr had served Bolingbroke as an esquire that does not necessarily mean that they had to like each other.

Whatever his feelings, Glyndwr remained decidedly neutral during the constitutional crisis of 1397. Considering his later actions, that must have been a hard position to maintain as the great events of that autumn were taking place almost on his doorstep at Conwy and Flint.

His position might have been unclear, or not easy to understand, but by his very inaction he was expressing acceptance of the status quo. That was surely how the other men of note would have seen it and we therefore make the assumption – and it is no more than an assumption – that Glyndwr maintained his support for Richard until the very end.[1]

However, during the twelve months between Richard's deposition and his own first foray into the world of rebellion Owain Glyndwr seems to have undergone a radical change of heart. By September 1400, he was no longer content to patiently and quietly sit out the turbulent times. He finally seized his chance to create an independent Wales.

The immediate spur might well have been a personal slight by Reginald Grey, Lord of Ruthin, followed by a snub from the new king, but from the beginning of his revolt Glyndwr was clear about his aim. He was intending to bring about an end to English rule in Wales.

He had sat and pondered this for many months. He had witnessed the chaos of English dynastic quarrels and the execution of men like his patron the Earl of Arundel. He had experienced at first hand the selfishness of the English nobility and now, fuelled by the bardic poems and prophesies that he had been fed all his life, he was spurred into action.

While it was time to actually do something about the situation in Wales, Glyndwr knew that his first target would be his neighbour and clear favourite with the new king, Lord Grey of Ruthin.

Before that, however, there was an important proclamation to be made. On 16 September 1400, over 300 men and women from all over Wales came to Glyndwr's house at Glyndyfrdwy to see and hear him presented to the people as the true Prince of Wales. It was an open and direct challenge to the Crown, as Henry IV, following the tradition established by King Edward I, had earlier that year already declared his eldest son Henry of Monmouth to be Prince of Wales.

Importantly, all sections of Welsh society were represented at the Glyndyfrdwy gathering. From carpenters and labourers to soldiers, churchmen and *uchelwyr*, they came from all over the country to proclaim him Prince of Wales. It was the start of what Glyndwr had always intended to be a people's rebellion.

His brother Tudur and his Hanmer relatives and in-laws were there, along with Hywel Cyffin, the Dean of St Asaph. Also present was a strange little man by the name of Crach Ffinnant. He was Glyndwr's personal prophet, his first name meaning 'dwarf' or 'scabby', the second being the area from which he hailed.

Crach Ffinnant had served with Owain and Tudur in Scotland back in 1385 and if Iolo Goch had become the house poet at Sycharth then Crach had manoeuvred himself into the position of house seer. Glyndwr, with his innate belief in prophecy, was notoriously superstitious and the presence of a man like Crach Ffinnant was important in the enterprise that was just beginning.

Evidence given at a court sitting in Oswestry on 6 October 1400 listed Owain's brother Tudur, his prophet, Crach Ffinnant, the Hanmers and dozens of the attendees, adding as a 'catch all' that many other Welshmen – unnamed but known – were also there: 'Treasonably plotting, conspiring and intending the death and disinheriting of the said Lord King (Henry IV) and the everlasting extinction of the said crown and regality of himself and all of his successors, the kings of England; the death of Henry, Prince of Wales, the first born son of our said king, of all the magnates and nobles of England; and also the death, destruction and the everlasting extinction of the whole English language.[2]

Glyndwr had probably chosen Glyndyfrdwy over Sycharth because of its location, remote and hidden, miles from any centre of population. It ensured that while dozens of supporters and would-be supporters were present, one particular group of people would *not* be there – the sheriffs, officials and officers of the English Crown.

By adopting the title Prince of Wales, self-proclaimed and rightful as it might be, Owain Glyndwr was making a statement to King Henry IV. He, not the English Crown with all its force and majesty, was in control of Wales and he was about to prove it.

With the investiture over it was time for Glyndwr to turn his attention towards the Lord of Ruthin. He and Lord Grey had been on bad terms with each other for some time. It had begun with a dispute over land and the boundary between Grey's territory and Glyndwr's. The area in question was common land known locally as The Crosses, but in the early part of 1399 Grey had seized it, illegally Glyndwr claimed. Rather than resort to violence, Glyndwr referred the matter to Parliament for an objective and honest judgement.

When a new Parliament met in the spring of 1400 Owain Glyndwr was appalled to find that its members were totally disinterested in his claim and rejected it out of hand. When the Bishop of St Asaph cautioned them that such reckless behaviour might cause an outcry amongst the Welsh the reply was curt: 'What care we for the barefoot rascals?'

Glyndwr made a further appeal to Henry IV but the new king, rather like his Parliament, dismissed it with just the most cursory of notice. He was on friendly terms with Reginald Grey; Glyndwr had been the protégée of the dead and disgraced Earl of Arundel and his value to Henry was minimal.

Things quickly went from bad to worse with Grey realising he held the whip hand over his neighbour. When Owain sent him a letter threatening that he would 'burn and slay' within his lands, Grey retaliated in the same fashion. In the original letter Glyndwr had apparently boasted that he had already stolen horses from Grey's land. This, Grey said, was criminal behaviour and he would refer the matter to Henry's council.

Glyndwr knew that, while his own appeal to Parliament and the king had been a disaster, Henry was far more likely to take Grey's referral seriously. Whichever way he looked at the problem, Glyndwr could see only further unhappiness and rejection.

That was not the end of the dispute. There is still a belief or myth that in the summer of 1400 the king sent Glyndwr a letter ordering him to join the force he was assembling to invade Scotland. The letter was sent via Reginald, Grey but the Lord of Ruthin held onto the summons. It appeared as if Owain was deliberately ignoring the king's summons – not exactly treasonous but certainly guaranteed to put Glyndwr in Henry's bad books.

Such behaviour was possible. Given the rancorous relationship between the two men, anything was possible. But why Henry should send a personal letter to Glyndwr through a man like Lord Grey has never been properly explained. If it did happen it is one more reason why Glyndwr and Grey hated each other so much.

On 18 September, just two days after he was proclaimed Prince of Wales, Owain Glyndwr struck. He and approximately 250 followers attacked and plundered the town of Ruthin. The place was full of farmers and merchants with their produce, all there for the annual St Matthews Day Fair which was to be held in a few days' time. What they could not steal the avenging Welsh burned or overturned in the mud and the townspeople ran in terror from the charging horses. It was, in the words of the English officials, a 'cavalry attack'.

With Ruthin sacked, Glyndwr might have been excused for sitting back on his laurels. If the cause of his rebellion was simply his dispute with Lord Grey, that is what he probably would have done. But Glyndwr had wider and deeper motives than simply paying back Reginald Grey. He had proclaimed himself Prince of Wales, and even now, at this very early stage, he was determined and intent on gaining independence for his people.

After Ruthin he moved on to challenge seven of the English boroughs: Oswestry, Welshpool, Denbigh, Flint, Rhuddlan, Hawarden and Holt. Glyndwr's technique was simple. He used speed, moving from one township to the next before anyone quite realised what was happening. Undefended and not expecting an attack, all of the towns fell easily and quickly, one after the other, to the rampaging Welsh.

Glyndwr's rising was destined not to be an isolated occurrence. At the same time as he was attacking Ruthin, his cousins, Rhys and Gwilym ap Tudor, also rose up in rebellion against the Crown on the island of Anglesey. It was immaculate timing although it is unlikely that the two rebellions were coordinated or planned to begin at the same time.

Rhys and Gwilym ap Tudor had been firm supporters of Richard II and they, like Glyndwr, resented both the coming of a new king and the appointment of his son, Henry of Monmouth, as Prince of Wales. That was not all. They had taken more particular offence at one of the king's recent actions. They were infuriated by Henry's decision to pass the control and management of North Wales to the Percy family of Northumberland – in particular to the young scion of the dynasty, Harry Hotspur.

The Percys were an ambitious, warlike family from the north of England. They were amongst the most powerful noblemen in the country, but prior to Hotspur's appointment they had had no previous contact with North Wales. To them it was an alien land, as wild as the Scottish territories that bordered their own possessions in Northumbria.

The Percys had a tenuous, not to say fickle alliance with the English Crown, always having seen themselves as separate from the nobles of England. They were, they believed, feudal lords of their own fiefdom where, to misquote an earlier adage about Wales, 'the king's writ did not run.'

Their relationship with the new king was no different and there was always the lurking thought that if Henry could usurp the throne they could easily do the same. It did not take a genius to see that there would be trouble ahead.

Nevertheless, Hotspur accepted his appointment in North Wales. It was done somewhat reluctantly it has to be admitted. It was certainly an unpopular move in the rest of the country and the two Tudor brothers on Anglesey, like many Welsh landowners, simmered with resentment. They were of the firm belief that any power or control over them and their lands in Anglesey must be carried out only by a native-born Welshman.

*****

While his cousins were marshalling their troops on Anglesey, Glyndwr's fortunes fluctuated wildly and rapidly. Within a few days of capturing most of the important towns in north-east Wales the tables were well and truly turned. On 24 September, Glyndwr's forces were defeated in what was little more than a skirmish outside the town of Welshpool.

In the wake of the defeat many of those who had so exuberantly proclaimed him Prince of Wales less than two weeks before, including his brother Tudur and little Crach Ffinnant, now threw their hands into the air and begged forgiveness from the king. It was early and significant proof for Glyndwr that acclaim was a fickle master.

The defeat seemed to bear out the views of Giraldus Cambrensis who, many years before, had pronounced stern judgement on the quality of the Welsh as fighting men: 'Their sole idea of tactics is either to pursue their opponents or else run away from them. They are lightly armed and they rely more on their agility than on brute strength. It follows that they cannot meet the enemy on equal terms or fight violently for very long.'[3]

Glyndwr's situation now seemed desperate. He had taken his chance and won a few victories, but as soon as he had come up against a well-organised and disciplined enemy his troops were shown up for what they were – a loose collection of individuals more intent on plunder than on helping Glyndwr achieve his somewhat more esoteric aims.

The rebellion seemed to be over before it had really begun. Quite where that left Glyndwr was not clear. His band of rebels had scattered, as was gleefully reported to the king: 'Friday immediately following, on which day they were defeated and scattered by Master Hugh Burnell with many other liegemen of the aforementioned King from the counties of Salop, Stafford and Warwick [...] and then they fled, seeking the mountains and the woods, and very many of the said rebels returned to their own manors, behaving just as if they had not been previously in the forests.'[4]

Glyndwr knew he could not return home and went into hiding. The king, however, was not content with what appeared to be an easy victory. He had never trusted the Welsh and what he now did was against all the advice of his counsellors. They recommended that the king should simply ignore what was going on in Wales. The Welsh were always fighting and squabbling with each other, so leave them alone and they would soon grow tired of murder and mayhem, at least until next year.

Henry chose not to listen. He assembled an army to wipe out the threat once and for all. Knowing that Glyndwr had been defeated outside Welshpool, Henry decided to concentrate his efforts against the Tudors on Anglesey.

In actual fact the king understood his enemy far better than his advisors ever did. He knew that if the insurrection – Glyndwr's as well as the Tudors – was not snuffed out very rapidly it would grow. Wales was a tinderbox waiting to ignite, the people angry and frustrated by English rule. It was not the time for kid glove treatment, he had to act quickly.

Henry threw his army along the North Wales coast, pausing at Bangor and Caernarfon before wheeling south towards Mawddwy and then back to the border town of Shrewsbury. There was some irresolute skirmishing during his long march and a number of bandit or guerrilla attacks by the local Welshmen but no pitched battle took place. Henry burned several homesteads and farms, pillaged the fields and barns, but the opposition was limited. The majority of the Welsh were risking no chances and had taken refuge in the hills.

The greatest difficulty faced by the king during his march had been the ever-changeable weather, particularly the rain which seemed to come vertically down from the sky. Even so he had impressed the locals by his show of force. And, all in all, it *had* been a pretty impressive performance by Henry, one that had hammered home his power and strength. That had always been his main purpose.

As he rode out of Wales the king might have been excused for feeling satisfied. He had made his show of force; it was an expedition which he felt should have cowed the populace, especially with the march culminating in the confiscation of Glyndwr's estates. There had been little real challenge to his authority and all the while Glyndwr remained in hiding with, as Adam of Usk described it, no more than seven men to keep him company.

Henry should have been content and yet he was still furiously angry. When he looked back on the rebellion and his response to it he could not help feeling that he had not been strong enough. He, more than anyone, knew how fickle public opinion could be.

Something harder and more punitive was needed and the Welsh must be obliged to suffer even greater indignities. Despite being newly ensconced as king, eager to show his strength and power, it is still hard to see why Henry felt this approach was needed.

Already, on 28 September 1400, eight of Glyndwr's rebels, who had been captured before they could flee to the hills, were executed at Ruthin. It was, Henry felt, not enough. Then in March of the following year he had made his solemn and dramatic hike through North Wales. It was still not enough. Even more draconian measures were required, the king decided, measures that would effectively reduce the Welsh to second- or third-class citizens in their own country. The result of his considerations was the series of infamous Penal Laws that were introduced in 1401 and 1402.

The laws were wide ranging and cruel but they began with a note of clemency. In March 1401, a pardon was extended to all those who had taken up arms against the Crown – apart from Owain Glyndwr and the two Tudor brothers, who were explicitly named as being outside Henry's clemency. Many others willingly took up the king's offer; it was their only chance. After that the iron fist slammed down.

Amongst other things the Penal Laws stated that no Welshman could now hold office of any sort, either in Wales or in any of the Marcher towns. He could not bear arms when out in public and could not purchase land either in England or in Wales. Welshmen were not permitted to become burgesses and, significantly, no Englishman accused of a crime could be tried by a jury of Welshmen. That pleasure belonged solely to the English. In future, as far as the law was concerned, a Welshman's word meant absolutely nothing.

There were to be no large meetings or assemblies – devastating for the bards of the country – and any Englishman who ever demeaned himself enough to marry a Welsh woman would immediately lose all his rights as a citizen. On the other hand a Welshman who wanted to elevate his position was now required to renounce his nationality. Any Welshman found within the walls of Chester after dark was liable for decapitation.

And so it went on. The laws were brutal and totally oppressive, but if Henry thought they would break the spirit of the Welsh he was gravely mistaken. Instead they gave the hidden Owain Glyndwr exactly the fillip he needed as more and more of his countrymen found the situation intolerable. Those men who would otherwise have been content tilling their crops or grinding their corn were being pushed into rebellion rather than docility and Glyndwr's mission was given new strength.

Perhaps more significantly, the Penal Laws showed just how big a divide there was between the Welsh and the English. The relationship had always been fragile, a conquered people could never be expected to maintain parity with their conquerors. But from the moment the first of the laws came into usage in 1401 it seemed that the English Crown – and therefore the whole English nation – was doing little more than widening the divide between the two peoples.

As the winter of 1401 gradually slipped away, Glyndwr lay in hiding somewhere in the Welsh hills and forests. Nobody knew where he was but clearly he was waiting, dreaming, planning.

Even to those who did not know him it was obvious that it would not be long before Glyndwr was ready to strike once more. Wherever he went, whoever he spoke to, the overriding message from the Welsh was one of unhappiness. Indeed, the growing unrest in the populace helped convince him, not that he needed any such convincing, that the desire for rebellion and, subsequently, for independence was still strong in Wales.

Spring brought with it renewed rebel activity. Guerrilla attacks on English outposts and farms increased alarmingly. These were largely independent outbreaks rather than organised attacks, but as with Scottish pirate attacks on the Llyn Peninsula that spring, Glyndwr was wise enough to take the credit. They reflected the mood of the people and sent a direct and chilling message to the English overlords – we will be coming, the message said, we will be coming soon!

Glyndwr's army of supporters was growing by the day. Now, though, support was not restricted to Wales but took in many of those who had left their native land to seek employment or education. The *Rolls of Parliament* for 1401, in curiously unemotional tones, makes the situation plainly obvious: 'Welsh scholars who had been residing in the universities of Oxford and Cambridge had left for their country; and that also Welsh labourers who had been living in various parts of the English realm had suddenly fled the said realm for their same country of Wales and had strongly equipped themselves with arms, bows, arrows and swords and other weapons such as they had not done before at any time since the conquest of Wales.'[5]

It was not just civilians, scholars and labourers who now joined Glyndwr. Archers and foot soldiers who had been serving with the king in Scotland began to leave the English army in their droves, all of them heading back to Wales and to a meeting with Owain Glyndwr.

The message for King Henry was clear. Despite that early defeat outside Welshpool Glyndwr was certainly not beaten. He would soon become active again. It was a disquieting time for Henry as the Welsh who were now beginning to join Glyndwr in ever increasing numbers came from his army, men who he might confidently expect to remain loyal to the Crown.

The Welsh attitude was something of an emotional response. It was as much about what Owain represented as what he had actually done – which, up until now, had been very little apart from sacking and pillaging a few towns. The mighty castles and fortresses of English oligarchy remained intact, untouched.

Both sides knew that the gigantic fortresses would be a target for the rebels in the coming year. It was not exactly a comforting thought for the king as he sat down to plan out that year's campaign. His position as monarch and ruler was fragile throughout England and particularly in Wales where Richard had always had a strong following. Henry was astute enough to see the problem – curing it was another problem altogether.

The medieval period was an age of superstition and strong belief, particularly in the matter of the divine right of kings. At the end of the day Richard was the rightful sovereign. Henry, in the eyes of many, was never going to be anything more than a usurper. The potential loss of significant and symbolic centres like the mighty castles of North Wales would be a psychological setback that Henry simply could not contemplate.

The king realised that he would have to work hard to contain the Welsh threat which was now, thanks to the Tudor brothers, presenting a two-pronged danger. And surprisingly, Henry's first real disaster of the year came not from Owain Glyndwr but from the least suspected direction, Rhys and Gwilym ap Tudor.

On Good Friday, 1 April 1401, the two Tudors seized the castle at Conwy. The English garrison, perhaps sixty or seventy men, were at worship in the church which lay outside the castle walls. Rhys and Gwilym, accompanied by forty followers, simply eased their way into the castle and barricaded it against the enemy. The amazement of the English soldiers when released from morning service to find their way back into the fortress totally barred can only be imagined.

Rhys and Gwilym ap Tudor held Conwy Castle for the next two months. The king's 'man on the spot', Henry Percy, had a degree of admiration for the way the castle had been taken and urged negotiation as the way forward. The king would have none of it and so a siege began.

It was against Percy's basic inclination. He had acquired the nickname 'Hotspur' because of his lightning fast reactions on the battlefield and because of strong hot headedness; siege warfare was an anathema to him. Nevertheless, he did as he was commanded, and as the weeks went past it seemed that the king had made the right decision to enforce a siege.

By June 1401, Rhys and Gwilym had reluctantly decided that they could hold Conwy no longer and asked for terms. They were granted a pardon from the king and allowed to march out with all their troops – apart from eight men who were to be randomly picked and handed over to the Crown for execution. The eight men, in all probability seized and bound while they were sleeping, quickly became martyrs for the cause.

By trickery and guile – or it may simply have been a misreading on behalf of the king –Glyndwr had managed to convince Henry IV that he had been responsible for the capture of Conwy Castle. It has never been clear how much he had known of his cousins' intent, and he was probably as surprised as Henry and Hotspur when he heard the news. Glyndwr was always a pragmatist, however, and knew exactly when and how to make the best out of any situation.

Capture of Conwy Castle meant that his reputation, both with the Welsh and with the English, grew yet again. As a warrior and as a war leader he was now huge in stature and standing. Glyndwr and the people of Wales were more than content – the king was furious.

Henry sent spies and agents to find him but Glyndwr knew the land and he knew the people. Henry's agents had no hope of laying their hands on the man who had now become the most wanted man in the kingdom.

For the next few months Glyndwr operated like a will-o-the-wisp, his troops moving from one location to another, attacking and despoiling wherever they appeared. For a brief period his soldiers even laid siege to Harlech Castle, only breaking away in the face of a large relieving army. For weeks on end Glyndwr led Hotspur's forces a merry dance.

It was not all success, however. In May 1401, Hotspur achieved a degree of revenge when he defeated a small rebel army near the mountain of Cader Idris. That same month John Charlton, Lord of Powys, managed another victory, this time over Glyndwr himself. The Welsh were scattered and fled, Charlton's men in pursuit: 'In this chase were taken certain prizes of the armour of the said Owain, certain horses and lances and a drape of cloth painted with maidens with red hands, as well as his henchmen [...] Of this painted cloth I send you a portion through the bearer of this letter.'[6]

Despite his defeat at the hands of Charlton, Glyndwr now moved south towards Cardigan. On the way he ran across an opposing army in a remote and almost inaccessible pass called Mynydd Hyddgen high in the Plynlimmon mountain range.

The English force of nearly 2,000 men, most of them from the county of Pembrokeshire, surprised the rebels and attacked first. Glyndwr saw the danger and immediately hurled his men at the centre of the enemy line. The result was a total rout and a victory for Glyndwr that was sorely needed. It sent waves of panic through the people of South Wales.

The English garrisons at Swansea and Kidwelly were immediately strengthened and in June 1401, King Henry decided that the time had come for him to once again take the lead. He would personally march an army into what had now undoubtedly become Glyndwr's territory and finish the problem for once and for all.

The king took time to assemble his army at Worcester, but by the end of September or beginning of October – late in the campaigning season – he was ready. This time Henry concentrated on the south of the country, driving deeply into Cardiganshire. Wisely, Glyndwr fell back before him, preferring the natural Welsh tactics of guerrilla fighting to standing for a pitched battle. That way, Glyndwr knew, lay only English victory.

Henry reached Strata Florida Abbey in the Cambrian Mountains as that year's rains set in. Wet and disgruntled, he decided to make the place his base. The abbey was one of the main centres of Welsh learning and culture, the monks almost automatically adhering to Glyndwr's aims and intentions, and the idea of displacing them from their warm and comfortable lodgings appealed to the more savage and vicious side of the king's nature.

That autumn was a time of great bloodshed and misery in the Welsh countryside, both the English and the Welsh suffering from the depredations of the rival armies: 'Owen Glendower, all North Wales and Cardigan and Powis siding with him, sorely harried with fire and sword the English who dwelt in those parts [...] Wherefore the English, invading those parts with a strong power and utterly laying them waste and ravaging them with fire, famine and sword, left them a desert, not even sparing children or churches.'[7]

Meanwhile Henry, now ensconced at Strata Florida Abbey, had a more subtle sort of punishment in his mind. He had no desire to kill holy men, but the monks of the Abbey needed to be taught a lesson and at least one was duly executed for treason. It was time, Henry thought, that the rebel Owain Glyndwr was put in his place. He would do it by degrading this place of learning and the people who lived close by, as Adam of Usk reported: 'The monastery of Strata Florida wherein the King himself was being lodged, and the church of which and its choir, even up to the high altar, they used as a stable, and pillaged even the patens; and they carried away into England more than a thousand children of both sexes to be their servants.'[8]

Adam, with his usual love of exaggeration, may have been enlarging on the number of children carried away into virtual slavery, but the use of the church as a stable, complete with horse dung and droppings, was real enough.

Glyndwr was not exactly innocent of committing atrocities himself. That autumn he killed or caused to be killed dozens, perhaps hundreds of Englishmen and their supporters, soldiers and civilians alike. Slow to anger, quick to act, he had been pushed to the edge of reason. And when he fought, one thing was abundantly clear – Owain Glyndwr would fight to the death.

There was, at times, almost an edge of mischievousness about Glyndwr's campaigns. That year he took particular delight in making off with the tents and horses of the 16-year-old Henry of Monmouth who was now campaigning on his father's behalf in Wales.

To Glyndwr the theft or the prizes of war – describe them as you will – were even better than defeating in battle the man who had dared to assume his title and position as Prince of Wales. For young Henry it was an insult that he, as the legally appointed English prince, bitterly resented but which he could do little about.

The king, isolated now at Strata Florida, was faced by a dilemma – stay in the monastery for the winter or retreat out of Wales. He chose to retreat, a strategy that was achieved with considerable loss of life as Glyndwr harassed his supply chain and the marching column at every opportunity. It was a long, slow trudge that seemed to take forever, but by the beginning of November Henry was safely ensconced back at Worcester.

As the year 1401 drew to a close Owain Glyndwr seemed to have garnered some sort of magical power around himself, a secret device or force that kept him concealed from the English king and hidden from his forces.

Already the suspicious English soldiers were muttering about Glyndwr the Magician and the illicit but effective pacts he had made with Lucifer. That suited Owain Glyndwr perfectly and he was happy to allow his reputation as a sorcerer to grow and develop.

Hidden by friends and supporters, Glyndwr's networks kept him informed of the whereabouts of the English and he would move easily between one sanctuary and the next before Hotspur, the king and other English leaders knew what was happening. It was infuriating for them. Small wonder they resorted to tales of Glyndwr's magic and demonic influence.

In desperation, Henry and his council even suggested that Hotspur should pretend to make gestures of peace, call Glyndwr to a meeting and then murder him. The proposal offended Hotspur's notion of chivalry. He was indignant that such a scheme could even be devised, let alone put to him as a serious proposition and immediately rejected it out of hand.

Meanwhile, with Henry now out of Wales, Glyndwr moved north again and organised an attack on the king's chief fortress at Caernarfon. It was to be a brief assault, one that resulted in a stalemate across North Wales.

There was an inconclusive battle at Tuthill and the Welsh did not manage to take Caernarfon Castle. Glyndwr had neither the siege engines nor the artillery to conduct an effective and protracted attack on a castle like Caernarfon. That would come later.

The time was not yet ripe and the significance lay not in the issue of whether Glyndwr took or did not take Henry's castle but in the fact that after a full year of fighting and marching across the whole of Wales he could even mount such an attack in the first place. It was simply proof that the Welsh were gaining in strength and confidence.

It was during this assault on Caernarfon that Glyndwr first unveiled his personal standard, a golden dragon on a white field. Although later superseded by the four dragons of the Princes of Gwynedd, this banner was particularly striking and gave immense credibility to the Welsh army.

Glyndwr moved on, before winter closed down the possibility of further action, to raid the lands of his enemy the Lord of Ruthin. Clearly he was looking for food to sustain his troops through the next few months: 'Owen and his men cruelly harried the lordship of Ruthin in North Wales and the countryside with fire and sword, on the last day but one of January, carrying off the spoil of the land and specially the cattle to the mountains of Snowdon.'[9]

With winter almost upon them and opportunities for campaigning now becoming greatly reduced Glyndwr filled his time by writing to the king of Scotland and to various leaders in Ireland in the hope that they might join him in breaking the bondage of the English nation.

The letter to the Scottish king was elegantly written but ultimately it was little more than a plea for an alliance. After stressing the common ancestry of the Welsh and the Scots and linking their descent to the Roman Brutus – a literary piece of fiction and myth that owed more to Geoffrey of Monmouth's imagination than it ever did to fact – Glyndwr made reference to an old prophesy. Once again this came from Geoffrey and predicted success for both countries if they would only work together.

He then asked the Scots to send him whatever reinforcements they could spare. Glyndwr did not expect too much – when all was said and done the Scottish armies were still waging a bitter war, as violent and draining as Glyndwr's, against the English Crown: 'I am very short of men-at-arms; It is for this reason, most esteemed lord and royal cousin, that I beg you, humbly and with bended knee, your royal majesty, please to send me a number of men-at-arms who, with the help of God, can help me to resist my and your enemies.'[10]

The appeal, like the one to Richard's old enemy Art MacMurrough of Leinster, fell on deaf ears. Further letters to the other Irish chieftains met with a similar response. It seemed that, for the moment at least, Owain Glyndwr would have to fight on alone.

Yet the idea of finding an ally against the English king did not go away. It was an idea that Glyndwr would return to in the future and was indeed something of a guiding principle in all of his foreign policy decisions.

Militarily at least, the year had been a good one for the Welsh rebel leader, but there was no doubt that the people – his people, his subjects, the people he was honour bound to protect – had suffered and suffered badly. With winter coming on, many of the labourers and subsistence farmers of Wales faced a bleak future, hardly knowing how they were going to survive until spring. And the really painful thing about the damage to their livelihood was that much of it had been caused by the forces of Glyndwr.

He had to find provisions for his army somewhere. Feeding and supplying a large force of men was probably more difficult than planning a battle, and with Henry controlling the sea lanes around Wales the Welsh farms were an obvious target. It was a ruthless approach, but, unfortunately for the Welsh farmers, a necessary one.

For the peasants life was difficult enough without the troubles and mayhem of the Welsh revolt, but now the consequences of rebellion came home to roost. Soon burned-out farms and destroyed provision stores, churned up fields and dead animals marked the landscape. They were scars from the wars of a Cain who was not the enemy but one of their own. The depredations of the English forces simply added to the woes of the Welsh people.

Some of the Welsh might have been pleased with all that Glyndwr had achieved, others might resent the misery he had brought to their world, but the real wonder was that none of them took the easy way out and gave him up to the king. The people would have known where he was hiding, known who supported him and who did not, but they said nothing.

Glyndwr's charisma apparently remained great even if his rebellion had condemned his people to such terrible poverty and hardship. The personality of the man must have been significant. Simply to catch and hold the affection of so many of his countrymen would have been an immense task.

And yet even now there are still those, as there were then, whose opinion on the character and personality of Owain Glyndwr remain decidedly negative: 'Ian Skidmore, Owain's distant relative and biographer, describes him as a psychopath who enjoyed killing. This, contrasted with what we know of his home life, suggests a split personality who probably did not give his wife an easy time [...] we can never know how happy their marriage was.'[11]

Glyndwr was probably no more of a psychopath than other freedom fighters like William Wallace or Giuseppe Garibaldi. In their own way they were all patriots fuelled by a burning desire to achieve their aims and would go to any lengths to fulfil their ambitions. What made Glyndwr different was the savagery of his campaigns and the length of the war that he waged. It was a brutal conflict that lasted for at least fifteen years, the final part of the conflict sliding into a series of skirmishes and guerrilla attacks that had no definite end.

Now, in that first terrible winter, the war seemed as if it was being fought against Glyndwr's own people as much as the English. Raiding crops, emptying storage barns and destroying houses not only gave his own men succour, it also prevented the English armies from laying their hands on much-needed assistance. Almost any means of damaging the enemy was acceptable in this early example of scorched-earth tactics.

If a blackened, burned-out countryside meant the people of Wales would suffer it was a price Glyndwr was willing to pay. He had suffered, his family had suffered, and he never bothered to ask what the people of Wales thought about it.

By the time of his death – whenever that actually was – Owain Glyndwr had been fighting so long and so fiercely that he knew no other way of existence. If he did have psychopathic tendencies it is difficult to know what triggered them.

It was a brutal age and while Glyndwr did attempt to create a more tolerant and democratic regime he knew that before anything significant could be achieved he would first have to impose his will by military force. Psychopath or freedom fighter, terrorist or man of the people, there were no half measures. Ultimately, people's views on Glyndwr depended on the perspective of each and every man or woman who crossed his path. Above all it depended on what they wanted out of the rebellion. Different perspectives lead to different stances and the real magic and mystery of Owain Glyndwr is that he managed to blend together so many of those different stances.

The best generals and leaders are not always the most loved. Glyndwr knew and understood that, but he seems to have managed the impossible, claiming respect and admiration from those who did not love him, adoration and unqualified love from those who might have been expected to just admire him. And regardless of what others thought of him, by December 1401 Glyndwr must have been content. What the years ahead might bring nobody could even begin to imagine.

Chapter Five

A Blazing Star

Early in the New Year of 1402 a blazing comet appeared in the skies above Britain. Long-tailed and as bright as the summer sun, it burned its way into the memory of the entire nation, and to those who watched its shimmering progress across the night sky it seemed as if this was a phenomenon that would last forever. More importantly it was, they said, an omen.

To the bards and mystics, to Owain Glyndwr and his supporters, to the men and women of the isolated hamlets and villages of Wales, the comet was not just an omen, it was a good one. It was, many believed, a symbol that signified the success of Glyndwr's mission to bring freedom and independence to Wales.

King Henry and his advisors undoubtedly thought the exact opposite but it hardly mattered. The superstitious nature of people at this time enabled them to turn the omen to whichever purpose they liked. And in 1402 it seemed as if the gods were indeed smiling on Owain Glyndwr.

The opening salvos of the 1402 campaign were hugely significant and impressive for him, proof positive that the events of the previous year had not been a simple glitch in the system. After successfully running off Lord Grey's cattle in January, Glyndwr continued to operate in North Wales, launching guerrilla attacks on English-owned farms and properties.

Then, in April he pulled off his greatest coup yet when he managed to capture and imprison his arch enemy and rival, Reginald Grey, Lord of Ruthin.

It was not as a result of a great battle or even a skirmish. Grey was tricked into leaving the safety of his castle at Ruthin, having been told that Glyndwr was skulking alongside the outer walls. The body of the Welsh leader would have been a significant prize to present to the king and Grey could not resist the opportunity. He raced out to capture and imprison his hated rival. Instead it was Grey who found himself surrounded, bound, and gagged, a prisoner of his great nemesis.

Grey was quickly spirited away from his domains and imprisoned in one of the few Welsh-held fortresses in North Wales, Glyndwr's Dolbadarn Castle at the foot of Snowdon. Mainly because of its location, Dolbadarn was as impregnable as Harlech or Caernarfon and Grey had little immediate prospect of rescue.

Having fallen into the hands of the one man on earth that he despised and feared, the Earl of Ruthin was undoubtedly concerned for his life. He knew that chivalry demanded at least a degree of leniency for men of rank and position but this was different, this was civil war. More importantly, he had fallen under the control of a man who was already well on the way to acquiring the reputation of a ruthless killer.

Owain Glyndwr, however, was as much a statesman as a warrior. It did not matter one jot how Grey had been captured or what tradition required of him, what mattered now was simply how he was going to use him. If killing Grey was the best option there is no doubt Glyndwr would have done so, but it soon became apparent that there was another option, one that was infinitely preferable.

Quite apart from the personal pleasure the entrapment of Lord Grey had given him, Glyndwr knew that this was a seminal moment in the rebellion. Grey was one of the most significant English leaders in the area. He was a close friend of Henry and to have this man in his power was worth a king's ransom to Owain Glyndwr, on a personal and political level.

Ransom was an important word in the power game of medieval politics. Traditionally, captured noblemen were ransomed for enormous sums of money – at least until Agincourt in 1415 when Henry V killed almost all of the French captives after the battle. For now, though, Lord Grey was about to become a very lucrative prisoner indeed for Glyndwr. *The Rolls of Parliament* recorded the moment:

> On behalf of Lord Grey of Ruthin – the said Commons requested our said lord the king that whereas Lord Grey of Ruthin was in a most wretched state, in a harsh and oppressive prison in Wales, and had agreed to pay 10,000 marks for his fine and ransom, namely 6000 marks at

Martimas following, and 4000 marks shortly afterwards or
else he would be put to death; may it please our same lord
to grant and give leave to Lord Roos and Lord Willoughby
[…] to ordain and make such arrangements for the said
finance and ransom.[1]

The king duly agreed and stumped up the money. Held captive for twelve
months, Grey was eventually released when the ransom money was paid
out. Henry cursed and fumed but Grey was a valuable ally; he was also a
personal friend and at that point in time Henry needed friends very badly
indeed. The king could do little else but pay what he regarded as bribery
money and try to look as magnanimous as possible.

The enormous sum of money, equivalent to nearly £100,000 in
today's currency, was larger than the annual income of most English
barons and earls. It bought much needed supplies and equipment for the
Welsh army, but, just as importantly, was the huge psychological boost
it gave to the Welsh soldiers and their families. They were now part of a
war, not just a rebellion.

On 22 June 1402, further Welsh success came at the Battle of Bryn
Glas near Knighton in the Marches. It was the most significant Welsh
victory yet, a substantial English army being scattered and several
prominent Marcher knights killed. Glyndwr's reputation as a soldier
soared. Perhaps just as significantly, by wiping out hundreds of rank and
file soldiers the Battle of Bryn Glas earned the Welsh leader a growing
reputation as a brutal and vicious force of destruction.

His standing as a ruthless leader was apparently aided by the
behaviour of the women in his train. According to legend, once the battle
was over these women moved silently but swiftly around the field of
combat, killing wounded soldiers as they lay on the ground waiting for
aid and mutilating the bodies of the dead. It was supposedly done in
revenge for atrocities committed by the English the year before. That, at
least, was the myth.

True or not, the story added to the fearsome reputation of Glyndwr
and the Welsh. Small wonder that a popular rhyme in vogue at the time
was used to frighten children in their nurseries:

Beware of Wales, Christ Jesus must us keep
That it makes not our child's child to weep.[2]

It was not just death and destruction that Glyndwr meted out. Edmund Mortimer, the most important of the Marcher Lords, was captured at Bryn Glas and Glyndwr must have been looking forward to another large ransom being paid into his coffers.

This time, however, King Henry refused to play ball. There is no clear reasoning behind Henry's decision. Always short of money and hard cash, it is possible that he thought Glyndwr had already had enough money from the Crown coffers, but more likely his decision was mixed up with the importance of the Mortimer family.

The Mortimers were one of the richest families in Wales. More significantly, the young nephew to Edmund Senior, another Edmund who was now languishing in captivity somewhere in Glyndwr's territory, had a far better claim to the throne than Henry. The boy Edmund was still an infant but it was what he could grow into that Henry most feared.

It remains supposition but that was probably the basis of Henry's refusal to pay a ransom for Mortimer. He would have been haunted by the one thought – why should he, as king of England, help the people who one day might become his rivals for the throne? Whatever the reason, Mortimer was mortified when he learned that Henry would sanction no ransom.

In light of Henry's decision, Edmund Mortimer must have been expecting execution, but Owain Glyndwr, while merciless on the battlefield, had no liking for cold blooded murder. He allowed Edmund to live, but rather than return to a king who had renounced and denied him, Mortimer chose to remain with Glyndwr.

By the autumn of that year Edmund Mortimer had married Glyndwr's daughter Catherine and become a fully-fledged participant in the rebellion. It was an amazing turnaround, and whatever Mortimer's real motives might have been, his change of heart and altered allegiance have to bear tribute to the personality of Owain Glyndwr.

*****

King Henry IV spent the early part of 1402 campaigning in Scotland, out of touch with events in Wales. Glyndwr, seizing his chance, extended his field of operations into the southern parts of the country. He rampaged into Gwent and Glamorgan and soon the south-eastern parts of Wales were under his control. Well over half of Wales was now in his hands and his band of supporters and camp followers ballooned out of all proportion.

Adam of Usk was openly fearful, writing that his heart trembled when he thought of the damage Glyndwr had caused to English rule. He went on to list the specific losses to the English Crown during this brief campaign: 'Backed by a following of thirty thousand men issuing from their lairs, throughout Wales and its marches he overthrew the castles, among which were Usk, Caerleon and Newport, and fired the towns. In short, like a second Assyrian, the rod of God's anger, he did deeds of unheard-of cruelty with fire and sword.'[3]

Fear and trembling, maybe, but Adam was still unable to keep the contempt out of his writing. Not even his poetical reference to the warlike Assyrians – who, like Glyndwr, came down like 'a wolf on the fold' – was able to lighten his mood.

However, from a military point of view it was warriors that Owain needed. He was not to be disappointed. Every day groups of dissatisfied Welsh soldiers absconded from the ranks of Henry's Scottish army and headed for Glyndwr's banners. Archers were particularly welcome.

Traditionally recruited from the lowest classes in society, archers had always occupied a rather precarious position in the armies of the time: 'The archer was considered well enough in war to slay Frenchmen and Scots but not, if you please, at the hunt to kill the king's deer – at all events, not until much later on in Tudor times.'[4]

In fact it was Owain Glyndwr, not the Tudors, who began to change that perception. Clever, and blessed with an innate understanding of tactics, Glyndwr soon began to realise that bows and bowmen were perhaps the most important part of his armoury against knights in chainmail armour. They would also be invaluable for use in the guerrilla campaigns and sneak attacks yet to come.

Interestingly, many of the archers who now came to fight with Glyndwr against Henry IV later went on to join the army of Henry's son during his campaigns in France. The same archers who had terrified the English in 1402 were there at the Battle of Agincourt in 1415 when Henry V won what was probably England's greatest ever victory over the French – this time on the English side.

By August 1402, the king was on his way back from Scotland, ready to wipe out the Welsh threat for once and for all. Before he left Scotland he had already sent word ordering his commissioners to organise three separate armies, each of several thousand men, to take on Glyndwr's forces. When he finally appeared preparations for the campaign were almost complete.

What Henry was intending was a triple attack that would come from three separate bases on the English-Welsh border. From Chester, from Shrewsbury and from Hereford the king's forces would hurl themselves into north, central and south Wales, all at the same time. This multi-pronged assault would pull Glyndwr's troops from one end of the country to the other. It was, Henry thought, guaranteed to succeed. Glyndwr simply did not have enough men to halt the three assaults.

Henry himself was to take command the northern assault, Henry Prince of Wales the central and the Earl of Stafford the south. It was reputed that there were as many as 100,000 soldiers gathered together for the invasion. The figure is probably a gross over-exaggeration, but even so the forces now facing Owain Glyndwr were formidable in the extreme.

Henry's armies marched at the end of summer 1402. Whatever the total number of English troops, Glyndwr was heavily outnumbered and knew that his only recourse was to retreat ahead of the English. Using traditional Welsh hit-and-run tactics, he would harry the three armies as they moved deeper and deeper into Wales.

It seemed a formidable task for Glyndwr but at that moment Wales's greatest and most renowned ally suddenly hove into view – inclement weather. The weather turned bad, exceedingly bad. The weather conditions that besieged Wales that year were such as men had never seen before. To the superstitious, in other words almost everybody in the medieval world, it was like the end of the human existence.

Rain, sleet, snow, thunder storms, all powered by winds that drove across the hills like a Biblical curse, not only demoralised the English but killed many of them. Men died from exposure, from drowning in the flooded rivers and from the inevitable fevers that accompanied such torrential downpours.

Mud, thick as cow dung, clung to the soldier's boots, caking their leggings and leather jerkins, making even the simple act of walking ten yards a virtual impossibility. Horses were bogged down and had to be pulled out of the morass by ropes while heavy and unwieldy armour was discarded as useless. Wagons carrying essential supplies slid and slipped across the terrain like children's toboggans gone out of control. Everywhere was chaos.

Those soldiers that were not disabled by the weather were thoroughly exhausted and no more able to fight off Glyndwr's lightning fast attacks on supply columns or isolated detachments than they were to control the sea and tides. Too tired to even eat or erect bivouacs, many of the soldiers of Henry's three mighty armies lay in their own filth and waited for the end.

As they lay, depressed and terrified, it was perhaps inevitable that the soldiers should curse Owain Glyndwr. He was, they decided, a magician who could control the weather as he wished. And now the Welsh magus had called down the powers of darkness on their heads. It was surely a spell that would not be broken or cease until they were all dead.

Faced by such arrant nonsense, and with the memory of those Welsh archers who had deserted him in Scotland, Henry was genuinely afraid of what might happen next. If he had lost so many men to desertion while on campaign in Scotland, what price the loyalty of his present army, particularly those Welsh archers and bowmen who remained in his employment?

The mood in the various camps was close to mutinous and Henry was not yet strong enough in his own position on the throne to withstand yet another setback. A mutinous army would have surely meant defeat, possibly even removal from the throne. Defeat to the likes of Owain Glyndwr was the last thing he needed. He had no option but to reluctantly call off the assaults and head back to the three original bases on the English border.

The retreat of the king's forces was an amazing success for the Welsh, albeit one that was achieved without the traditional series of battles and lamenting widows. Any successes King Henry had managed to gain lay not in the number of battles won or Welsh soldiers killed but only in the number of cattle he was able to cut out and take back to England. From a military perspective the three-pronged attack had been an utter disaster.

Even Adam of Usk, in his vacillating *Chronicle*, was unable to quite remove his tongue from his cheek when describing the end of that year's campaigns: 'In this year the king, with one hundred thousand men and more divided into three bodies, invaded Wales in war against Owen. But he and his poor wretches keeping close in their caves and woods, the king laid waste the land and returned victoriously, with a countless spoil of cattle into his own country.'[5]

Right: The Great Seal of Owain Glyndwr, probably the only accurate likeness we have of the last true Prince of Wales. (Public Domain)

Below: The Madness of Charles VI, a French painting from the time showing the onset of Charles's strange illness and affliction. (Public Domain)

A detail from Jean Froissart's *Chronicle*, showing archers and soldiers during the Battle of Crecy. Froissart's *Chronicle* has long been a major source of information on the Hundred Years' War and the chivalric code of the times. (Public Domain)

PENNON, *said to have been taken in Single Combat by* DOUGLAS: *from the celebrated* HOTSPUR.

The pennant of Glyndwr's friend and ally Henry 'Hotspur' Percy. (Phil Carradice Collection)

Right: An artist's impression of the death of Llewelyn the Last in 1282. (Public Domain)

Below: Cannons were a new weapon during the fourteenth century. This shows the cannon balls for the massive Mons Meg cannon at Edinburgh Castle. The weapons and armament used by Prince Henry during the war with Glyndwr would have been much the same. (Public Domain)

Above: Siege artillery in action – people were terrified of the sound of the cannonades, a new form of psychological warfare. Notice the use of archers to supplement the cannons. (Phil Carradice collection)

Left: The arms of Glyndwr's arch-enemy Dafydd Gam. (Public Domain)

DAVID GAM.

John Speed's map of Caernarfon, circa 1617. Little would have changed since Glyndwr's days when he was desperate to take the stronghold. (Phil Carradice Collection)

A monument commemorating the Battle of Hyddgen, one of Glyndwr's great victories. (Public Domain)

Above: The Peasants Revolt, a detail from Froissart's *Chronicle*. The bravery of the young King Richard II was remarked on by almost everyone. (Public Domain)

Left: King Henry V in traditional pose. Much of his skill as a warrior was learned during his campaigns against Glyndwr. (Phil Carradice Collection)

Mynydd Hyddgen in Mid Wales, scene of one of Glyndwr's victories against the forces of King Henry IV. (Public Domain)

The dragon banner of Owain Glyndwr. (Public Domain)

Above: A portrait of Glyndwr, one that owes more to the artist's imagination than it does to a true likeness. (Public Domain)

Left: The statue of Glyndwr that now stands in Corwen. (Phil Carradice Collection)

Owain Glyndwr, as imagined by the poet and artist William Blake. (Public Domain)

King Richard II, brave but foolish, a man who eventually became one of the most disliked kings of England. (Public Domain)

Above: St Mary's
Church, Monnington-
on-Wye – burial site
for Owain Glyndwr,
perhaps? (Phil
Carradice Collection)

Left: Strata Florida
Abbey, despoiled
by Henry IV during
his campaigns
against Glyndwr.
(Public Domain)

STRATA FLORIDA ABBEY.

All that now remains of Sycharth, once the home of Glyndwr before it was destroyed by Prince Henry. (Phil Carradice Collection)

Aberystwyth Castle, a key strategic post in the Welsh rebellion. (Phil Carradice Collection)

Left: William Wallace, Scottish freedom fighter. (Public Domain)

Below: A Victorian view of Ruthin – little has changed since Glyndwr's day. (Postcard view)

An artist's impression of King Arthur defeating the Saxons – the image of Owain Glyndwr as Arthur reborn was crucial in maintaining Welsh support for the rebellion and war of Owain Glyndwr. (Public Domain)

Glyndwr's Parliament House in Machynlleth. (Phil Carradice Collection)

Glyndyfrdwy, now despoiled, where Glyndwr was proclaimed as Prince of Wales. (Phil Carradice Collection)

Harlech Castle, where Glyndwr set up his court and lived in great style. It's capture by Prince Henry was one of the turning points of the war. (Public Domain)

The death of Hotspur, an artist's impression. (Public Domain)

The coronation of Henry IV, taken from Froissart's *Chronicle*. (Public Domain)

Henry Percy, Earl of Northumberland, father to Hotspur and one of the three men – along with Glyndwr and Edmund Mortimer – who signed the Tripartite Indenture. (Public Domain)

HENRY V.

Henry V, as a young Prince when he was still fighting against Owain Glyndwr. (Public Domain)

The real victor was undoubtedly the weather but when bards like Iolo Goch and Gruffudd Llwyd got to work they conveniently overlooked this factor and composed celebratory odes that lauded Owain and his skills. Iolo, as might be expected, was particularly fulsome in his praise:

> Behold a world caused by English arrogance!
> Very often have I wished
> to have a lord – full of eagerness for a blade –
> from amongst ourselves.
> A mighty feat – everyone knows who:
> the fair, brave and fear-inspiring weapon of Glyndyfrdwy.[6]

At that stage in his life and career it really did seem as if Owain Glyndwr could achieve anything he set his mind to. Independence, surely, was just a matter of months away.

*****

Even in the 'off season' for campaigning Glyndwr was not prepared simply to rest on his laurels. He had begun his campaign against the English and there was still work to be done.

Happily exploiting his new companion in arms, his son-in-law, Edmund Mortimer, Glyndwr was soon scheming for the coming year. Mortimer put him in touch with the most dynamic and dangerous of English soldiers, the young Harry 'Hotspur' Percy. Previously enemies when Hotspur was serving the Crown as Henry's chief lieutenant in North Wales, there had always been a degree of respect between the two men, each of them admiring the other's military abilities.

The Percy family had never been close to the king, but 1402 marked a low point in their relationship, thanks largely to Henry's refusal or inability to pay them for their services. Over and above the issue of money, Hotspur, the son and heir of the Earl of Northumberland, was unhappy with the king's military tactics and disposition of troops. More importantly, he was furious at Henry's decision not to pay a ransom for Mortimer.

There was good reason for Hotspur's anger. To start with he was married to Edmund Mortimer's sister and that made the captive nobleman his brother-in-law. This, in turn, created a complicated but potentially all powerful and dynamic connection between Glyndwr and Mortimer from Wales and the Percy family from Northumberland.

It was not just the family connections, it was far more important than that, as Henry clearly saw. The inter-weaving of these powerful family relationships represented what was a potential threat to his position as king.

Hotspur's family connections with the Mortimers, even though they came through marriage, gave him a claim to the throne, should he care to exploit it. Hotspur was a well-regarded, well-liked figure in England, the antithesis of Henry himself. If it ever came to a popularity contest Henry was in no doubt which one of them would emerge triumphant. It was not something that Henry was ever liable to forget.

Hotspur was exactly the sort of dynamic individual that people were drawn to, a man of honour who would act as he saw fit in order to defend his family and the country. At this distance it remains unclear if Hotspur did actually have designs on the throne, but regardless of his intentions, he was someone who Henry recognised as posing a very real danger to his position.

That autumn and winter the news from North Wales, as far as Henry was concerned, was not good. To begin with, it appeared as if his concerns and fears about the Percy family were going to be realised. The young Hotspur, it seemed, was in the process of changing his allegiance, and, in the fickle world of medieval politics, abandoning his previous alliance with the king.

He was now appearing to show support, even friendship for Glyndwr, the man he had fought and had once beaten in the early stage of the rebellion. A formidable warrior, Henry would not have been best pleased at the possibility of Hotspur now facing him in the field.

Hotspur had already begun to gather together a powerful army ready for the new campaigning season – something that Henry had certainly not asked him to do. When and if these soldiers were linked with those of Glyndwr and Mortimer they would undoubtedly prove to be the strongest military force in the kingdom.

At the moment it was all still supposition on the part of the king. Hotspur had not technically declared for Glyndwr, at least not yet, and could easily change his mind depending on the incentives he was offered. But Henry trusted no one. It was a character trait that only grew more intense as the king got older and spent more time on the throne.

A usurper who had claimed ultimate power in the kingdom by nothing more than military strength, Henry was acutely aware that what he had done to Richard others could do to him. Suspicion became second nature to an increasingly morbid and paranoid Henry Bolingbroke. It was a character trait that Glyndwr and his new allies saw they could exploit.

That winter Edmund Mortimer began a highly effective propaganda campaign against the Crown, addressing letters to the ruling monarch and statements to the public under the ruler's given name Henry of Lancaster or Henry Bolingbroke. The title of King Henry IV was never used.

It was a deliberate insult to the man who was his sovereign ruler and in the mood of the times was tantamount to the most treasonous of behaviour. It was as if he was denying Henry any right to the throne and regarding him as a mere interloper. It was a minor matter but it infuriated Henry and pleased Mortimer no end.

Also during those winter months Mortimer and Hotspur began to spread the rumour that Richard II had not died. On the contrary, he was still alive and well, in hiding somewhere in the country or possibly even abroad.

Richard had, as Henry knew only too well, been removed from the Tower of London soon after he had been deposed. Taken by boat down the Thames, he had been imprisoned in Pontefract Castle where he had since died. But Henry also knew that many of his subjects would be taken in by the lie and would soon start looking for Mortimer to return the deposed Richard to the kingship. Forget how unpopular he had been, Richard was the rightful monarch and he, Henry, was merely a usurper.

In the increasingly torpid and murky world of Henry's court the practicalities were ignored. Questions like where on earth had Richard been living, why had no one seen him for two or three years, and what was his purpose in staying hidden might well have been in people's minds, but that was where they stayed. Rumour was everything and the increasingly paranoid Henry, who had given orders for Richard to be murdered in 1400, could do absolutely nothing to prevent them, not without giving the game away.

That summer the English people were confused. Was Richard alive or was he dead? And if, by any chance, Richard *was* actually dead, people asked, what then? Mortimer had an answer to that particular conundrum. He would, he declared, simply place his nephew Edmund, the young Earl of March and the rightful monarch, on the throne in his stead. Either way he would remove Henry and most assuredly support Glyndwr's position as Prince of Wales.

It was all a diplomatic and political nightmare for Henry; a degree of uncertainty that spread as swiftly as the Black Death beyond the royal court and into the towns and villages of the country. Its effects were soon obvious.

Henry's supporters in Wales were growing increasingly nervous. They had seen Glyndwr's incursions at first hand and they had also witnessed some fairly inept reaction from the Crown forces. This was hardly the sort of security that King Henry had promised to his subjects.

The people knew that when Glyndwr came – and it was now a matter of *when* rather than *if* – he would come with fire and bloodshed. Appeal after frantic appeal was made to Henry. All of them, like this brief plea from Jankin Havard in Carmarthenshire, were dripping with fear and panic: 'I pray that you will not be false to us, that you will send to us word within a short time whether we shall have any help or not [...] I write at Dinefwr, in haste and dread.'[7]

The wheeling and dealing of that winter period shows Owain Glyndwr at his statesmanlike best. He opened negotiations with the French, and, while there was no full-scale alliance, Charles VI, the king of France, did begin to show an interest in Welsh affairs and, in particular, the Welsh rebellion.

As far as Charles was concerned Wales could well be used as an additional base for his armies. In the same way as Scotland had and was still being used, it would be a good platform from which to attack and discomfort the English. Taking the war to the English rather than allowing them to campaign each year in France certainly had an appeal to Charles.

In July and August of 1402, French privateers began making repeated attacks on English merchant vessels in the Irish Sea and in the western approaches. As an island nation Britain had always depended on merchant shipping to bring in items like fine cloths and spices. They were not essential items but the English in particular had grown used to having them. Sudden deprivation would hardly do much to aid Henry's popularity with his people.

The attacks were not coordinated and the privateers were largely free agents, able to strike and move on as they wished. That was not a problem for Glyndwr; any confusion and chaos they could cause was more than welcome. The situation did not get any easier in the New Year.

Early in 1403 a small Breton squadron of warships defeated a similar group of English vessels in the Channel and went on to cause havoc in Plymouth, Jersey and Guernsey. French ships arrived off the Isle of Wight and, briefly, even managed to put troops ashore. It might not have been an invasion but the very fact that foreign troops had landed in Britain caused anguish and confusion amongst Henry's subjects.

The raiding privateers and buccaneers were certainly troublesome to the English king, who needed peaceful and open seaways to supply his fortresses like Harlech, Aberystwyth and Beaumaris. Wales was relatively small and there was barely a point of the country that was not within a few hours ride from the coast. Many other castles, inland as well as around the coast, relied on the sea to keep their supply chains open and operating.

Beaumaris Castle on Anglesey, the last and most perfect concentric castle to be built in Wales, had been under siege for some time. The defenders fought heroically, but with the king unable to provide adequate supplies and reinforcements the end result was inevitable. It finally fell to the forces of Glyndwr and the Tudors early in 1403. This was despite the fact that its situation on the south-eastern coast of Anglesey should have made supplying it relatively simple. Command of the sea lanes had yet again proved the crucial element in siege warfare.

The fall of Beaumaris Castle was a major victory for the rebels, reinforcing the power of the Tudor brothers on the island. The fortress was to remain in rebel hands for the next two years.

For the first time gifts of weapons and other materials were now being made from the French to the Prince of Wales. They were a drop in the ocean to the French but hugely important to the needy Welsh who were happy to receive whatever gifts were on offer.

The greatest benefit of the gifts and the privateer attacks, however, came not in the practical nature of products that now changed hands but in the psychological effect of a great nation like the French actually helping tiny Wales in her fight against the English Crown. Glyndwr knew that the motives behind the French generosity were far from altruistic, but as far as the Welsh were concerned that was irrelevant; what mattered was that the Glyndwr rebellion was beginning to attract international interest.

Meanwhile the king and the English Parliament were like hapless children, helpless to do anything more than pass another series of anti-Welsh laws. In many ways the new laws were even more counter-productive than the original set. One of the new laws declared it illegal for the English and Welsh to engage in any sort of trade with each other. But even that was a pretty toothless piece of legislation as an illegal smuggling racket between the two countries quickly developed.

And so the year ground to an end. It was cold but at least the rains had stopped, proof positive – or so it seemed – to the battered and depressed English soldiers that now, when they had left Wales for the season, Glyndwr did not need the elements to batter them. It seemed that he really could control the wind and rain.

It is tempting to picture Glyndwr sitting comfortably at home in Sycharth during that Christmas of 1402, fire blazing in the hearth and only the occasional hunt for rabbits and hares to break the sonorous languor. This would be the last festive time he would ever spend at his family home so why should he not enjoy the moment?

Sadly, of course, the image is mere conjecture, albeit something that conforms to the romantic appeal of the period and the man. It is no more than what we want to see and would like to have taken place.

Reality would have been very different. Home would have been the obvious place to search for the Welsh rebel. Hard as it might be to accept, Glyndwr probably spent that Christmas in a cave deep in the forests or high up in the hills. If he was lucky he might have enjoyed a few days in one or other of the houses of his supporters. Home would never have been a likely prospect.

From a political and more practical perspective Owain Glyndwr was fast approaching the height of his career. Soon times would change and the zenith of the man's power and position would slip past and be gone forever. But what a zenith it would be.

Chapter Six

The Glory Years

The two climactic years of 1403 and 1404 were, in many respects, ones of glorious success for Owain Glyndwr, and yet, amongst all of the victories and high points, there were more than a few disasters as well. It was a rollercoaster period when his fortunes, like those of his rebellion, fluctuated wildly.

The year 1403 began with Glyndwr's forces yet again besieging Harlech and Aberystwyth castles. Glyndwr's successes of the previous year meant that both fortresses were now deep in rebel territory and only managed to remain in English hands because of their close proximity to the sea. Henry's ships regularly provided the castles with food and other supplies while Glyndwr, lacking in any real form of maritime aid, was unable to intercept the supply convoys and prevent them relieving or assisting the two castles.

In March 1403, the 16-year-old Henry of Monmouth, future King Henry V of England, was appointed his father's chief officer in Wales. It was a role previously filled by Hotspur, but by passing on control of the country to his son, Henry IV was clearly keeping things 'in the family'. He had learned something, it seemed, from the familial gathering of Glyndwr, Hotspur and Mortimer.

The young Henry of Monmouth, the Prince of Wales as the English insisted on calling him, much to the fury of Glyndwr and the Welsh, was a military genius who later went on to prove his ability in campaigns against the French. But he was also a ruthless warrior with a savage streak that belied his youthfulness. He would kill – livestock or people, it hardly mattered – burn, destroy and pillage at will. Wales was just the place to develop that simmering streak of sadism.

As if to celebrate his new position, at the end of March Henry drove deeply into Glyndwr's home county of Powys. Finding Glyndwr absent, he promptly burned and raised to the ground the house at Sycharth.

He then repeated his act of wanton destruction by doing exactly the same to Glyndwr's properties at Glyndyfrdwy. Crops, woodland and barns were also levelled at the same time.

Unfortunately for Henry – but luckily for Glyndwr – the king was busy in Scotland, waging a long-running campaign against his enemies north of the border. It meant that, for the moment at least, Wales was hardly number one priority for him. No matter how much the heir apparent might plead, Henry IV refused to send him reinforcements and the siege engines he so desperately needed.

That inevitably meant that the young prince was unable to exploit his successes in Powys. With Harlech and Aberystwyth under siege this would have been the ideal moment to launch a counter offensive against the besieging armies, catching them in the rear when their attention was fixed on the walls of the castles they were attacking.

It didn't happen and Henry knew that if he remained in Wales with an underfunded, under-supplied and badly equipped army it would lead only to disaster. Reluctantly, he was forced to abandon the campaign and retreat across the border to Shrewsbury.

Then, on 19 July 1403, Harry Hotspur finally did what everyone had been expecting of him for the past few months – he openly declared for Glyndwr. Hotspur raised his standard at Chester in what had always been a royal enclave, effectively snubbing his nose at the monarch and declaring that he did not recognise him as king. It was a double blow for Henry. Not only had he lost the most capable of his allies but Hotspur's ringing announcement had deprived him of one of the lynchpins of his strategy in the north.

Henry had always relied on the lords of Northumberland to help him in his campaigns against the Scots. The Percy clan was a strong, warlike family that had been in control of the northern territories for many years. As long as they were managing the security of the border regions Henry knew that he could safely turn his attention elsewhere.

Now with the defection of Hotspur – and that effectively meant the whole Percy family – the situation in the north looked suddenly quite parlous. Hotspur's father, the Duke of Northumberland, and his uncle the Earl of Worcester were both famous warriors, men experienced in battle and in the political manoeuvring of the times. They, like Hotspur, would have to be dealt with.

Henry reacted with an unaccustomed alacrity and energy that were totally out of character for him. Knowing that Glyndwr was still somewhere in the southern regions of Wales, he marched towards Hotspur who, according to his informants, had recently left Chester and had now set off to intercept the Prince of Wales at Shrewsbury.

The king had to strike fast, before Glyndwr returned to the north. Owain was then at Kidwelly where he had attacked the castle but so far had managed only to set fire to the gatehouse of the giant fortress. In response to an appeal from Hotspur, he had already dispatched 4,000 advance troops to help him. It would not be long before Glyndwr himself marched to join him.

There was another problem for the king. Hotspur's father had recently left Northumberland to join his son and was fast approaching Chester. Once Hotspur's army was reinforced it would have been too formidable a unit to challenge, even for the English king, and therefore speed was crucial. Hit hard, hit first, was the only way to take out Henry Percy.

Hotspur responded to the challenge with his usual reckless self-belief. Henry was of no account as a warrior, Glyndwr had proved that, but his son was an altogether different prospect. He needed to be defeated – in fact he needed to be killed. And so he continued his progress towards Mid Wales.

Hotspur's decision to fight before his troops were fully marshalled was typical of his instinctive and mercurial behaviour. In this respect he could be said to mirror, or rather foretell, Nathan Bedford Forrest, the famous American Civil War General who, when asked the secret of his success, replied 'I gets there firstest with the mostest.' This time, for Henry Hotspur, 'getting there firstest' was a technique that was to prove fatal.

In fact Henry IV arrived at Shrewsbury in advance of Hotspur and joined forces with his son. On 21 July 1403, the king's army and Hotspur's met at the village of Berwick, just a few miles outside Shrewsbury. Accounts of the Battle of Shrewsbury differ, many saying that the contest lasted all day, others that it took just three hours. Either way it was a bloodbath.

Early on in the fighting Prince Henry was wounded by an arrow in his cheek, the bolt lodging itself six inches into his face. For many men the wound would have put them out of action for several weeks, but not Henry. On the battlefield, the arrow head was removed by the surgeon digging into his flesh, without any form of anaesthetic, and leaving a long jagged scar that stayed with him until his dying day. Then Prince

Henry went blithely back to join his troops in the combat: 'And after there had fallen on either side in most bloody slaughter to the number of sixteen thousand men in the field of Berwick [...] two miles from Shrewsbury, victory was declared for the king who had thus made the onslaught. In this battle the said Lord Percy, the flower and the glory of Christendom, fell, alas, and with him his uncle.'[1]

However long it lasted, the battle was clearly very bloody. In addition to the thousands of men-at-arms who fell during the combat over 300 knights were also killed and the outcome was in doubt right to the end. At one stage a shout went up that the king had been killed. Many say that it was Hotspur who gave the shout, 'Henry Bolingbroke, dead. Henry Percy, king!' It was quickly proved untrue. Then, within minutes, another shout went up, this time claiming that Hotspur had been downed. 'Henry Percy, dead,' was the call. And this time the call proved to be absolutely true.

Hotspur, in the brunt of the conflict, had been shot in the face and killed. He fell almost at King Henry's feet. After that, Hotspur's forces lost heart and just melted away, leaving the two Henrys in control of the field. The whole campaign, from beginning to end, had been, for Henry Bolingbroke at least, the most decisive moment so far in his reign.

The death of Hotspur was a bitter blow for Glyndwr's Welsh rebels. Hotspur had enjoyed a mystical reputation as a soldier, almost equal to Glyndwr, but now that power and strength had been removed. To further discomfort the Percy clan, two days after the battle the captured Earl of Worcester was executed.

King Henry was inclined to celebrate his victory. He decided to parade his forces through South Wales, but in the end did not stay long enough to enjoy the moment. Ever fearful of the Scottish threat, he soon left Wales in the hands of his son and headed north to alleviate the problem there. Wherever he looked, it seemed, there was nothing but pain and grief for his regime.

The death of Hotspur was not the disaster it might have been and Henry actually gained little from it. Glyndwr had lost an ally, but Henry Percy Senior, the dead man's father, was soon on the scene at the head of a large body of northern troops. The elder Percy was considerably less impulsive than Hotspur. The threat to the Crown's position in North Wales had not yet gone away.

Matters did not look much better for him in the south west. That July Glyndwr and a considerable force of rebels suddenly materialised in the

Tywi Valley to begin one of the most effective forced marches of the whole war. It was to be a swift and merciless campaign with Glyndwr mirroring the route of an expedition taken by Llewelyn the Great many years before.

In a stunning and lightning-fast foray, Owain achieved one blistering success after another. Marching south, taking poorly defended manor houses and English garrisons as he went, he soon found himself outside the strongly fortified town of Carmarthen.

The town, which guarded the approaches to the staunchly royalist Pembrokeshire, had long been an English stronghold in the west and had been recently reinforced by troops from across the border. Nevertheless, the town and its castle quickly fell to Glyndwr and his lieutenants, men like Rhys Ddu from nearby Cardigan. Then, after garrisoning the fortress with troops from the local area, Glyndwr marched on to other equally significant objectives.

Within the space of a few months the castles of Careg Cennen, Dryslwyn, Llansteffan and Newcastle Emlyn had all been taken. None of them were particularly well defended, being held by a couple of dozen soldiers at best, but each and every capture was great for Welsh morale.

Then Glyndwr turned back on himself, headed east and set about destroying English possessions in Gwent and Glamorgan. The town of Abergavenny was sacked and burned before he switched his attentions to Newport and Cardiff. Both towns and their castles were soon in his hands.

Owain Glyndwr did not have sufficient strength in depth – a euphemism, perhaps, for not having enough men – to leave his conquests in safe hands. Most of them were abandoned or left empty within a few months of their capture. The important thing was that each of them had fallen to him, granting the Welsh a psychological victory that was worth far more than any echoing great fortress that would take many men to defend. The exceptions were Harlech, Aberystwyth and, if possible, mighty Caernarfon. They were symbolic of English tyranny and to capture them would be a real blow to the solar plexus of the English Crown.

In line with that thinking, while he was busy in the south Glyndwr's supporters in North Wales renewed their siege of Caernarfon. In November 1403, the attackers were joined by a French fleet which gave an added dimension to their siege. Even so, much to King Henry's pleasure, the castle managed to hold out.

In September the king had launched yet another brief campaign into Wales, his fourth personal entry into the Welsh war. Leaving Hereford behind him, Henry was soon burning his way across the country before, yet again, violent and drenching rains set in. Trying to ignore them, he sallied past Brecon and arrived outside Carmarthen. The Welsh simply sat and waited. Sure enough, inside a fortnight the king had gone, heading back to the warmth and comfort of Hereford.

That brief attack in 1403 was to be the king's last incursion into Wales. In future, he decided, he would leave fighting the Welsh to his son. A truly gifted soldier, Prince Henry had no more luck against Glyndwr and his guerrilla fighters than his father.

As the year ended the strength and reputation of Owain Glyndwr had never been higher. Yes, he had lost the support of Hotspur, but virtually all of Wales was now in his grip and Englishmen and women across the country and on the border shivered in fear at the sound of his name.

Magician, demon, warrior and warlord, Owain Glyndwr was now the stuff of nightmares. In 1404 nothing much would change – in fact things only got worse for King Henry of England.

*****

In May 1404, after months of siege and almost continuous assault, the castles of Harlech and Aberystwyth were eventually taken by Owain Glyndwr. Despite repeated attempts, the Welsh besiegers had failed to batter their way into Harlech, which, regardless of everything Glyndwr threw at it, stood proud and defiant on its sea-girt rock. And so Glyndwr reverted to the well-tried tactics of old – he would starve out the defenders.

It was a long, slow process which many of the besieging soldiers felt could be ended by a swift assault. Glyndwr stuck to his policy of besieging the castle. It was only when disease broke out, decimating the defenders and taking away their will to fight on, that the castle finally surrendered. Glyndwr promptly took possession, made the place his 'seat' and installed his family inside the fortress walls.

Aberystwyth Castle was taken at about the same time. The exact date, like so much else from the period, is unknown. Despite its picturesque position and superb views out over the sea, Aberystwyth Castle had always been vulnerable to attack. If he was going to hold the place – and it seemed that he was – Glyndwr would have to make modifications and fill the castle with a strong garrison.

Unlike his other conquests, Owain Glyndwr had every intention of holding on to Harlech and Aberystwyth. They would become symbols of Welsh resistance and were fortresses worthy of any man in his position.

Harlech quickly came to be regarded as the capital of the new Wales. There Glyndwr established his court and for a few short months was able to pose and parade around like a king before his courtiers and visiting dignitaries. The castle rooms and galleries were furnished to a high level with wall coverings and paintings, all chosen to reflect Glyndwr's rise to glory. Poets and story tellers, churchmen and pilgrims wandered the corridors while envoys from countries as diverse as France and Spain gave Harlech Castle an exotic and romantic feel. Feasts and jousting tournaments were held in the castle grounds, mirroring the stories from legend, stories that the bards were happy to repeat again and again.

No longer could Chroniclers like Adan of Usk sneer at the 'miserable Welsh' who conducted such low, despicable sneak attacks before running back to their caves in the woods. Now Wales had a monarch, a man to be proud of, a man who had fought and beaten the English. All it now needed for this picture to be complete was a parliament: 'Owen and his hill men, even in their misery, at Machynlleth, usurping the right of conquest, and other marks of royalty, albeit to his own confusion, held or counterfeited or made pretence of holding parliaments.'[2]

With his position now more secure than it ever had been Owain Glyndwr set about organising the apparatus of government. It was the right move at the right time and clearly showed the Welsh leader as someone who was considerably more than a simple guerrilla fighter.

In July 1404, he called four men from each commote of Wales to meet with him in a parliament at Machynlleth. The position or site of this, the first Welsh parliament, was carefully chosen in the centre of Glyndwr's territory. He knew that he was safe there but he was also making an important statement – this is my land, all of it, and you can do absolutely nothing about it.

This was no pretence, as Adam of Usk tried to label it. Calling a parliament was a genuine attempt at creating a democratic unit of representation for an independent country. To help or aid him in his plans Glyndwr was able to call on several capable men. These included Gruffudd Young, who was appointed as his chancellor, and John Trefor, the Bishop of St Asaph. Together they laid plans for the creation of an independent state governed and driven by a broad nationalistic ideal.[3]

There is an often repeated story that Glyndwr's implacable enemy Dafydd Gam managed to slip into the Parliament Hall at Machynlleth where he attempted to assassinate Owain. He was, according to the legend, overpowered and captured before he could do any damage. He was then ransomed for a large sum of money.

The story is of somewhat dubious authenticity, however. Apart from anything else Gam had already proved himself such a nuisance that Glyndwr, ruthless when he had to be, would have had him executed on the spot.

The significance of Glyndwr's first parliament should never be underestimated. Apart from a second such gathering at Harlech the following year, no Welsh parliament sat again until twentieth-century devolution created the Senedd which sits now in Cardiff Bay. The very process of calling a parliament showed how serious Glyndwr and his advisors were about creating a Welsh state and nation, and at the head of it stood Owain Glyndwr. This was no rabble rouser, no idle dreamer; this was a man who had clear plans for the future.

And yet Glyndwr knew that it was not enough just to dream and lay plans – or, for that matter, to conduct guerrilla campaigns, no matter how effective they might be. In order to be fully free of England he would have to fight traditional wars and stand in the field against a fully-fledged and experienced army of professional soldiers. To do that he would need allies.

Glyndwr's first parliament was attended by representatives of the king of France, along with envoys from Spain and Scotland. A treaty or agreement had already been thrashed out between Wales and France when Gruffudd Young and John Hanmer, representatives of Glyndwr's government, had sailed for the continent earlier in the year. Now at Machynlleth, in the summer of 1404, that treaty was formally signed and acknowledged.

Glyndwr understood only too well that the French would aid him only as long as it suited them. Charles VI of France, like all medieval rulers, was pragmatic in his actions and alliances. Astute and intelligent as Glyndwr was – and blessed with an innate perception of international diplomacy – he could see that for the moment an alliance suited Charles very well. Both parties, Welsh and French, were conscious of the old adage, 'My enemy's enemy is my friend.'

Neither Charles nor Glyndwr could afford to antagonise the other. They both needed the alliance and they both needed the reassurance of a strong and powerful ally at their shoulder. It was at the first parliament that Glyndwr was formally acknowledged as Prince of Wales, an important point as previously he had been merely self-proclaimed. Now everyone, his lords and captains, and, in particular, the envoys of France and Spain, were there to give witness to the event.

The treaty was simple enough. The two nations formally agreed to make war on Henry IV and not to sign separate peace agreements. It was to be a fight to the finish, in theory at least.

The French saw the alliance as an extension of their war with England, opening up another front which would further split Henry's forces. Glyndwr wanted to make use of French sea power and also to employ numbers of French men-at-arms in the more formal battles he knew he would soon have to fight.

It was an opportune moment for such an alliance. Henry, having lost the support of the Percy family in the north, was more vulnerable than ever. With Glyndwr active in the west he would have to fight a war on two fronts – three if you count the seemingly endless campaigns in France and English-held territories like Aquitaine.

With fortresses like Harlech and Aberystwyth under his control, a parliament organised and running and a formal alliance with a foreign power, it had been a good period for the Welsh. Owain Glyndwr was now supremely confident about his position. Almost all of Wales was in his hands or under his influence. Only a few great castles in the north and the county of Pembrokeshire in the south west stood out against him. He had achieved great things but already people were asking how much further he could go.

*****

For the rest of the year Glyndwr continued with his successful hit-and-run tactics, burning and looting English possessions in South Wales, across the Marches and along the coast. Woebley Castle in the south was badly damaged by his forces and Bangor Cathedral was burned.

His successes did not always go without criticism. In addition to the burning of the cathedral at Bangor, several Welsh towns had been subjected to looting and destruction by both sides, Carmarthen and Brecon amongst them. The inhabitants had no reason to love and support either the Welsh or the English.

As far as the ordinary Welsh farmers and labourers were concerned the power of the English might appear to be broken or at the very least severely dented. The trouble was that it had been replaced by a degree of terrorism from Glyndwr and his followers that seemed to know few limits.

Welsh men and women died as easily as English and very often no one really knew who the perpetrators were. Whether it was from a Welsh arrow or an English lance, death came easily and brutally to the ordinary people of Wales.

Glyndwr had developed a policy of destruction, a scorched-earth tactic that was designed to make the country untenable for the English. Unfortunately it did not help the Welsh either. With English soldiers doing exactly the same it meant that life in Wales was not always the idyllic and pastoral experience that we are often led to believe.

The English, of course, could afford to wait, to see out the troublesome war. Henry might be criticised by Parliament for the money that was being wasted on military campaigns in Wales and Scotland but he knew that if he just gritted his teeth and got on with fighting the rebels the adverse comments would eventually go away.

Owain Glyndwr did not enjoy such a luxury. Each death, each burned house or farm, bit slowly but surely into his reserves of support. There was the added problem that Glyndwr had to feed his troops and plunder or pillaging was the quickest and easiest, maybe even the only, way of solving this logistical nightmare.

And yet, despite the strong anti-Glyndwr lobby, there was also a huge groundswell of support from people right across Wales. In a world of polarised opinion there was a simple choice, love him or hate him: the people of Wales did both. It was the *potential* of what he was offering rather than what had been achieved that was Glyndwr's greatest appeal. That remains a dichotomy that was rampant at the time and continues to exist today.

However you look at it, by 1404 Owain appeared to have gained a powerful foothold both in material possessions and in support from the

Welsh peasants. Its base may have been rooted in fear, of Glyndwr as much as anyone, but he was undoubtedly a man of the people, promising them – in deeds if not in words – a better future.

The church had always been a strong backer of Glyndwr's rebellion, both the Bishop and the Dean of St Asaph being particularly virulent and vocal in their condemnation of English acts of barbarity. It was an important element of cooperation, offering Glyndwr an educated and theoretical level of support which might otherwise have been missing.

John Trefor, Bishop of St Asaph, was one of the most influential of Glyndwr's supporters. He, along with Gruffudd Yonge, was instrumental in penning the famous Pennal Letter of 1405, and in giving the uprising its remarkable literate base. In turn that undoubtedly helped with the credibility of Glyndwr in the eyes of foreign rulers and provided the rebellion with a degree of intellectual provenance to what Owain was trying to achieve.

Church support went further and deeper than that. Glyndwr enjoyed particularly strong support from the Cistercian and Franciscan monks who had established themselves in monasteries like Strata Florida, Llanfaes on Anglesey, and Llantarnam near the old Roman legionary camp of Caerleon. Sion ap Hywel, Abbot of Llantarnam, was one of Glyndwr's most fervent supporters, dying for the cause in spectacular fashion in May 1405.

The great monasteries of Wales were, in the main, seething hotbeds of support for Glyndwr, and one of the reasons that Henry had so enjoyed desecrating the abbey at Strata Florida. There is little doubt that at one time or another Glyndwr sought and received sanctuary at one or more of the great religious houses of the country.

The *uchelwyr* of Wales, leaders of the various communities across the country, were another powerful group of supporters. However, their motives were often questionable and Henry IV, Prince Harry and the other English leaders were conscious of the words of Giraldus Cambrensis, written many years before but nonetheless still acceptable to their minds: 'The Welsh people rarely keep their promises, for their minds are as fickle as their bodies are agile. It is very easy to persuade them to do something wrong, and then just as easy to stop them once they have started [...] The only thing they really persist in is changing their minds.'[4]

It was a damning comment that people in power remembered. It was an opinion that persisted for many years, and without being too defensive, probably still exists today in some quarters. Luckily for Owain Glyndwr not every member of the *uchelwyr* class was as fickle as Giraldus believed. The two Tudor brothers from Anglesey were dynamic leaders, *uchelwyrs* to the bone and forerunners of a dynamic dynasty, but there were many others as well.

Men like Gwilym Gwyn, Rhys Ddu and Rhys Gethin were always ready to fight alongside Glyndwr. Perhaps the most notable of them all was Henry Dwn of Kidwelly. In August 1403, he led an assault on the town and castle of Kidwelly, burning the houses and laying waste to much of the land around the area.

Glyndwr had to acknowledge that not everyone was as loyal or as committed as Henry Dwn, Rhys Ddu and the rest. The *uchelwyr* as a class were enormously conscious of their positions as community leaders. Many of them would support Glyndwr while it was expedient to do so. When times changed their alliance and friendship could easily change as well.

Gwilym ap Gruffudd of North Wales was a prime example of the two-faced nature of many of the *uchelwyr*. Sly and self-interested, Gwilym ap Gruffudd cared about one thing only – his future. Glyndwr knew it, of course, but also knew that he had no choice. He needed Gruffudd's support.

In Glyndwr's glory years Gwilym was an active and unashamed supporter of the rebellion, but when the fortunes of the Prince of Wales began to turn Gruffudd quickly changed sides. He did it without shame or compunction.

In the years after Glyndwr's death he married an English woman, disinherited his children from a previous Welsh marriage and formally levied the king to declare him English. He inherited or was given much of the land seized from Glyndwr's supporters before dying peacefully in his bed in 1431.

Other Welsh noblemen opposed Glyndwr from the start, a stance that was at least an honourable one. These were men who felt they owed an allegiance to the English Crown. The old knightly code of chivalry was strong with them but they were also pragmatic and, looking ahead, could see only defeat for Owain and his rebels.

Dafydd Gam was one of the leading supporters of the king in Wales. He came from a landed, well-established family in the Brecon area and was a descendent of the Norman De Bohun line. His real name was Dafydd ap Llewelyn ap Hywel but he was awarded the name Gam

(Welsh for lame or deformed) because of a physical disability – and, of course, for his inveterate opposition to the Welsh national hero.

Dafydd Gam took a lead role in the later English victory at Pwll Melyn in May 1405, before being captured and ransomed by Glyndwr's forces in 1412. He went on to serve Henry V, dying at the Battle of Agincourt in October 1415, one of the few English casualties. He appears in Shakespeare's *Henry V* as the character Fluellen.

The one thing that could be said about men like Dafydd Gam was that Glyndwr at least knew where he stood with them. That was not possible with people like Gwilym ap Gruffudd – or, for that matter, with his supposed French allies.

The first real involvement of the French came soon after Glyndwr's parliament in Machynlleth. That summer a fleet of nearly 100 sail, under the command of Jean, sire de Rieux et Rochefort, Marshal of France and Brittany, left France to attack the coast of Britain.

There was great excitement in the Welsh ranks when they heard about the coming of the French fleet. Now, at last, Glyndwr would have what he had always needed – ships to harry the coast and castles of the English, to destroy their supply chains and to give him easy access to the other parts of Europe.

Unfortunately, the French had too many 'old scores' to settle and this was payback time in a very big way. None of the French sailors or their leaders knew when or if such an opportunity would ever come again. With that in mind, Jean and his commanders decided to concentrate their efforts on the southern coast of England where the pickings were greatest. The area was certainly richer than even the most arable and wealthy parts of Wales, and loot, it appeared, was central to the thoughts and intentions of the French force.

The decision could be justified – even if only barely – by the contention that this was where the French attacks could hurt the English most. That was true enough, but it did not help the Welsh to cope with the disappointment.

Within a few short weeks the French had raided and looted many small ports and towns on the Devon coast. There was, as Jean had expected, panic amongst the townspeople. Nobody knew where the French would strike next.

Dartmouth was set alight and all but destroyed. French pockets were well and truly bulging with loot. It was a tactic that might well annoy and frustrate Henry but it had little real effect on conditions in Wales. It was also an enterprise that could never be more than short lived. The south coast of England was a vulnerable area but it was also easily reached and reinforced. After the first half dozen attacks reinforcement of the coastal towns of Devon and Cornwall was exactly what the English did, and when resistance finally proved too strong the French Fleet simply reversed course and headed home.

Arguably, they could have turned their attention to Wales but for some reason chose not to sail to the aid of their allies. It was a lost opportunity, but Glyndwr hoped better cooperation would be achieved next time.

Even then there must have been a sliver of doubt in his brain – were the French really interested in helping the Welsh in their rebellion or was the alliance little more than a grand gesture that had already passed its period of usefulness? It did not bear too much analysis and Glyndwr would have been a fool to place too much emphasis on French support.

Despite the poor performance of the French ships, Glyndwr's name and reputation continued to be feared throughout the Principality. King Henry was inundated with requests for help, the terror in people's letters being almost palpable: 'May it please you to reflect that it will be a great disgrace to lose a country which your noble ancestors have won [...] Written in haste – in great haste – at Hereford.'[5]

The urgency of the above appeal is almost disrespectful but that is how the Welsh rebellion was now affecting the king's supporters. If there was one phrase to sum up the attitude of the English supporters and soldiers in Wales it had to be the simple but heartfelt plea, 'Do something!'

By the end of 1404 Owain Glyndwr stood at the height of his power. His achievements had been magnificent and now, with the help and support of the French – albeit the rather questionable, disinterested French – there was no reason to believe that he would fail to go on and achieve his ultimate aim. In December 1404, an independent and secure Wales, free at last from her English overlords, seemed to be a distinct possibility. The whole world, it seemed, lay at Glyndwr's feet and there was, it appeared, nobody and nothing to stop him.

Chapter Seven

The Year of the French

The years 1403 and 1404 had shown Owain Glyndwr at his statesmanlike best. It was a skill that he would have to display again in 1405.

He began the year by developing an idea he had previously discussed with Edward Mortimer and Harry Hotspur. Knowing that in the long run he had neither the manpower nor the equipment to defeat Henry IV on his own, Glyndwr had always favoured the idea of strong allies. That was the purpose behind the previous year's treaty with France, but allies were also available within Britain.

Glyndwr had lost the strong right arm of Henry Hotspur at the Battle of Shrewsbury but it was not the grievous loss that might have been supposed. His death brought an altogether different dimension to the rebellion.

The young warrior, dynamic and thrusting as he was, had always been hot headed, and against such an innately powerful nation as the English that was always liable to spell disaster. It was also against the natural instinct of Owain Glyndwr himself, a man who had always preferred to think a problem through before taking action.

Diplomacy was certainly not the forte of the young Henry Percy, but his father, also called Henry, was an altogether more controlled and far-sighted individual. For many years the elder Percy had maintained a degree of independence from the English Crown, carefully treading the line between rebellion and total subservience – never an easy task in the medieval world. And now he was ready to extract revenge for the death of his son.

Henry Percy was one probable ally. The other was Glyndwr's son-in-law Edward Mortimer. He had been supportive since changing sides and joining the Welsh rebels two years earlier but Mortimer was no mere lieutenant to Glyndwr. He was a powerful nobleman in his own right with land, soldiers and money of his own. His connections alone made him the ideal 'Third Man'.

On 28 February 1405, Glyndwr, Edward Mortimer and Henry Percy formally signed what was called the Tripartite Indenture. Its aim was simple – to dethrone Henry IV and divide England and Wales between them. The indenture was based on friendship, the friendship of good and loyal comrades who would 'lay aside all fraud and deceit' in order to achieve their goals.

According to the indenture agreement, once Henry was removed the country was to be split into three separate kingdoms. Owain was to receive all of Wales, but, importantly, the boundaries of his empire were to be greatly extended:

> Owain and his heirs shall have the whole of Cambria or Wales, within the borders, limits and boundaries underwritten, divided from Loegria, which is commonly called England; namely from the Severn coast where the River Severn leads from the sea, going down to the north gate of the city of Worcester; and from that gate directly to the ash trees commonly called Onnenau Meigion which grow on the high road from Bridgnorth to Kinver; thence directly by the high road [...] as far as the head or source of the river commonly called the Mersey.[1]

Effectively, in addition to all of Wales, the agreement handed him most of modern-day Cheshire, Shropshire and Herefordshire. Percy was to take the north of England, Mortimer the south. The boundary between the lands of the two Englishmen was to be along a line abutting Glyndwr's Wales and passing east just below Market Bosworth, through Northampton to the North Sea coast.

Interestingly, the intended division of Britain was to follow the advice of a prophecy supposedly made by Merlin, the ancient and legendary magician of King Arthur. Merlin had apparently defined how the island of Britain was to be best divided up and Glyndwr in particular saw no reason to deviate from the wishes of the old magician.

Mortimer, Percy and Glyndwr were all superstitious men and here, in the Tripartite Indenture, prophecy was being used to make the seizure of power a legitimate action. It was in many respects a justification for what they were doing, and while all three men were not above manipulating prophecy and myth for their own ends, they all had an implicit belief in the power of soothsayers, magicians and wise men.

Despite popular opinion, Owain Glyndwr never claimed to be Y Mab Daragon, the son of prophecy or destiny, but it was certainly an appellation that was awarded to him after his death. Even so, he had an incredibly strong regard for prophecy and fate, so much so that he would not act or do anything of significance if the omens were not favourable.

In the early days of the rebellion his personal prophet, Crach Ffinnant, was always consulted before any major steps were taken. That need continued. In 1403 – some accounts say 1404 – Glyndwr is also known to have consulted Hopcyn ap Tomas of Ynys Forgan, perhaps the most renowned sage in the country, about the likelihood of success in the coming campaigns.

It was not just Glyndwr. Belief in prophecy had become something of a craze in the medieval period, reaching a height during the reign of Richard II, and was to return with a vengeance during the early days of the Wars of the Roses. Richard had gone, his regime and his management style wiped out by Henry Bolingbroke, but it has to be remembered that Glyndwr was very much a child of Richard's reign. And, of course, he was a Celt with all of the mystic Celtic visions and dreams associated with the ancient people of the west.

At the end of the day his attitude was simple – he believed in spirits, in prophecy and in myth. It was, therefore, perfectly logical to justify the removal of Henry IV, just as Bolingbroke had removed Richard, and acknowledge the subsequent planned division of the country as inevitable by invoking the prophecy of Merlin.

*****

The year 1405 has always been known as 'The Year of the French', the time when French assistance would bring the long-held aim of Welsh freedom to a positive conclusion. It was a year of hope and exhilaration for the Welsh, a year of promise and celebration, but ultimately it was a year of disappointed dreams and failure.

Charles VI of France, already becoming known as Charles the Mad, was drifting in and out of periods of insanity when, amongst other afflictions, he believed that he was made of glass. On those occasions he would let no one near him in case they should shatter his body.

However, in his lucid periods the French king was already thinking about abandoning his warlike stance and making peace with Henry. He was beginning to formulate, in his head at least, a peace plan that would get him out of this costly war with England.

Things did not quite begin like that as Charles had already made tentative moves in his campaigns against the English. The previous year, between August and October, Charles d'Albret, first cousin of the king, had led an expedition against Anglo-Gascon Aquitaine. The Aquitaine was then, apart from Calais, the only English possession left in mainland Europe and to reclaim it for the French would be a major achievement.

Over the next few months many towns and fortresses fell into French hands. They had either been stormed or 'bought off', sold by self-serving English officers for considerable amounts of money. A second offensive was soon being planned for 1405. Charles VI might be thinking about peace but that was for the future and for the moment the war continued.[2]

As the New Year dawned Charles came under increasing pressure from his more aggressive brother, the Duke of Orleans. As a result the French king finally realised that he had no option other than to put his forces to work, particularly on the English mainland. For Owain Glyndwr it was not a moment too soon as events in South Wales had taken an unfortunate turn for the worse.

That spring, Prince Henry of Monmouth had inflicted a serious defeat on Glyndwr's supporters at Grosmont in the Welsh Marches. Henry was an absent commander, being ensconced a dozen miles away in Hereford when the battle was fought, but he did manage to garner the plaudits, taking much of the credit for this victory over the Welsh rebels.

On 11 March 1405, outside Grosmont Castle in Gwent, men of Henry's command succeeded in putting to flight a significant number of Glyndwr's supporters. The men of Gwent were enthusiastic enough but were no match for the better trained and better equipped English soldiers.

The town of Grosmont was then an important trading centre, being the third largest settlement in South Wales behind Carmarthen and Abergavenny. It also boasted a large castle, one of the famous three castles – Skenfrith, White and Grosmont – which had been built in the early days of the English conquest to defend this part of the Welsh Marches.

According to Prince Henry a rebel force of some 8,000 men attacked and burned part of the town. Henry immediately despatched Lord Talbot with a small force of foot and cavalry along with knights like John Greyndour and William Newport to assist him. Despite being greatly outnumbered by the rebels, their aim was to halt the enemy incursion.

Henry's report to the king, his father, was succinct and to the point. In it he was proud and egotistical as only a successful adolescent, full of his own importance can possibly be: 'By the aid of the blessed Trinity your men won the field and vanquished all the said rebels and killed by reliable account on the battlefield at their return from pursuit, some say 800 and some 1000, on pain of their life.'[3]

If Henry's figures are correct – and they do appear to be a little exaggerated – that would make the Battle of Grosmont an enormous defeat for Glyndwr. Accurate or not, the defeat and the casualties incurred certainly brought Glyndwr up short. He had not been present at the battle but he knew that his fight for independence would not sustain its momentum if he began to suffer more defeats like Grosmont.

He was right to worry. On 5 May 1405, his troops suffered a second setback, their most grievous defeat yet. Despite being stopped in their tracks at Grosmont, the rebels regrouped and, under the command of Glyndwr's brother Tudur and son Gruffudd, launched another offensive in the south east. This time they were aiming for the castle at Usk, a significant citadel in that part of Wales.

Glyndwr had already burned the town of Usk some time before, causing untold damage for the householders and the farmers in the region. None of the townsfolk would have been pleased to see his troops returning, even though Glyndwr himself was then many miles away in North Wales.

The battle began with Gruffudd launching an attack on Usk Castle. The assault was repulsed and the Welsh army retreated to the north. They were pursued by Henry's troops from the Usk garrison under the command of Sir John Greyndour, Richard Grey and Sir John Oldcastle. Foremost in the pursuing host was Dafydd Gam, eager as ever to make his mark.

Legend has it that the local knowledge of Dafydd Gam and John Oldcastle, both men from the area who knew every track and pathway over the hills, helped the English forces in their pursuit of the fleeing rebels. Gruffudd's troops were chased into Monkswood Forest, north-west of Usk, where, close to the mountain of Pwll Melyn, they were systematically cut down and destroyed. Gruffudd was captured and his uncle Tudur killed. Adam of Usk was suitably triumphant in his vituperative account of the Battle of Pwll Melyn: 'Griffith (Gruffudd), eldest son of Owen, with a great following, made assault, in an evil hour for himself, on the castle of Usk [...] (The king's forces) sallying forth manfully, took him captive and pursuing his men even to the hill country of Higher Gwent, through the River Usk, there slew with fire and the edge of the sword many of them, and above all the Abbot of Llanthony, and they crushed them without ceasing, driving them through the monk's wood, where the said Griffith was taken.'[4]

The battle, following so closely on the defeat at Grosmont, had cost Glyndwr dearly. In addition to around 1,500 dead, many of his supporters were taken prisoner. According to Adam of Usk a total of 300 of these prisoners were immediately executed in front of the castle, others sent to captivity in London. Amongst those to make the journey eastwards was Gruffudd who was held for six years in the Tower of London before dying in the prison, probably from plague.

The death in battle of his brother Tudur was a loss that hurt Glyndwr deeply. They had always been close, despite Tudur accepting the king's pardon back in 1401. He had since reverted to his brother's side, and while not the same man of action and diplomacy as Owain, he was a battle-hardened veteran.

The two brothers were apparently very similar in appearance and, for a brief moment, after the body had been decapitated and the head presented to the English commanders, it was believed that Glyndwr himself had been felled in the battle: 'The spirits of the English were sadly damped when the absence of a wart under the left eye, a distinguishing mark of Glyndwr, proclaimed that they joy was premature and that it was the dead face of his younger brother on which they were gazing.'[5]

The wart was actually on Glyndwr's forehead rather than under his eye but the lack of any growth anywhere on the severed head was enough to convince the English that this was not Owain Glyndwr but his brother.

The Abbot of Llanthony, Sion ap Howell, had been a supporter of the rebellion since its beginning. His death at Pwll Melyn was both tragic and unnecessary. He was cut down while he was tending to the wounded – of both sides – and taking no part in the actual fighting.

It is possible that another of Glyndwr's great supporters, Rhys Gethin, was also killed in the battle. Doubts and confusion have been expressed over Rhys – who exactly was he, where did he come from and so on. There are at least two strong candidates for the identity of the man, just as there are two possibilities for the site and time of his death.

Rhys, who had played a significant part in Glyndwr's victory at Bryn Glas in 1402, was apparently Owain's standard bearer – probably an honorific or ceremonial role. He was also at the forefront of the action when the castles of West Wales were taken in 1403. We simply do not know much more than that about the man. He was killed in 1405, but whether it was at the Battle of Grosmont or the Battle of Pwll Melyn remains unclear.

The results of the double defeat were, predictably enough, disastrous for Owain Glyndwr and his supporters. Writers throughout the years have seized on the defeats as the start of Glyndwr's decline as a power in Wales and have waxed lyrical about their effect: 'The result of these two defeats was almost magical. Within a week the bubble had burst. Owain's undisciplined troops had melted like snow in the sunshine. Each man had hurried to his home, while their leader was a fugitive hiding from his pursuers in rocks and caves.'[6]

Edward Laws, the writer of the above quotation, was typical of the romantic but not always strictly accurate style of recording. Owain was not present at either of the battles, which did not take place within a few days of each other, and he was not forced to take shelter in mountain caves – not this time at least. Even so, the extract does manage to catch the despair that must have fallen across Glyndwr's forces when they heard the news of Gruffudd's capture and Tudur's death.

As if these defeats were not enough, in June Beaumaris Castle was retaken by the forces of King Henry. An English army from Ireland landed on Anglesey and after taking the castle set about looting and pillaging across the whole island. It was undoubtedly a low point for Glyndwr's rebellion.

*****

Matters began to improve in August 1405. On the first day of the month Glyndwr's second parliament was convened at Harlech Castle. If nothing else, calling the parliament showed that Owain Glyndwr had no intention of rolling over and dying. His spirit and the spirit of the rebellion were still strong despite the recent setbacks, setbacks on a national and on a personal level.

The parliament was attended by ambassadors from France, Brittany, Scotland and Castille, displaying the international support that still existed for Glyndwr. He immediately startled his supporters out of their undoubted mood of despondency by announcing that the French were at last coming. Owain Glyndwr was not making a prophecy, he was telling the truth – King Charles of France had finally been jolted out of his lethargy and was about to honour his commitment.

A French fleet comprising 140 vessels had already left Brest, leaving the port on 22 July. Crammed onto the decks of the ships were just short of 3,000 soldiers, a force that was made up of 800 men-at-arms, 600 crossbowmen or archers and 1,200 light infantry and cavalry. Three days after Glyndwr announced that they were on their way the armada appeared in Milford Haven and the troops began to disembark.

Within days of establishing themselves on shore the French were met by 10,000 Welsh troops. Owain Glyndwr, it seems, was amongst them, having been granted money and soldiers by his parliament. At the time, joining with the French was seen as a great opportunity to achieve victory over Henry. Only now, with the benefit of hindsight and in light of the coming events, does it appear that this was actually something of a last throw of the dice.

It was unfortunate that many of the horses of the French army had died or become unwell on the voyage and some delay was necessary in order to replenish or replace the cavalry mounts. When everything was organised, however, the Franco-Welsh force set off. Their target was England.

First, however, there were English occupied fortresses to take care of in Wales. In quick succession the towns of Haverfordwest and Tenby were taken, but the combined force failed to take the castles in either of the towns. They had more success at St Clears on the road to Carmarthen, and then, by agreement rather than by assault or act of war, Carmarthen itself fell into their hands.

More importantly, the town and castle of Cardigan were captured when Glyndwr decided to swing north and head up the coast. Strategically this was a great blow to King Henry as, together with Aberystwyth and

Harlech a little further up the coast, it gave Owain vital control of the sea lanes – in particular the Irish Sea – around Wales.

The combined force marched on, crossing the broad belly of Wales and finally penetrating into England by means of the Teme Valley. The Franco-Welsh force drew up on Woodbury Hill outside the village of Great Witley and paused in their advance. They were still some seven or eight miles short of Worcester and the pause was meant to be no more than a brief respite, a time to draw breath and check weapons.

Glyndwr, ever conscious of his beloved myths and prophecies, was intending to confront the English at Onnenau Meigion, on the road to Bridgnorth, the six ash trees that traditionally marked the border of Wales. This was where, according to a legend attributed once again to Merlin, the great eagle (Glyndwr) would defeat an army from the east (the English). Glyndwr believed the story implicitly and his march through Wales was leading him ever closer to Onnenau Meigion.

Unfortunately for his plans, the English suddenly appeared, drawing up a mile away on the adjacent Abberley Hill. Glyndwr was still a dozen miles short of his proposed battle site. The news that a French and Welsh Army was now in England had spread alarm throughout the country. No one could remember when a French Army had pushed so deeply and so decisively into England and King Henry immediately dropped what he was doing and rushed to Worcester where he took command of the English force.

Henry and Glyndwr were finally face to face and the battle, when it came, would undoubtedly suit Henry more than it would Glyndwr. It would, as they both knew, be a traditional contest of arms with knight against knight, man-at-arms against man-at-arms. This was clearly going to be the final battle.

As it turned out this was not even close to being the final battle. It was, however, the supreme anti-climax. Quite simply, nothing happened. For eight days the two armies sat and stared at each other and neither one made any attempt to break the stalemate.

The total lack of movement from either side has never been satisfactorily explained. Some historians have suggested that it was not two great armies that faced each other, just small scouting parties or small pickets of skirmishers. The main armies were well behind the advance guard, they say, out of harm's way.

As the information about the stand-off has come mainly from French sources there may have been an element of truth in the belief. Ever conscious of what would be said when they returned home, the French commanders would have been seeking to explain away their reluctance to attack a foreign army in a foreign land.

The French knew that their Welsh allies were not exactly at their best in open combat and, therefore, the bulk of the fighting in any face-to-face encounter would come down to them. They certainly had more to lose than their opponents. Cut off, isolated and far from home, defeat would have meant many months, years even, in English prisons.

It is more likely, however, that the reluctance to engage emanated from the Welsh. Owain was unhappy at the prospect of a pitched battle. That was not his style, not the type of combat for which he was rightly famous. The two recent defeats in the south had shown him that in a traditional encounter, where training and tactics, armour and discipline were the qualities that really mattered, he was at a decided disadvantage. His forces were sorely lacking in all of those elements. He did not really know the quality of the French soldiers and his own men were much happier in the hit-and-run campaigns that had brought them so much success in the past.

And then, of course, the prophecy in which he implicitly believed had declared that victory would come to Glyndwr at Onnenau Meigion, not some hill outside Worcester. He had waited too long and now Henry and his army stood between him and his objective.

Glyndwr knew that he was a long way from home and, despite being 13,000 strong, his army was still outnumbered. His supply lines were already tenuous, open to sniping guerrilla attacks. He and his commanders probably felt as vulnerable as the French. To fight now, in the wrong frame of mind, would have been against all the laws of warfare. Victory would have been impossible, defeat would have been disastrous.

Clearly Henry Bolingbroke was thinking along similar lines – in his case defeat would have been even more calamitous. He knew he was unpopular with the people of Britain, who still resented his sudden and unexpected rise to power. He was only too well aware that there were people out there just waiting for him to slip up yet again. Defeat by what was still regarded as 'the French army' would have surely meant the end of his reign.

Two reluctant commanders, two reluctant armies – there was only one possible result. After eight days Glyndwr gave the order and his Franco-Welsh contingent wheeled around and headed back into Wales. The English watched them go before turning and making their own way off the battlefield that had never been.

Viewed now, Glyndwr's decision not to risk battle at Worcester was perhaps the greatest mistake of his military career, perhaps his political one as well. The opportunity to win a great victory over Henry never came to him again.

Who would have emerged victorious remains an imponderable, but for small nations like Wales wars are not often won by guerrilla tactics alone. At some stage there always has to be a major confrontation. Owain Glyndwr had missed his opportunity.

*****

Henry made one final attempt at military victory that year. In September 1405, he brought his forces to Coity in South Wales where, for some time, Glyndwr's men had been besieging the castle.

It was a half-hearted attempt by the king to break the siege and it failed. Little is known about the action but it seems that Henry was once again frustrated by poor weather as much as by the local Welsh forces. He quickly gave up his attempt and retreated to Hereford in some disarray, leaving behind his baggage train which was quickly ransacked by the rebels, their prize yielding vast quantities of much-needed weapons, clothing and money.

Then, for Glyndwr at least, came a moment of utter disbelief. On 1 November, the feast of All Saints, a large number of the French troops that had marched with him into England suddenly left his side and went home. There was no warning, no discussion, they simply left.

The reason for their abrupt departure has never been made totally clear, but the French were undoubtedly concerned about the strength of the English defenders. They had seen them during the stand-off at Great Witley, witnessed their numbers and their weapons, and probably had doubts about their ability to defeat such a host.

The French departure was an unexpected blow and it left Glyndwr high and dry. Twelve hundred lightly armoured soldiers along with 500 crossbowmen under the command of a Picard knight named le

Begue de Belay remained alongside his army but it was clear that they, too, were not intending to stay long. When, early in the New Year, the last of the French contingent followed their comrades back home, Owain Glyndwr was once again facing Henry alone.

Glyndwr should have known that the French were 'fair weather' friends. Their performance in the various campaigns – at sea and on land – should have told him that they were at best half-hearted in their support. They needed a strong and dynamic leader who could direct their operations. Poor, mad Charles VI was not the man to provide that leadership.

The departing French had made promises of sending a new army to Wales but such a force never materialised and it was soon obvious that there had never been any intention of sending more troops. As R.R. Davies has written, 'the truth is that Wales no longer figured as an important item on the French agenda.'[7] It is an accurate statement but there was more, a lot more, to the sudden departure of the French forces.

Traditionally, French soldiers had only ever been provided with very basic rations and had always been expected to pillage or live off the land during their campaigns. Wales, it quickly became apparent, was not the best of environments to aid such tactics. It was cold, it rained constantly, the wind was like a knife and what crops there were had been left to rot in the fields. The people were already half-starved and had little to entice the raiders.

On the broader political front Charles VI had finally got his way and peace negotiations were in progress. The last thing Charles needed while talks were being held was the thought of an invading French army on English or Welsh soil. The negotiations ground on, slowly but surely. A halt to hostilities, temporarily as it turned out, was formally declared between England and France towards the end of 1407.

Promised military help for Glyndwr from the Scots had not materialised and in late 1405 Prince Henry began to implement an economic blockade that was, in the long run, far more effective than any military campaign he might have mounted.

Henry's tactic was simple but highly effective – he would identify key ports and blockade or attack them so that Glyndwr could not get supplies through. It may not have been the romantic style the English prince had been looking for but it was highly effective.

Over the next few months Glyndwr's forces found themselves increasingly short of rations and weapons as the blockade began to bite. The effect was slow to materialise but in the long run it was a hugely important factor in the eventual defeat of the Welsh rebels.

It is hard to know the state of Glyndwr's mind during the final troubled months of 1405 but he must have been devastated by the way events had turned out. He was no great ponderer or reflector on events of the past, what was gone was gone, but he would have been far more concerned about what might happen in the future. The capture of his brother-in-law John Hanmer and his personal secretary, Owain ap Gruffudd ap Rhisiart, by the English that winter added to Glyndwr's woes.

He had known all along that he would not be able to defeat Henry and the might of England without foreign aid. That notion had been central to all his actions, the basis of all his statesmanship and strategy, but the French had now abandoned him and the Scots, his other potential allies, were soon to have their own worries.

In March 1406, English pirates operating off Flamborough Head captured the future King James I of Scotland. James, an 11-year-old boy, was on his way to France where it was felt he would be safe from the English and from internal enemies. That would have been a correct assumption – if he had been allowed to get there.

The pirates duly handed James over to Henry – for a price, of course – and the young boy spent the next eighteen years of his life in captivity. He was a more than useful pawn in the game of international politics and Glyndwr would now look in vain for help from the Scots.

Abandoned by his allies, forced to pillage and raid the lands of his own followers in order to feed his soldiers, by the end of 1405 things were looking decidedly bleak for Owain Glyndwr and for the future of the Welsh rebellion. With winter almost upon them the chances for any last-minute success against English forces was highly unlikely.

If there was one saving grace it came in the shape of Aberystwyth and Harlech, the two great castles that had fallen to the Welsh rebels a few years previously. Both of them occupied important positions, one in Mid Wales, the other in the north, and both held commanding locations on the coast which allowed the rebels easy access to the sea lanes and travel to the continent.

The castles were not just significant fortresses, though. It was what they symbolised and stood for that was important. As long as they remained in Welsh hands there was always hope.

Despite his military misfortunes Owain Glyndwr was still a significant presence in Wales. He was recognised almost everywhere as the Prince of Wales and even had a great seal made to emphasise the point. The inscription around the outside of the seal declared that he was 'Owain, by Grace of God, Prince of Wales'.

The phrase 'Grace of God' was important. God had ordained Owain to be prince and that was not just a challenge to the king of England, it was a statement that declared his status and his rank amongst the people he claimed to lead. Henry could challenge that statement – but only if he dared.

Chapter Eight

The Pennal Letters

If ignominious retreat from Worcester had damaged the reputation of Owain Glyndwr, Henry IV, the other 'non-participant' in the event, seemed no worse off than he had been before.

The traditional view, long held by academics and the public alike, is that Henry had achieved nothing out of the confrontation but had risked nothing either. That is not strictly true. Admittedly, Henry did not launch an immediate attack when he came face to face with his enemy, but he had good reason to sit on his ridge and wait.

With the two armies hunkered down and gazing at each other it was for Glyndwr, the invader, to take the offensive. Henry could afford simply to wait for the rebel army to make its move. Given the situation, the king was able to take a defensive stance where, if necessary, he would fight from fixed positions against an enemy that was floundering across open ground towards him. Militarily it was the correct option.

Not only that – it can be argued that it was Henry's presence at the head of his army, his numerically superior army, outside the village of Great Witley that had caused Glyndwr to turn around and head back into Wales. Simply by being present on the battlefield in command of his army Henry had put his crown up for grabs. In that respect he had actually risked a great deal –everything in fact.

The non-battle of Great Witley was surely one of the greatest examples of military brinkmanship in the whole of the fifteenth century. 'Come on, then, it's your move,' a modern-day warrior chief might have told Glyndwr. With Glyndwr failing to make that move it was time now for Henry to enjoy the fruits of his very bizarre 'victory'. To some extent that is what he did, at least until time and nature stepped in.

From 1406 onwards the king increasingly began to take a back seat – particularly in military matters – as ill health and depression began to make a profound effect on a man who was already possessed by sullen moods and self-doubt. Never the life and soul of the party, and not one-tenth of the soldier his son was to become, Henry IV began to fade. It was a slow process but by the end of the decade Henry IV was a virtual passenger in the field of government.

As the decade wore on, Prince Henry, whose economic blockade of Wales had at last shown his qualities as a leader of men, began to assume a more central position in the seemingly endless campaigns against Glyndwr. No longer a callow teenager, he was now battle hardened, happy and anxious to take control. If anything he had grown even more ruthless.

As far as becoming king was concerned, he would have to wait for several more years, though, if Shakespeare is to be believed, he did at least try on the crown before his father died. Fiction, yes, but it would certainly fit Prince Henry's character. Militarily, however, with his father increasingly disabled, it was all there for him – glory, fame, blood and power.

Meanwhile, King Henry was slipping further and further downhill. Adam of Usk provided a graphic description of some of the ills that befell Henry IV in the final years of his life: 'He had been tormented for five years by a rotting of the flesh, by a drying up of the eyes, and by a rupture of the intestines […] there ensued such a growth of lice, especially on his head, that he neither grew hair nor could he have his head uncovered for many months.'[1]

Glyndwr, of course, knew none of this. He was battling hard to survive, but increasingly the fates appeared to be against him. Prince Henry's economic blockade was proving to be increasingly effective, grinding down the Welsh will to continue fighting.

Henry's tactics were simple. They involved taking key positions, such as harbours and fortresses, which would have a major impact on the infrastructure of the rebellion, and then sitting on those recently gained positions. That was clearly preferable and militarily more effective than chasing Glyndwr across country that he knew like the back of his hand. It was clearly an astute move that hurt the rebel forces and caused the English forces least trouble.

The recapture of Aberystwyth and Harlech Castles was crucial to this strategy. They were symbolic but they were also strategically important centres with easy access to the sea, places that needed to be cut out of Glyndwr's supply system. In the months and years ahead Prince Henry would devote considerable time and energy to achieving exactly this.

Henry was undoubtedly helped by large parts of Wales visibly withdrawing their support for Owain. This happened in the lordships of Caerleon and Usk immediately after the double defeats at Grosmont and Pwll Melyn. However, easily the most damaging of these strategic 'turnabouts' took place on the island of Anglesey.

Long known as Mon, Mam Cymru (Mon, the mother of Wales) Anglesey was something of a vital element in supplying grain for Glyndwr's troops and so became yet another target for Prince Henry's blockade. The island had already been ravaged by the English in 1405, but in January of the following year Henry sent by ship a further 400 soldiers from Chester to the port and castle of Beaumaris. Destruction of the island's farms and fields continued.

Soon even more English soldiers were despatched to Anglesey. It was systematic occupation that ground down or eliminated the will to resist, and, as Prince Henry expected, by the end of the year the population had had enough. On 9 November 1406, representatives from the islanders made a plea for pardon from the king. Graciously, mercy was granted but everyone on Anglesey had to pay a huge fine to the English Crown for the simple privilege of living in peace once more. King Henry was exacting an enormous toll but obviously the islanders felt it was worth the price.

*****

At the beginning of 1406 the loss of Anglesey still lay some months away in the future. At that stage losing control of the island was not something to be even contemplated. That January and February Owain Glyndwr had other matters on his mind, and what he had planned was hugely significant, strategically at least.

Still trying to mould a country and a nation around his dreams and ideas, Glyndwr called a meeting of the leading Welsh figures of the day, clergy and laymen alike, at the tiny church of Pennal, near Machynlleth. The past few months had seen his rebellion, his movement to create an independent Wales, stalling or being stymied by the English.

This gathering, Glyndwr believed, would get things moving forward again. It was not going to be a military gathering: this was to be a far more important matter of state. The meeting took place in March 1406.

Glyndwr had received a letter from Charles VI of France urging him to pledge his allegiance to Pope Benedict XIII of Avignon. It was an easy enough favour to ask but Henry IV – and, therefore, all of England – had remained a supporter of the rival Pope Boniface IX, ensconced in the traditional seat of the pontiffs at Rome. Charles, who was a firm supporter of the Avignon Pope, was now urging Glyndwr, as Prince of Wales, to change sides and declare for Benedict.

The Great Schism, the establishment of the two rival popes, had existed since 1378. It was a ridiculous and confusing situation, each of them claiming to be the true head of the Church. The peasants and labourers of Europe had no vested interest or concern about which of the two men was the rightful representative of Christ on earth and simply accepted what their kings and lords decreed without debate or discussion.

In the academic centres of learning like Oxford, however, there was considerable unease. The schism led to what has become known as the Age of Doubt. Critical scholars like Roger Bacon and John Wycliffe were urging people not to accept blindly but to explore and discover the truth for themselves. Lollardy, which grew out of Wycliffe's beliefs and ideas, existed in Britain for over 200 years as a pre-Protestant religious movement until it was subsumed by the Reformation of Henry VIII.

Wycliffe's words had a deep effect on those able to think logically and without fear of heresy, and the Lollards became a centre of controversy that stretched way beyond their original objectives. Their influence was not limited to the shores of Britain and in the wider domain led to war across Europe. Countries like Bohemia fought for many years for the right of its people to worship in their own way.

As far as the schism was concerned it meant that, inevitably, the kingdoms of Europe became polarised, their leaders supporting one Pope or the other. Uncertainty reigned in the religious and secular worlds.

For Glyndwr, despite his firm religious convictions, the situation had now become a political rather than a spiritual matter, an opportunity to reclaim some of the ground he had lost when the French soldiers had left his army to return home. What could France offer him if he decided to change his allegiance to Pope Benedict?

Not only that, this was also an opportunity for Glyndwr to further develop the apparatus of government and to build the structure needed if Wales was to become a truly independent state. This was more than just a pragmatic seizure of opportunity; it was another chance to create a nation.

After considerable discussion and debate, on 31 March 1406, the Welsh 'think tank' – comprising the leading Welsh churchmen, intellectuals and theologians of the day – put forward a number of ideas which, in 1406, were revolutionary and even now seem light years ahead of their time.

These ideas were enshrined in two letters, the Pennal Letters as they were known, which Glyndwr sent to Charles, outlining the conditions on which his Parliament would agree to recognise Benedict XIII of Avignon as Pope and head of the Church.

The letters were written in excellent Latin and were probably composed by Gruffudd Young, Glyndwr's chancellor. He was the last of several churchmen to serve Glyndwr in a political capacity, having acted as his chancellor and been sent on important diplomatic missions. His time at Glyndwr's side was drawing to a close, however, and in 1407 Young was made Bishop of Bangor by Benedict XIII, the newly supported Pope.

The first Pennal Letter, addressed directly to King Charles of France, expressed an agreement on behalf of all the people of Wales – his subjects as Owain called them – that they would, in the future, recognise Benedict as the Supreme pontiff: 'Confident indeed in his right and intending to agree with you as far as is possible for me, I recognise him as the true Vicar of Christ, on my own behalf, and on behalf of my subjects by these letters patent […] I pray and sincerely beseech your majesty to have these letters sent to my lord, the supreme pontifex.'[2]

The most significant of the various conditions Glyndwr/Young went on to outline was that Benedict should permit the creation of an ecclesiastical province in Wales, a province that was totally independent and free from the oversight and jurisdiction of the Archbishop of Canterbury. This province, the Welsh Church as it would be termed, would embrace the existing four bishoprics of Wales and those parts of England that Glyndwr confidently expected to become his as part of the Tripartite Indenture.

The church of St David was to be at the head of this ecclesiastical province, the other Bishoprics of Llandaff, St Asaph and Bangor to be subordinate to the West Wales see. The yet-to-be-claimed areas of England – Hereford, Bath, Coventry, Lichfield and Exeter – would also, when Henry was displaced as king, be assimilated into the Welsh Church and be subordinate to St David's.

Glyndwr had considerably more in mind. This was his chance to make radical reform within what he and the Welsh clergy saw as an unworthy church. It was one chance in a million and Owain Glyndwr was going to take it.

Outlined in the Pennal Letters were other conditions. In future only Welsh speakers would be appointed as bishops and priests in Wales, thus ensuring the essential closeness of the people to the representatives of the new Welsh Church. Distance between the clergy and their congregation had long been an issue in Wales. This was one way of eliminating that problem.

The letters also advocated the creation of two Welsh universities, one in the north, one in the south. It was more than a simple altruistic desire to see his people educated. Glyndwr knew that by creating two universities along the lines of Oxford and Cambridge he would be establishing high quality educational establishments which would soon be producing the administrators and civil servants that his regime and the country desperately needed.

There would be no more grants made by Welsh parishes to English monasteries and colleges. This would ensure that Welsh money would be spent on Welsh institutions; the lack of such a cash injection into Welsh churches, colleges and monasteries had been a long held grievance.

It was a far-sighted and imaginative programme which, had it been allowed to come to fruition, would have radically changed the course of Welsh and English history. Even now it seems to have been an erudite and well thought-through missive. Even so, at the end of the second Pennal Letter Glyndwr could not resist having one last swipe at his old enemy and nemesis. There was one final thing Glyndwr wanted the Pope to do for him: 'Benedict shall brand as heretics and cause to be tortured in the usual manner Henry of Lancaster, the intruder of the kingdom of England, and the usurper of the crown of the same kingdom, and his adherents, in that of their own free will they have burnt or caused to be burnt so many cathedrals, convents and parish churches; that they have savagely hung, beheaded and quartered archbishops, bishops, prelates, priests, religious men, as madmen or beggars or caused the same to be done.'[3]

It was all a dream, one destined never to achieve reality. The setbacks that had afflicted Glyndwr in 1405 were not minor problems that could be easily rectified. They were monumental disasters that showed the

Welsh and the English that the world was changing yet again. And Owain Glyndwr, it seemed, was being sidelined and left behind.

Benedict was happy to accept the changed allegiance of the Welsh but Glyndwr's star was waning – rapidly. Regardless of his dreams and schemes, he had neither the opportunity nor the freedom to implement his far-sighted plan.

*****

Despite the significance of the Pennal Letters, 1406 was not a good year for Owain Glyndwr. Across the length and breadth of Wales, whole regions and hundreds of men began withdrawing their support for his cause.

It was a strange sort of withdrawal, hardly one expected given the mood of the times. Nobody, not even self-seekers like Gwilym ap Gruffydd, ever betrayed Glyndwr to the English authorities. They simply withdrew their active support and got on with their lives, hoping against all hope that things might yet change again. The thought that their continued support might just be what was required to change matters probably never entered their heads.

In some cases the change of heart was due to military setbacks, as demonstrated in the south east after defeats at Pwll Melyn and Grosmont. It was the old story – the king could afford the odd defeat, Glyndwr could not.

Flintshire was another county that quickly decided to call it quits and pay homage to the king after Hywel Gwynedd, leader of the rebellion in the area, was killed in battle in March 1406. Over 1,000 men from Flintshire duly appeared in front of Sir Gilbert Talbot, the chief justice of the king, to beg forgiveness for their support of Glyndwr and agree to the payment of a communal fine.

By the end of the year Gower and large parts of Cardiganshire had also reverted to the Crown. Glyndwr seemed powerless to stop the rot. No matter what success he might achieve – and he still managed to pursue the fight – more and more of his supporters continued to drift away. The decision in November of the year by the Anglesey population to submit to Prince Henry was yet another blow, this time a heavy and debilitating one.

Rhys and Gwilym Tudor from Anglesey had remained active supporters of Glyndwr and both were outlawed by Henry IV in 1406.

As outlaws they forfeited their lands – much of which went to the infamous Gwilym ap Gruffydd – but the two brothers continued the fight.

Rhys was captured in 1406 by authorities in Welshpool and spent several years in prison at Chester before finally being executed in 1412. His body, hanged, drawn and quartered, was duly exhibited at various places as a warning to the people. Gwilym Tudor was undoubtedly luckier – he was pardoned by the king in 1413.

In February 1406 Prince Henry decided to strengthen his forces at Caernarfon Castle, the garrison being quadrupled in strength. A naval force was also deployed to the town in order to protect the Menai Straits and strengthen communications with the castle.

It was the start of a 'protection policy' with additional troops soon being sent to strategic points like Caernarfon in the north and Strata Florida Abbey in the south. Despite its religious function, Strata Florida was fortified with 480 men-at-arms and archers who happily made themselves at home in buildings once inhabited only by monks (and, of course, the horses of the king). Slowly but surely the net was being tightened around Owain Glyndwr.

It is reported that on St George's Day 1406 Glyndwr fought a pitched battle against English forces and was decisively defeated. It is said that he sustained casualties of over 1,000 dead. The exact location of the battle is unknown, which leads one to question the validity of the story. Apart from anything else Owain Glyndwr was an intensely superstitious man – would he really have risked everything by fighting on the name day of England's patron saint?

Whether or not the St George's Day battle took place, Glyndwr's campaigns continued throughout 1406 and 1407. He was not yet ready to give up, but by now their focus had changed somewhat. Now the campaigns were no longer set military exercises, they had morphed into raids on English properties in Wales and along the border. They would continue as long as there was hope and belief in ultimate victory. Arguably, the ferocity of both sides grew even more intense as the rebellion entered its final phase.

The *Rolls of Parliament* for 1407 gives an indication of the ferocity of Glyndwr and his supporters, even in this, the least productive year of the revolt. The English border town of Shrewsbury apparently suffered badly at Glyndwr's hands: 'The town and its inhabitants have been greatly impoverished and ruined [...] the traitor and rebel Owain Glyndwr has burned eight villages within the franchise of the said town, as well as its own suburbs right up to the gates, to the great destruction of the whole town.'[4]

It was not just burning towns and villages. In their raid on Shrewsbury, Glyndwr and his men took sheep and cattle, beer and other foodstuffs, ruining the victuallers of the town. There were many other border raids as winter closed in on one of the most depressing periods of the rebellion.

The New Year of 1407 brought little relief for Glyndwr. It was a harsh winter and the main task now was trying to keep his family, his army and his supporters warm and fed. He managed to find some relief in the castle at Harlech even though the place was now a mere shell of what it had been in the early days of Glyndwr's power. The majesty and the glory of Harlech had by now all but vanished.

The castle, like all other parts of Wales, was suffering from food shortages thanks to the effectiveness of Prince Henry's continued blockade and there was little time or money for the jousting and feasting that had made the place so welcoming in the past. The poets and bards might remain but the foreign emissaries had long vanished.

Both Aberystwyth and Harlech castles were besieged by the forces of Prince Henry during 1407. These were on and off affairs, long lasting but not constant. Little progress was made by the attacking troops, but as long as Henry and his men were encamped outside the two castles there would be no relief or supplies for the people trapped inside.

For the defenders, hunger grew and sickness spread. Even to the most extreme of Glyndwr's supporters it was clear that it would only be a matter of time before the fortresses fell. Nothing would make them give up, however; they would hold on until the last.

The winters of 1407 and 1408 were perhaps the harshest in living memory, which only added to the sufferings of the Welsh people and, of course, to those of Glyndwr and his supporters. The English soldiers in the countryside shivered, just like the Welsh, but at least they had food in their bellies, and as long as Glyndwr was stuck inside Harlech castle they could light fires with impunity. There was no doubt about who had the advantage.

*****

In the late summer of 1407 Prince Henry was back at Aberystwyth. This time he meant to take the castle by storm and in order to achieve his aim he had been reinforced with 600 men-at-arms and 1,800 archers. Perhaps more importantly, his army was also now equipped with several new-fangled cannons and artillery pieces.

The development of siege guns, something of a brand-new secret weapon in the medieval world, had been deliberately exploited by the English Crown, master gunners from the Tower liaising with experts on the Continent in order to come up with the best weapons possible. The rationale behind developing and using cannons is easy to see: 'The bow was easy to shoot but hard to master – and master it you must if you were going to shoot an Artillery bow effectively. The gun on the other hand could be handled moderately competently after only a relatively short period of training.'[5]

Cannons were hugely effective against the stone bulwarks of the castles which, until now, had always been regarded as almost unconquerable. Indeed, so powerful and brilliantly constructed were these giant fortresses that many of them were garrisoned by as few as a dozen men. In total contrast it would have taken hundreds of soldiers to besiege or storm the citadels.

There were tactics for taking the castles, the most effective, even if it was the most time consuming, being to lay siege. This could take many months but once food ran short and disease broke out within the castle walls the defenders really had no option other than to surrender. That was fine, as long as time was not an issue. Otherwise it came down to frontal attack and that was always hugely expensive in terms of men and equipment.

The traditional technique of mining beneath the foundations of walls and towers in order to cause them to collapse was both time consuming and dangerous. It is easy, therefore, to see the value of the new artillery pieces. Guns gave attackers an altogether different perspective – apart from anything else the gunners could see where their cannonballs were striking.

It is not clear how involved Prince Henry was in the development of effective artillery, but given his interest in all manner of warfare it is highly likely that he was at least consulted. For the moment, gunpowder had to be imported – it was not until 1412 that it was first manufactured in England – and that made artillery an expensive if vital component in warfare. Use sparingly seemed to be the unspoken advice from gunners and from the king.

Nevertheless, Prince Henry intended to make full use of his guns at Aberystwyth. Apart from anything else he and other commanders wanted to see just how effective these new weapons really were and what, if any, were their drawbacks. Developing cannons was one thing, using them in combat was a different matter altogether: 'It is evident that steps were being taken at the latter end of the reign of Henry 1V to prepare for future operations by improving the artillery, and a great advance was made when gunpowder was first manufactured in England.'[6]

When it began, Henry's assault was furious. With his new cannons and siege engines, sent around the coast by ship from Bristol, his attacks were backed up by the archers who maintained a heavy and constant fire across the battlements.

Amongst Henry's siege artillery was a massive 5,000-lb brass cannon named *Messager* along with a similar iron cannon called *Neelpot*. There were several smaller weapons to back up these monstrous new guns. It was perhaps lucky for the Welsh defenders that both the *Messager* and *Neelpot* exploded during the siege, causing damage to any of Henry's divisions within striking distance and putting the guns out of action. At least two of the smaller cannon also exploded with shot in their barrels.[7]

Apart from the practicalities of loading and firing these massive pieces of artillery, their construction was such that they had to be carefully managed and handled. A maximum of seven or eight shots a day was all that could be safely fired; go over that number and self-destruction was likely, as Henry and the other commanders at Aberystwyth could testify.

Despite the exploding cannon, the Welsh position seemed hopeless. So hopeless in fact that the commander of the garrison, Rhys Ddu – one of Owain's most trusted and reliable of lieutenants – felt that he had no option other than to ask for terms. Henry was happy to agree.

On 12 September 1407, Rhys and Henry signed a truce agreement. It was effectively an armistice that would last for the next six weeks. Neither the attackers nor the defenders would use that time to reinforce or resupply their troops, but after the six weeks of truce hostilities would recommence. Glyndwr or some other Welsh commander would then have just seven days in which to raise the siege.

If the attempt to relieve the Aberystwyth garrison failed, the castle would be handed over to the English. Rhys and his men would then swear loyalty to the king. It was all very courteous and gentlemanly, in keeping with the rules of chivalry that were then widely accepted.

When Prince Henry informed his father of the plan the king was delighted at what was surely a successful enterprise. This would mark the beginning of the end for the troublesome Glyndwr, he felt, and even made arrangements to come to Aberystwyth himself in order to be present for the forthcoming surrender – no mean undertaking given his state of health.

It was unfortunate for Prince Henry and the king that Owain Glyndwr had other ideas. Rhys took advantage of the armistice to ride to Gwynedd, where Glyndwr was then in hiding, and inform him about the situation. If he had expected acquiescence from his leader Rhys was to be disappointed. Glyndwr was furious and gathered together his forces and set off for Aberystwyth, muttering dire threats about what he would do to Rhys Ddu if the castle fell to the English.

If Glyndwr was angry, Prince Henry was incandescent with rage. Rhys Ddu had broken the terms of the armistice, his defenders had been reinforced by Owain Glyndwr of all people and all of the sacred rules of chivalry had been torn up and disregarded. With winter fast approaching, Henry had no alternative but to call off the siege and head back across the border to England, vowing vengeance. Behind him the Welsh celebrated.

Raising the siege of Aberystwyth Castle was an example of Owain Glyndwr at his dramatic best. Dynamic, committed and brave, he had risked everything on his personal judgement. He knew about Henry's artillery and siege engines but believed in his own ability to overcome these weapons – and, of course, he believed in fate.

In the best traditions of medieval warfare he had made a hurried forced march south to keep the citadel in Welsh hands. And Prince Henry, despite his cannons and men in overwhelming numbers, had been humiliated.

While Henry went home to lick his wounds, Glyndwr set about reinforcing and repairing the castle. In the rest of Wales, however, the situation was not so favourable.

Gilbert Talbot, with 400 archers and hundreds of foot soldiers at his beck and call, was on the march through Caernarfonshire and Merioneth, collecting fines from those Welsh rebels who had surrendered and were now claiming pardon from the king. It was really rubbing salt into the wounds but the king and Prince Henry knew how to hit a man when he was down. It was not so much the process of collecting money that shocked the Welsh people but the fact that Talbot could now do it with impunity. Two years before, Talbot and the king would never have dared to take such risks.

On Anglesey John Mainwaring was now the military commander, dozens of men-at-arms and archers at his disposal. What had once been a Tudor/Glyndwr enclave was now solidly behind the Crown. Everywhere, it appeared, the forces of the English king were in the ascendancy. And that made the relief of Aberystwyth Castle so much more important. The English were not invincible, it seemed to say. It was only a temporary respite, however; everyone knew that Henry would be back.

In November 1407, Glyndwr received another blow when the long expected truce between England and France was finally agreed. Indeed, the build up to the truce had been so long and so protracted that Glyndwr and many others with vested interests on one side or the other might have been excused for believing it would never happen.

By the autumn of 1407 the situation in France was nothing short of chaotic. Charles was having increasingly regular attacks of madness. In his most intense moments of insanity he believed he was made of glass and then no one could see or touch him, not even his wife or the Dauphin, his son.

In November the strong man behind the throne, Louis, Duke of Orleans, brother to the king, had been assassinated when riding, unprotected, through the streets of Paris. It was a brutal attack that brought home the fragility of his situation to Charles – if this could happen to Louis it could just as easily happen to the man made of glass.

At first nobody knew who had committed the assassination but then John the Fearless of Burgundy admitted his guilt. He was the logical candidate. John was hardly expecting a pardon from the king; this was a pure statement of intent. There was deep unrest and virtual civil war in the country and it did not take a great statesman to see that Owain could clearly expect no further help from that quarter.

And so the year spluttered to an end. Despite some notable moments, it had been a difficult time for Glyndwr, and to many of the more objective observers it seemed as if the Glyndwr rebellion was running out of steam. That, certainly, was what the English king felt.

131

It would be fair to say that Glyndwr's successes over the six years of the rebellion had been huge and for this he deserved great credit. But those successes were as much about England's weakness as they were about the strength of Wales and Owain Glyndwr.

Quite apart from the growing threat of Owain Glyndwr, since coming to the throne Henry had faced rebellions, war with both Scotland and France and a Treasury that, at times, seemed almost bankrupt. Lack of money was always one of the king's major problems; throughout his reign he fought a constant battle against bankruptcy.

His health had not improved and there was always the prospect of the troublesome barons deciding, one day, to take matters into their own hands. Henry knew that it would not require much for them to depose him just as he had deposed Richard II.

By the end of 1407, however, Henry had begun to solve at least some of his problems. He was beginning to feel more secure, more comfortable, and with that security behind him he had established himself more firmly on the throne. Much of that security, of course, came from more stable foreign relationships.

By now England and France were at peace – for a while at least. The Scots, ever conscious that their king was in English hands, had subsided into a sullen acceptance of the situation. Like the French, they were never entirely happy with their powerful neighbours and Henry's kidnapping of James did little more than delay the inevitable conflicts that would eventually come. But for Henry, peace with Scotland and France was an important element in the security of his country.

With peace came full coffers – no longer would valuable tax money be laid out to fund English armies on the Continent. Henry could allow himself a brief moment of relaxation. It was not exactly triumph but it was an awareness of a job well done, regardless of the challenges.

Nobody doubted that this security was a temporary arrangement, particularly where the war with France was concerned. The French threat would be back. Henry, as much or perhaps more than anyone, knew that to be a fact. But for now it was time to take advantage of his weakened enemies while he could. England's strength and power were growing, the country beginning to rise to a position where in a hundred or so years it would occupy a role of world importance. Henry was hardly able to look ahead and plan a future for his country that would have been beyond his imagination. His interests were somewhat more limited and disputes on his borders, particularly with the warlike Welsh, were much more of an issue for him.

For Glyndwr and his supporters, who by the nature of their ideals and dreams were confined to an even smaller canvas than Henry's, the future looked ominous. The rebellion had already morphed into a war, but even so it was going to require careful management in the months ahead.

Chapter Nine

A Losing Battle

The three months from January to March 1408 saw Wales frozen like an igloo into a snow-shrouded landscape that refused to melt and give back to the world the first green shoots of spring. Until April a frozen sheet of ice covered the land, making any sort of military exercise a virtual impossibility. Conditions were so bad that the early part of the year was known, almost universally, as 'The Great Frost and Ice'.

Glyndwr and his supporters were used to conditions like this – well, almost – but even they decided against the idea of campaigning against the English in such weather. They would wait for warmer months and the balmy days of a Welsh summer. But not Henry Percy, the 1st Earl of Northumberland and father of Glyndwr's redoubtable ally, Henry, or Harry, Hotspur.

Percy had been at odds with the king since 1402 when Henry IV had demanded that Scottish prisoners captured by the earl should be handed over to him. As usual the monarch was short of money and ransoming these Scottish noblemen, rather than allowing Percy to do it, was a sure way of raising quick capital.

When Henry fought and killed Hotspur, Percy's beloved eldest son, at the Battle of Shrewsbury it did not take a prophet or one of Glyndwr's seers to realise that vengeance would soon be on the cards.

Glyndwr, Percy and Edmund Mortimer had already sealed their pact, the Tripartite Indenture, pledging to assist each other in bringing down Henry IV. However, the agreement did not stop any of them from acting alone. This was something which, in the dead of that terrible winter, Henry Percy now decided to do. It was a gamble more in the style of his son Hotspur than the older earl, but it was a risk that he was willing to take. He took it knowing that it would be perhaps his last attempt to seize the crown.

In February 1408 the Earl of Northumberland sat down to plan an attack that would finally help him to topple Henry. He was hopeful that

Sir Thomas Rockley, High Sheriff of Yorkshire, would join him in the venture. Instead, Rockley remained loyal to Henry and immediately began gathering together an army to oppose the rebellious earl.

Neither side had been able to lay their hands on good quality troops, which meant that the armies that were soon gathered together were made up of part-time soldiers, tradesmen, gamekeepers and gentlemen of leisure. Percy appealed to Glyndwr for troops and weapons but Owain had troubles of his own, and besides, who really wanted to fight during the time of 'Great Frost and Ice'. Unfortunately for Percy, no Welsh soldiers were forthcoming.

On 19 February the two armies drew up on Bramham Moor, three miles west of Tadcaster. The battle began just after 2pm and was over in less than an hour and a half. Fought in a driving snowstorm, the soldiers were battered by a wind straight off the Arctic ice cap. It was a brutal and bloody melee with little thought given to strategy or tactics. Squadrons or columns of men literally chopped their way forward, slashing and killing their opponents before the same thing happened to them.

Against all the odds Percy's forces were routed. Panic set in and they were decimated, cut down as they ran, leaving Rockley in total command of the field. Rockley's army, in direct contrast to Percy's, suffered almost no casualties at all.

Henry Percy was killed leading a desperate rearguard action. His comrade-in-arms, Baron Bardalf, was mortally wounded and died later that night. Percy's body was quartered and his head sent to London where, for several years, it remained on the railings at the Tower, a dreadful warning of the fate that would meet all would-be rebels. His lands were appropriated and distributed amongst the followers of the king.

After the battle a number of rebels were executed, including the Abbot of Hailes. The reason for this seems to be that, regardless of whether or not he wielded arms, he had appeared on the battlefield in full armour. Gruffudd Young, the former Bishop of Bangor, was spared execution because he was wearing his vestments.

The Battle of Bramham Moor was yet another blow for Owain Glyndwr, one that he really did not need. Henry Percy was an important member of the triumvirate who had so gleefully signed the indenture two years before. Now he was gone, leaving just Glyndwr and his son-in-law, Edmund Mortimer, to keep battling against the English king.

Glyndwr's world of fighting for freedom and independence had been suddenly changed from a glorious venture into a desperate battle for survival. Everything he had created and dreamed about over the past few years appeared to be fracturing before his eyes.

The Tripartite Indenture was in tatters. From a situation where Glyndwr had been clearly in control, now he was able to do little more than react to problems and situations as they arose. There seemed to be little chance now of Owain adding large swathes of western England to his kingdom of Wales. He would, a gleeful King Henry decided, be lucky to last out the year.

*****

Glyndwr, of course, had other ideas. Things may have been going badly wrong for him but he still harboured the notion of a great alliance with the French. Who else? The French were the implacable enemies of England and could surely be called on to help anyone opposed to the English Crown. It was a basic tenet, an idea that had governed political thought and manoeuvring for many years – and it was decidedly wrong.

Even so, the idea prevailed. As a result of this mistaken belief, in May 1408 Glyndwr sent two envoys to Paris to appeal for help in his struggle. The names of the envoys are not known although it is likely that they could have been the ever-loyal, ever-willing Gruffudd Young and Bishop John Trevor.

Whoever the ambassadors actually were, their mission ended in failure. Charles VI was still suffering from bouts of insanity and France remained in utter chaos. It was neither the time nor the place to ask for help, not when France itself seemed about to implode. Charles, in one lucid moment, did in fact pledge to send troops to aid not just Wales but other English rebels as well. Then he lapsed back into his madness and they never materialised.

Whether or not it was as a result of the French unwillingness to assist, at the end of May Glyndwr ensconced the bulk of his army in the upper Conwy Valley. It was a remote spot, well away from prying eyes and the unwanted attentions of English troops. In the meantime Owain remained with his family at Harlech.

That summer Prince Henry's thoughts turned once more to the mighty castles at Aberystwyth and Harlech. They remained in Welsh hands and to Henry, who could not forget his defeat the previous year (one that was an unbearable insult to his father and to him) it was time to redress the balance. It was as much a political as a military move: 'Without these (the castles) Glyn Dwr might lack legitimacy internationally, and be more easily cast as one of a number of rebels or pretenders that plagued Europe's thrones throughout the period. In addition parliaments held in the woods perhaps lacked the required majesty or appeal for envoys of foreign crowns. Safely held ports and castles told those powers that they would be able to extract their forces when required.'[1]

If it was vital for the Welsh to hold onto the castles, but it was equally as important for the English to take them. For those with foresight and an understanding of the political scene it was clear that the future of Glyndwr's whole rebellion hinged on the retention or the loss of the two castles.

Consequently, in the summer of 1408 Henry resumed his siege of Aberystwyth. Again and again his cannons battered the walls of the castle while archers made sure that no one dared to put his head above the battlements. Day after day, week after week the siege continued and eventually – the exact date is uncertain but it was possibly in September or October – Aberystwyth Castle fell to the forces of Prince Henry.

It was perhaps the bitterest blow Glyndwr had yet suffered but he had little time to mourn or wallow in self-pity. Prince Henry, flushed now with success, simply gathered up his siege engines and headed for Harlech.

Harlech Castle had been under siege since Gilbert Talbot had invested the place early the previous year. The garrison had suffered grievously in the siege, many of the defenders dying from starvation, even though the presence of the Welsh 'royal family' might have been expected to bring more provisions. No matter who was in residence, food was not forthcoming, though death and terror certainly were.

Henry brought with him from Aberystwyth all the horror and destructive powers of his revolutionary new artillery pieces. With these new miracle weapons he intended to finally finish off Glyndwr's home base.

Harlech's defenders fought, as they always had, with desperation. The attackers' best weapon, however, was not a regular and much repeated assault by foot soldiers and archers but the grinding insistence of blockade – in other words starving out the garrison. Even so, there were many attacks, particularly once Prince Henry arrived on the scene. English soldiers often managed to reach the castle walls, but despite their new weapons, they could not get over them.

Harlech was a well-situated fortress, sitting high on a rock overlooking the coastal plain below. Strong towers and walls were supplemented by the crucially important 'way to the sea', a protected walkway that ran 200yds from the foot of the castle to the water's edge. This vital walkway gave cover for men hauling provisions from any ships that had managed to run Henry's blockade. There were not many.

These days the area below the castle is covered by high sand dunes and a golf course but in 1408 the sea was a great deal closer to the castle walls. There was also a deep, protective moat, 30-50ft wide, on the south and eastern flanks. All in all it meant a powerful and almost impregnable fortress – the key word is 'almost'.

By the winter of 1408 Henry's force outside Harlech had grown to over a thousand archers and foot soldiers – and, of course, despite the cannons lost at Aberystwyth the previous year, he still had a large portion of his siege artillery intact and available for use.

As might be expected, the battery of cannons was a force to be reckoned with. They had proved their worth at Aberystwyth and the defenders must have looked on the giant, unwieldy shapes on the plain below them with a mixture of awe and horror. However, this lethal artillery unit suffered another significant blow when the giant cannon known as *The Kings Daughter* – or *Kyngesdoghter* as they spelled it – exploded and, like its sisters the year before, was totally destroyed.

The rest of the cannons continued to fire at the castle walls. The effect of the guns was terrifying for those on the receiving end, both the giant cannons and the occasional arquebus or hand gun held by the soldiers (or arquebusiers as they were known). The artillery pieces gave many of the defenders their first experience of modern warfare. It was the noise they made as much as the effect of the cannonballs and round shot that terrified them. Psychological warfare had reached a new level.

Warfare, whatever its specific style or nature, was certainly changing. When military commanders finally realised the true value of artillery the art of successful warfare became a matter of economics as much as tactics: 'A good gun would last many years in use where an Artillery Bow might last one battle, perhaps even a campaign but often considerably less.'[2]

Owain Glyndwr had no cannons. If he could have captured one of the king's guns he might have been able to turn it against the enemy – that was if he could find trained artillery gunners – but there is no record of anything like that ever happening during Glyndwr's war.

Other than that it was a case of sticking to the artillery bow of the famous but increasingly outdated Welsh archers. The pinnacle of English – and Welsh – archery had arguably been reached at the Battle of Crecy in 1346, the same battle in which cannons were used for the first time. For a brief time cannons and longbows were used side by side in the wars of the medieval period.[3]

Despite the loss of *The King's Daughter* Prince Henry proceeded with the siege of Harlech Castle. Day after day the bombardment went on and for the desperate men and women inside the castle there was not even the relief of a good meal and a flagon of porter when the day's hostilities were over. Nerves were shredded and casualties, from hunger and from the cannon and archery assaults, increased steadily. Relief became an impossible dream.

Glyndwr could see that the end was near and knew that he had to make a momentous decision. He could not risk capture and if the English had ever broken into the castle he would probably have ended his life himself. The whole rebellion depended on him staying alive and free. He was now faced by a terrible choice, to stay at Harlech or to leave. Knowing his importance to the revolt, there was only one decision – he chose the latter.

At some stage that winter Edmund Mortimer had died, probably from starvation. The exact date of his demise is unknown. Mortimer was the second member of the Tripartite Indenture plotters to perish and Glyndwr knew that if there was to be any sort of change in the upper echelons of English power and control he had to remain at large. That was essential to retain any chance of Welsh independence. The struggle would go on: that was what Mortimer would have wanted.

Reluctantly, Owain was forced to leave his wife, Margaret Hanmer, and his daughters behind, trusting in the chivalry of the English to treat them well. It would have been a soul-rending decision and what Margaret thought about it we will never know. No matter how much it hurt him, however, Owain Glyndwr was never above making the hard, unpalatable decision.

He gathered together his weapons and the few supplies the castle could spare, then slipped silently down 'the way to the sea' and boarded a small boat. The oars dipped into the waves and Owain Glyndwr was spirited away from the clutches of Prince Henry.

With him were his son Maredudd and a few faithful followers. In a case of romance over reality it is easy to picture Margaret Hanmer at this time. She might have remained in her rooms but more likely she would have stood on the walls of Harlech Castle, watching her husband and her favourite son disappear into the distance, wondering if she would ever see them again.

Soon afterwards, in the early months of 1409, Harlech Castle surrendered. Even though Glyndwr had escaped, the English celebrated this capitulation as the ultimate victory. In London there were celebratory bonfires and even a victory parade through the streets of the city.

Margaret Hanmer and two of Glyndwr's daughters – including the now widowed Catherine Mortimer – were taken into captivity and sent to London where they were lodged in the Tower. With the main Glyndwr women went three of Catherine's daughters, Owain's granddaughters. Rendering them all into captivity was a sacrifice that Glyndwr knew needed to be made. He did not expect their fate to be quite so appalling.

Between 1411 and 1413 Catherine Mortimer, her three daughters and Glyndwr's son Gruffudd all died in the Tower of London, probably from a combination of the plague and starvation. Owain's wife, Margaret, escaped their fate by a hair's breadth. Somehow she was released or disappeared from captivity some six months before the plague hit and subsequently disappeared from history – not unlike Owain Glyndwr himself.

*****

After slipping out of Harlech Castle, Owain Glyndwr went into hiding. He would continue with his war for several more years, mostly guerrilla campaigns or lightning-fast raids across the border into England. To the English it was annoying, even infuriating, but no more than a persistent wasp that could cause a limited amount of irritation before being idly swatted down.

From 1409 onwards Owain Glyndwr found that he was being forced into fighting the typical hit-and-run Welsh style of war that his men fought so well. It was at least something, some form of defiance, but when looked at objectively such actions were little more than throwbacks to the early years of his rebellion. They were relics of his days before the two castles, before his parliament, before his alliance with France. They were successful but they were not where he wanted to be.

Glyndwr was still a power to be reckoned with, but the loss of Aberystwyth and Harlech Castles had certainly damaged his reputation. His grandeur – the grandeur that had powered the royal court at Harlech – had withered in the wind, leaving him not so much a Prince of Wales as a simple bandit chief. He had had limited hope of foreign aid before, now it was non-existent.

Without Aberystwyth and Harlech his credibility was zero. Perhaps equally as important, perhaps above all else, every successful leader of revolution or rebellion has always required one crucial element – they have all needed a capital. A capital was something more than just a base; it was a venue, a physical town or city or castle that would show would-be allies that the rebels were serious and powerful. Harlech had been that capital. Now it had gone.

To all intents and purposes Glyndwr's rebellion – at least as far as the English were concerned – was over. It did not stop Owain continuing to take the fight to Henry. That was something that even the king, now increasingly fragile and sick, could not fail to see. Something needed to be done.

In December 1411, Henry issued a formal and all-embracing pardon to all of those who had opposed him during his reign, either in England or in Wales. Only two people were omitted from this pardon and specifically named as being outside the king's gracious forgiveness: one a troublesome and persistent pretender by the name of Thomas Trumpington, who was not concerned with the Welsh rebellion, and the other the arch-revolutionary Owain Glyndwr.

Even if Glyndwr had wanted to give up, to put down his sword and lance and settle back to a relaxed and sedentary old age, that was now impossible. Henry's pardon for everyone excluding Glyndwr ended the possibility of peace and forgiveness as surely as the executioner's axe. Surrender now would mean Owain being publicly arraigned, then hanged, drawn and quartered, a fate that no one would ever willingly embrace.

If he didn't know it before, Glyndwr knew now that his only course of action was to keep fighting until the end. He would probably have wanted that anyway, and there are many who believe that the thought of capitulating, of bending his knee before the king and pledging forgiveness and loyalty never even entered his brain.

Gone were the heady days of the bards and the wandering minstrels, but poets were still around and did still manage to sing the praises of Glyndwr, even if there was now little money for their art. Llewelyn Ab Y Moel, a poet, guerrilla fighter and loyal supporter of the Welsh prince, was even reduced to writing in praise of the forest where he and Glyndwr probably hid in the days after the fall of Harlech:

> Faultless nature, it was very good for me
> to have you to keep me safe:
> a radiant bower, a cozy shelter,
> a pleasant, tightly-woven, snug thicket.[4]

Glyndwr's exact whereabouts over the next few years remains unknown. He surfaced occasionally, making raids and eliciting strong orders from the Crown for the noblemen of North Wales to take action against him, but where he lived is unknown. He moved constantly, always one step ahead of the hunters, flitting like a mercurial will-o'-the-wisp between one part of Wales and the next.

Glyndwr's support base within Wales was still vast and there were hundreds of people who would have provided him with food and shelter. It would hardly have been home and certainly not luxurious but the shelter provided by his people was safe and it was comforting.

This was his time as a hunted outlaw. It was the legend that stuck with Glyndwr until the very end – Owain sheltering in a mountain cave, bending over the fire for warmth, always listening for the approach of Henry's men. There might well be an element of truth in the idea but it was certainly not the whole picture.

The image of the battered warrior, defeated but never beaten, remains an essential element of the Welsh character. Glyndwr fits it perfectly. In hiding he is a combination of Robin Hood and that other Welsh folk hero Twm Sion Cati, with perhaps a few shards of King Arthur thrown in for good measure. He is a man who has fought a good fight, a man let down, abandoned – but never a man without hope. And for those final few years of his life hope was almost the only thing that Owain Glyndwr was left with.

In 1410 he mounted one last campaign of major proportions. It was a raid into the border county of Shropshire and it went wrong from the beginning. Glyndwr's forces were outnumbered and outclassed. Two of his main supporters, Rhys Ddu from Cardigan and Philip Scudamore (Skydmore) of Gwent, were isolated, captured and taken to London and Shrewsbury respectively for imprisonment and trial.

Rhys had been a persistent thorn in the Crown's side, having held Aberystwyth against Prince Henry for several months. His capture was yet another severe blow for Glyndwr. At this stage in his war with the English he could hardly afford such a loss.

Together with Rhys ap Tudor, still imprisoned in Chester, Rhys Ddu and Philip Scudamore were found guilty and in 1411 sentenced to be hanged, then drawn and quartered. Their severed heads were then displayed as a warning against treachery and rebellion, on London Bridge and on Welsh Bridge – the road leading into and out of Wales – in Shrewsbury.

None of the three condemned men ever seriously considered revealing Glyndwr's place of hiding, although they were undoubtedly offered clemency for such information. Not even in the final and extreme torture of execution did they betray their prince.

*****

Despite his recent defeats and major military setbacks Owain Glyndwr remained a powerful presence. Defeated he may have been but the English were still very wary of him, both as a soldier and as a motivator of men. Put simply, they were afraid, afraid of the man and of the continued possibility of unrest. In some areas, they believed, even the mention of his name could spark riots in the Welsh countryside. The dark magic of Owain Glyndwr, the magus who had controlled even the weather during so many gruelling campaigns, lived on.

In 1411, in order to guard against further outbreaks, Henry IV agreed to send a thousand extra soldiers, mainly archers, to North Wales. Their task was to help protect English possessions along the vital arterial highways from Wales into England, and in particular to guard the road back across the hills leading to Ireland.

At a time when archers were paid the princely sum of two shillings a day for their services – foot soldiers the lesser sum of two pence –

just paying those troops cost the Crown a small fortune. The alternative, Henry felt, was too dangerous to contemplate. He certainly did not want to go down in history as the man who had abandoned the Anglo-Welsh citizens of Wales to their fate.

When extra expenditure – items such as quartering and provisioning the troops – came to be added to the bill the cost of providing the extra soldiers would have been somewhere in the region of £8,000 to £10,000. By the standards of the day it was a phenomenal sum of money, one that arguably could, and probably should, have been put to other uses. A fortune, then, to protect the English from an already defeated old man.[5]

A year later more soldiers were sent to Bala and to Merioneth amidst fears that the revolt was about to break out again. In 1410 yet another small fleet had already been despatched to the Menai Straits, patrolling the waterway to ensure that Glyndwr did not return to the attack by sea. Wherever you looked there was military activity. It appeared as if no expense would be spared in order to ensure Glyndwr did not bother anyone again. Fear in the English ranks remained palpable.

Apart from sending in soldiers there were other methods employed to keep the country safe. Above all there was always the option of paying 'protection money' to Glyndwr's supporters, as officials from Pembrokeshire and Oswestry chose to do. It seemed an easy way out of the problem, and money well spent, although how much Owain was involved in this practice and where the money went once it had been handed over remain unclear.

In 1412 Owain Glyndwr achieved what was to be his last major success, even though he was not directly involved in the matter. While he was sheltering somewhere in the hills of North Wales his rebellion continued and in the south of the country his followers achieved one of their most notable successes yet.

Early in the year Glyndwr's arch-enemy, Dafydd Gam, was captured by a band of Glyndwr's supporters. The news soon reached Owain in his North Wales hideout. He must have been pleased at this late success, perhaps even more so by the huge ransom Gam provided when he was released in August 1412.

Gam, incidentally, was given permission by the king to apply a special tax on the people of his lordship in Brecon in order to recompense him for the ransom money. It was a considerable sum, another example of how Glyndwr's rebellion hurt the Welsh almost as much as it did the English.

The levying of that tax showed how well thought of and admired Dafydd Gam was in the English court. Yet Gam and many others knew that at the height of his powers it was exactly the type of draining pressure on the Welsh labouring people of Wales that Owain Glyndwr would have strenuously opposed.

It remains something of a tragedy that by 1412 Glyndwr had neither the strength nor the opportunity to help the working men and women of his country. Instead, he simply withered away – if that is not too poetical a phrase – and was never seen again after the release of Dafydd Gam. Whether that was due to death, to military impotence or to shame has never been decided.

Glyndwr had always been something of a champion for the Welsh working classes. He had a genuine respect for them and for their back-breaking honest toil, a respect that many others in his position in society could not begin to understand, let alone feel.

When Iolo Goch wrote about that staple man of the countryside, the ploughman, he commented that, 'There is no life, no world without him.' To those who had the ability to look beyond the obvious subject of the poem it was a barely concealed metaphor that was aimed at far more than just the man behind the plough.

On one level – the direct, descriptive level – the image was meant to symbolise the simple labourer, but it was also a glorification of Glyndwr and all that he represented. That was the mystical or magical level, making Iolo's poem an altogether deeper and more intense piece of work. In particular it highlighted Glyndwr's feelings for the men and women on the lowest rung of the social ladder, people without whom society would simply dissolve.[6]

How the money raised by Gam's capture and ransom was used is not clear. It is unlikely that much of it went to Glyndwr, at least not personally, but his troops, still loyal and willing to act on his instructions, would have received some of the proceeds.

The capture and ransoming of Dafydd Gam was a symbolic event. Looked at now, after many hundreds of years, it sums up the two sides involved in Glyndwr's long-running war. On the one hand there were the men who kidnapped Dafydd Gam, loyal to the end and dedicated to supporting their prince even at the risk of losing their lives. Then there was Gam himself, a fervent supporter of the English monarchy and a man as dedicated to his cause, his beliefs, as any supporter of Owain Glyndwr.

Two poles, destined never to meet or agree – that was the essence of Glyndwr's continuing war, two ideologies that were light years apart. There would be no backing down, not until the final trumpet call was sounded.

That did not mean there were no peace proposals or attempts to end the war. There were several, and when they did arrive on Glyndwr's lap such proposals always seemed to originate from the English Crown. He never made any appeal, direct or otherwise, for peace and clemency.

Perhaps the most serious attempt at making peace, an overture towards achieving a compromise that would by that stage have helped everyone, Welsh and English alike, was actually made by the English Crown and government in 1415.

By then Prince Henry had become Henry V. The new king was a man who was respected, even if he was not liked, by Glyndwr and his followers. Everyone saw Henry V as a potentially great war leader who was likely to cause chaos in the Welsh ranks. That made little impact on the Welsh decision to go on fighting.

By 1415 most of the decisions in the Welsh camp were being taken by Maredudd, a curious piece of synchronicity to the earlier situation in the English realms of power when Prince Henry had taken over much of the governance of state from his father. Nothing much seemed to change in the Welsh camp, however. Glyndwr's son was as opposed to the English Crown as his father ever was.

Taking a back seat was not exactly an abdication on Glyndwr's part, but Maredudd was young and fit. Physical and emotional health was a vital element in the perpetual war against the English.

By now, though his dedication remained, Owain had lost most of the drive that had propelled his early revolutionary ardour and subsequent career. He was happy to offer advice, to use his vast knowledge to assist Maredudd, but crawling through the heather and undergrowth of the Welsh hills, and running like a gazelle from English patrols was a young man's game.

Maredudd, like his father, had suffered, seeing his family members – men and women alike – cut down in the prime of their lives, and had no love of the English. Yet it made no difference how Maredudd felt.

Glyndwr was uncompromising and would have nothing to do with any agreement that required him to apologise for his actions and pay homage to the new king.

Glyndwr's attitude, and his rejection of the peace proposals was, to some extent, understandable. He had always had to be dogmatic and rigid in his approach to the English overlords. Anything else would have led to immediate defeat.

What remains an astounding feature of the rebellion is that all of Owain's main followers continued to support him when, for the sake of a few meaningless words, they could have retired peacefully to their houses and families, free from persecution by the king. Such was the loyalty that Owain Glyndwr was able to engender, even at the end of a long, bitter and ultimately unsuccessful rebellion against an unbeatable foe.

And so the conflict went on, an interminable struggle that saw men killed and houses burned almost every single day. There is no exact date for the end of Glyndwr's war. From his point of view it probably went on until the day he died.

For the English the actual fighting was more or less over by 1412-13, although the fear that rebellion might be resurrected remained strong in the English ranks. As if to reflect that fear, the movement of soldiers between the borders of England and the western parts of Wales continued for several more years.

It was a strange time, hope and reality melding together in both the Welsh and English sides of the divide. In a confused and contradictory report *The Rolls of Parliament* for 1414 made an explicit comment, declaring that the war was over but then went on to outline continuing problems: 'Since the rebellion in Wales recently put down by you, our sovereign lord, and by your forceful government, many of the rebels with others who are their adherents, have come into the counties of Shropshire, Herefordshire, Gloucestershire and others adjacent to the same land, with force of arms and in a warlike manner.'[7]

The *Rolls of Parliament* went on to describe the activities of the Welsh raiders: highway robbery, looting, pillaging, burglary, even kidnap which, with the prospect of ransom money at the end of the exercise, was always extremely popular amongst the rebels. Travellers were afraid to venture out on the highways, it was declared, and people, despite sheltering behind locked and bolted doors, felt totally unsafe at night.

So, was the conflict over? It appeared not. As long as Glyndwr was alive, or was thought to be alive, hiding somewhere in the hills of Wales, the spirit of rebellion and the desire for independence were the ever-present companions to the men of the rebel army.

Glyndwr had always been a stubborn fighter and it may well have been that, after long years of war and bloodshed, he knew of no other way to behave. His character had been forged on the battlefield – once he had abandoned the cosy hearth for the sword and lance there was simply no other way for him to go.

By 1412 he could certainly have had few, if any, hopes of victory. Those days had long passed and by 1413-14 he was simply being a hard-nosed and stubborn old man who was refusing to back down and admit that his moment had gone.

And yet, on the other hand, he may well have been looking to the future, knowing that his name would come to have special meaning to the people of Wales. If that was indeed the case it would have given purpose to the final years of the conflict. We will never know which way his mind was turning

However he was feeling, the English certainly helped to perpetuate his memory and his legend. Glyndwr the magus, Glyndwr the fearless warrior, Glyndwr the mutilator of men's bodies – the attributes or curses went on and on. Fighting the French or the Scots was easy compared to the mystical madness of Glyndwr and his forces.

As late as December 1413, there was significant fear in the English court that the Lollards – strong religious opponents of the established Church – might gather together under Sir John Oldcastle from Herefordshire, march into Wales and join forces with Glyndwr. Like so many other half-truths and fantasies that were woven around Owain Glyndwr – not to mention the Lollards – there was little or no substance to the rumour.

To the end of his life Owain Glyndwr apparently still had the magic ability to terrify his potential opponents. It was a tribute to the success of his campaigns over the past twelve or so years since the revolt first began and even now it leaves the modern reader marvelling at how close he came to success.

Chapter Ten

The King is Dead, Long Live the King

King Henry IV died on 20 March 1413. Ill health had forced him to take a greatly reduced interest in the politics of England for the previous three or four years, leaving the management of the country to his son. If ever there was an opportune moment to sit back and take stock of his life, to consider what he had achieved, this was surely it.

With Glyndwr seemingly running out of steam and France placated if not defeated, Henry must have allowed himself at least a few moments of self-satisfied contentment. Perhaps for the first time in his reign the king could afford to relax a little or at least not push himself too hard, knowing that young Henry would control affairs of state.

It was a situation that the young Prince Henry had eagerly seized. It was not the real thing but it would do until true succession occurred. And each time he looked at his father, older and sicker every day, it appeared to the prince that the succession could not be long in arriving. Now, at last, in the spring of 1413 his time had come.

Even now nobody is really sure what had been wrong with Henry IV, but acute and disabling attacks of some grave and mysterious illness had laid him low on several occasions during his time as monarch. The first of these had come in 1405, returning on average every two or three years. The last of the attacks was the fatal bout that finally killed him in 1413.

For several years the king had also been afflicted with a painful and disfiguring skin disease which meant he could not bear to be touched or even looked at. It may have been some form of leprosy or psoriasis but there were many who believed it was God's punishment for a usurper who had not only seized the throne to which he had no right but had also killed the previous incumbent.

Despite everything King Henry IV died a disappointed man. It had been prophesised – and he firmly believed in the prediction – that he would die in Jerusalem, presumably while on a crusade to the Holy

Land. In actual fact he passed away in the Jerusalem Chamber of the Abbot's House in Westminster Abbey, thus making speculation about his fate at least partially correct.

Whatever the cause of Henry's health problems, his son Prince Henry was finally crowned king a few weeks after his father's death. Now recognised as one of the finest military leaders England had ever known, Henry's immediate reaction to the war in Wales was one of conciliation. It was Henry at his pragmatic best.

He did not want war with the Welsh. He had fought them too long, often without success, and had suffered from the climate of the country and from the doughty strength of the Welsh warriors. He already had other aims in mind – like conquering the French and making himself, as his forefathers had been in the past, the acknowledged king of both England and France.

Owain Glyndwr and his rebellion had become, in young Henry's eyes, little more than a troublesome itch. But it was an itch that had the propensity to grow quickly into a rash and then into an open sore if it was not dealt with quickly and efficiently.

If Henry was going to campaign in France it would be wise to leave Wales happy, contented and secure behind him. His father had made the mistake of fighting wars on several fronts at the same time. He had led armies into Scotland and into Wales as well as continuing the long-running war with France. The various campaigns had, arguably, ruined not only the country's economy but also the king's health.

Henry V had seen his father's difficulties at first hand and was well aware how damaging such diverse military activity could be. He needed to be able to devote everything to the matter of winning in France. That was his aim, his clear priority.

Henry V was not just a fighter, he was also a skilled tactician and had developed a well-thought-out strategic plan. He began by establishing his authority as king, clearly believing that it was easier to adopt a softer, more humane approach in the wake of a hard and dramatic start than it was the other way around. Go in hard, come out soft, he decided, would be his motto with the Welsh.

Accordingly, on 10 March 1414, acting on Henry's instructions, the new Earl of Arundel, assisted by two other justices of the peace, held Crown Courts at Bala, in the very heart of Glyndwr country: 'Six hundred men of the district went on their knees before the three justices and swore on the Scriptures to be loyal subjects of the King of England and never to rebel against him.'[1]

Bringing that number of Welsh men and women to heel was a deliberate and effective way of establishing his credibility. 'I am king,' he seemed to be saying, 'you need to obey me.' It worked.

It may have worked for Henry, but for Glyndwr it was yet another severe blow. Bala and its environs were close to his now burned-out house and holdings at Glyndyfrdwy. This was where the rebellion had begun but now dozens and dozens of the men he had counted as 'his people' had admitted defeat and pledged their allegiance to Henry.

Many of the men who had bowed the knee to the English Crown at Bala had, in the past, been soldiers for Glyndwr. They were experienced and hardened veterans and many of them now enlisted as archers and foot soldiers in Henry's army which, in the summer of 1415, took ship for France. They needed the wages – two shillings a day for archers, who could resist that?

Fighting for the king was certainly better than a tenuous career as a rebel outlaw where wages and money depended on who and what you captured. And what better way could there be of proving your loyalty to the new king than agreeing to fight for him?

Having wielded the iron fist, Henry now chose to soothe the battered brows of the Welsh. In July 1415, just a few weeks before he set out for the Continent, Henry V issued orders for Gilbert Talbot, the long-time supporter of the English Crown, to begin negotiations with Glyndwr regarding surrender and an end to hostilities. There would be a pardon for him and for other rebels still outside the law.

It was a major sea change. Henry IV had excluded Glyndwr from any possibility of a pardon. Now his son, Henry V, was happy to include the Welsh leader in this sudden reprieve. All that was required was for Owain to offer his obedience to the king. Predictably, there was a negative response – in fact there was no response at all.

Glyndwr would not submit. Let Henry pursue his dreams of glory, Glyndwr had suffered too much at the hands of the English to even contemplate capitulation. Too much blood had been spilled and there was no way that could ever be forgotten. To Owain Glyndwr the war was not over, and it would never be over as long as there was breath left in his body.

Henry shrugged his shoulders, consigned Glyndwr and the Welsh to the backburner and went off on his brief but momentous conquest of northern France. Adam of Usk, desperate to get back into the monarch's good books after several years in the doldrums thanks to Henry IV and the machinations of the two popes in Rome and Avignon, was fulsome in his praise of the new king's achievement: 'And against him came his adversaries of France to the number of sixty thousands of the nobles and men of rank, nigh Agincourt in Picardy. Battle was joined and blessed by God, the victory fell to our king, on whose side only seven and twenty were slain.'[2]

Amongst the twenty-seven English dead, Adam announced, was Glyndwr's old nemesis and bitter rival, Dafydd Gam. Legend declares that Gam was knighted as he lay dying on the field of battle, though this is unlikely, and Adam, who would have eagerly seized such a moment of sentimental loyalty, does not mention it.

There was much that Adam skirted around in his brief account. French casualties, he gleefully recorded, included numerous barons and counts, 1400 gentlemen and 7,000 commoners. However, he did not mention the dozens of high-ranking prisoners Henry had executed immediately after the first stage of the battle. Nor did he report on the skills of the Welsh bowmen, skills that effectively won what had seemed to be an unwinnable battle for King Henry.

His war over and Paris and the French crown within his grasp, Henry V, the warrior king, duly returned to England. There he would pick up the role of kingship once more.

*****

Henry had spent 1414 and 1415 fighting the French. Glyndwr had spent it waiting and watching from somewhere in the Welsh hills. He had launched no campaigns or raids while Henry was otherwise engaged – he was, in fact, simply sitting in isolation and growing older by the minute. Arguably, he was just waiting to die. He was now rapidly approaching the age of sixty and in the medieval world that was considered decidedly ancient.

The average life expectancy of a man at that time was around forty to fifty – which meant that Glyndwr was already operating on borrowed time. The stresses and strains of conducting a long-drawn-out war against England would probably have added to a premature aging process, making Glyndwr feel and act nearer to seventy or eighty than his actual age.

No matter how he felt, Glyndwr's name still remained a byword for courage. His reputation was as great as it had ever been and no one ever entered the dark and sinister woodlands or traversed the towering mountains of Wales without uttering at least one silent prayer to keep them safe from the bandit and outlaw Owain Glyndwr.

By 1415, however, Glyndwr had disappeared from view. In fact, the last sighting of him occurred in 1412. He was still alive the following year when, as late as February 1413, news of his whereabouts was relayed to Prince Henry, in the days before he became king, by an English government spy. But after that there was nothing, not a word, not a report, nothing.

There was rumour, of course, and there were threats about what he might still do. They came, not from Glyndwr but from the rumour machine that always seemed to operate around the Welsh leader, untraceable, impossible to pin down but nonetheless terrifying because of that.

Glyndwr's disappearance was strange, it was even bizarre, but he had vanished as suddenly and as effectively as if the ground had opened up and swallowed him. The odd sighting, the occasional glimpse of him on the hills or in the forests might have been expected, but for the next two or three years there was nothing, not one report on his activities, not one word of his plans or presence.

To all intents and purposes Owain Glyndwr could have been spirited away by the magical powers he was supposed to possess, or by the demonic forces that, as far as the English soldiers were concerned, he was alleged to serve. He might equally as well have been dead, so barren and fruitless were the records of his old age.

Nobody is really sure if he lived on or if he had actually died quietly in the hills or woods of his native land. Speculation and hope tend to lead the way when judgements come to be made, particularly judgements based on limited information, and even now they remain at the forefront in any discussion of Glyndwr's final years.

From the moment of his disappearance the rumours grew gradually into legend, replacing the actuality of Glyndwr and what he had achieved. Some of them were wild and impossible, some containing what might have been a shade of truth. The bards and storytellers were rather more circumspect but somehow quite precise in their reporting of Glyndwr's fate: 'Owain disappeared on the Feast of St Matthew in the autumn

(1415). From then on the place of his disappearance was not known. A great many say he died; the seers say he did not.'[3]

The rumour machine was one of the results of people not knowing the truth. In the wake of Owain's disappearance it was inevitable that people's imaginations, those of friends and foes alike, should begin to run riot. For Owain's supporters it was not exactly an unwelcome response, one that could be exploited and put to great use in the future.

Glyndwr had been such a significant figure for over ten years that to suddenly find him gone from public gaze was at best disquieting, at worst unbelievable. There seemed to be no rhyme or reason to this sudden chasm of silence that now gathered like a cloak or the swirl of an autumn mist around the name and reputation of Owain Glyndwr.

As the years, then the centuries, passed the legends only grew in significance. In some quarters Glyndwr was reported as having fled Wales, the idea dating back to a Welsh language work of 1833. According to that pamphlet, at the end of summer 1415 Owain bade farewell to his soldiers, informing them that he was about to travel to the Continent to find and enlist help. He never returned and was now to be found living, in some luxury, in France where he was happy cosying up to his former allies.[4]

Another story had him hiding in the mountain vastness of Snowdonia where the English dared not follow him. If it was true it would hardly have been the most comfortable of existences, but it certainly suited the image of the old Welsh warrior.

Perhaps the most fantastic of all the stories, but still the most lasting – thanks mainly to the flowing pen of forger, professional fantasist and practiced liar Iolo Morganwg – stated that he was hiding in a cave in Gwent where he would wait for the next thousand years if need be. He was not dead but sleeping and listening for the call to arms. Different versions of the story place Glyndwr's cave in different locations: it was all part of the legend.

So where was he? It is a question that has puzzled historians for the past 600 years and no one has really come up with an answer. Like the beginning of his life, Glyndwr's demise remains clouded in mystery. There is, however, still an awful lot of room for serious speculation.

All of his sons, with the exception of Maredudd, had been killed in battle or had died in captivity, and Maredudd, like his father, was now a hunted outlaw and fugitive. None of Glyndwr's sons had children, which meant that when Owain died it would be the end of his line.

His son-in-law, Edmund Mortimer, had perished during the defence of Harlech Castle. Two of his daughters, along with three grandchildren, had ended their lives in the Tower of London or other places of captivity. That left just his three surviving daughters: Alys, Jonet (or Janet) and Margaret.

After leaving the Tower of London, Glyndwr's wife, Margaret Hanmer, had 'gone to ground'. She was probably already living with one or the other of her daughters in the Welsh Marches and it has been suggested that after his disappearance Owain did exactly the same. If that is true he would have had to be in disguise – masquerading as a family priest and personal tutor for the children as some reports were quick to suggest.

Glyndwr's spy system must have been good, even at this stage. Capture in the house of one of his daughters would have meant arrest, not just for him but for all of the family. Easy enough to slip out the back way should the enemy approach, but even if his warning system did operate as effectively as that, it must have put an immense strain on the nerves of everyone involved.

There is a legend amongst the Scudamore family of Kentchurch Court – still in residence 600 years after Glyndwr's death – that when he was staying there he gave orders for a fully saddled horse to be kept directly below the window of his room. That way, if soldiers appeared he could leap from his window and make a quick escape – although what such a jump would have done to the limbs of a 60-year-old man remains imponderable. It is a lovely story but there is no way of proving or disproving the veracity of the tale.

It is doubtful that Henry V ever instituted a serious search for Owain Glyndwr. Having returned from France with his honour and his reputation enhanced, he now had Wales more or less under control and his reputation as a warrior – a Welsh-born warrior from the town of Monmouth – certainly stood him in better stead than his father.

As long as Glyndwr was silent and still, causing no problems wherever he was, Henry appeared to be happy. He had somewhat larger and more important targets in mind. After all, what did the Prince of Wales signify when the kingship of all France lay within his grasp?

Other suggestions take us in the opposite direction. Writers and historians, perhaps influenced by the chroniclers, have sometimes come up with more flamboyant ideas about Glyndwr's end: 'Tradition has it that he (Glyndwr) was at the last left absolutely alone, when he is supposed to have wandered about the country in disguise and in a fashion so mysterious that a wealth of legend has gathered around these wanderings [...] It was rumoured that he escaped in the guise of a reaper bearing a sickle. The prevalent opinion was that he died in a wood in Glamorgan.'[5]

That 'prevalent opinion' came, of course, courtesy of the pen of the imaginative Iolo Morganwg and first saw light of day several centuries later. Iolo's aim of perpetuating the Welsh and Celtic love of mythology, conjuring up an image of a people wallowing in their glorious past, led him, naturally and inevitably, to the cave in the wood. Arguably, it is as good a bet as anyone else's, but, of course, it depends on your own stance, your own purpose behind perpetuating the myth of the magical Owain.

A peaceful final few years in the house of one – or all, in turn, one after the other – of his surviving daughters seems much the more likely ending for the man who had once held all of Wales gripped in a vice of terror. Whether or not that is true, it still leaves us floundering about in the dark regarding the motives behind Glyndwr's disappearance.

He had seen so many of his friends and comrades killed in the wars with England that he must have been hardened to death. He had put his own life on the line and expected his supporters to do the same. That was not lack of care or concern; it was the way things had to be if there was ever going to be a chance of Welsh victory.

Metaphorically at least, Owain Glyndwr had endured and shared in the agony of men like Rhys Ddu and Rhys ap Tudor. Faithful to the last, his two lieutenants had continued to support him even when the possibility of success had all but gone. In 1411 he had seen them condemned to being hanged, drawn and quartered, perhaps the most awful of all medieval punishments. There had been little sign of a pardon for them and for a man of Glyndwr's temperament that would have been infuriating.

But there was also a personal concern. Owain Glyndwr was not afraid of dying; he could not have fought such a long and bloody campaign if he had been. And yet he had no desire to suffer the same fate as Rhys Ddu or Rhys ap Tudor, and the thought of his head being spiked onto the railings of the Tower of London to be abused and laughed at by the rabble was an anathema to him. It would also have been decidedly unappealing to his loyal followers.

So perhaps – and yet again we are in the realms of conjecture – his disappearance was a deliberate plan or tactic. Perhaps Glyndwr staged the whole thing. A disappearance was certainly a great deal less messy than a final battle. Luck was always a major component in any medieval struggle and the possibility of being captured was at least as great as the alternative – death at the end of a soldier's sword or lance.

Unlike Lord Grey of Ruthin, or Dafydd Gam, Glyndwr knew that in his case capture would not be ended by the payment of a ransom. Capture would be brief and brutal but it would be followed by a trial that could only have one possible outcome. And after that would be the total humiliation of public execution. If anything was going to signify an English victory it was surely that.

With no battered or mutilated body to display, however, it would have meant there was no definitive ending to the war – and no ending to the war would have meant a total lack of victory for England. The Welsh would, in a strange, oblique fashion, have triumphed in the conflict. They would, at least, have claimed the win.

So the idea of disappearing from public view had an undoubtedly practical purpose. Glyndwr was always a skilled general, knowing when to stand, when to retreat, and for him disappearing from view would have had a far more welcome finality than the alternative option – crushing defeat in the face of superior numbers.

There was also the prospect of building his legend. Superstition was rife in the medieval world and Glyndwr was probably more susceptible than most. He made many decisions and judgements on the advice of his prophets and seers, men such as little Crach Ffinnant who, in the early days of the rebellion, had accompanied him everywhere, interpreting signs and omens for his lord. To leave his people with the image of a man fated to fight to the last, whatever the result, would undoubtedly have had an appeal. Glyndwr's imagination was almost as strong as his belief in the supernatural world.

There was more. There was also the eternal loser's perpetual dream of glory. His disappearance signified not failure or retreat but the simple fact that that Owain Glyndwr would return. At some stage, no one knew where or how or when, he would be back. After all, he was the Welsh magus, wasn't he? All that he needed in order to return was a people who believed in him and in his cause – an independent Wales.

Accepting Henry's offer of a pardon would have been dangerous, no matter how well intended the offer might have been. Kings die and future sovereigns might not have taken such a lenient stance as Henry. The pardon could always have been revoked. Henry himself might someday change his mind and decide that Glyndwr was too dangerous to leave at large.

Apart from anything else there was always the possibility that the offer of a pardon was never anything more than a trap. Hadn't Henry IV once suggested just such a solution to the youthful Harry Hotspur all those years ago? His son might well be pursuing a similar tactic.

Even if the offer was genuine, did that mean safety for Glyndwr? He had fought Henry before, many times, and knew how ruthless he could be if the situation demanded it. Henry V had already demonstrated his pragmatism and lack of care for the formal rules of chivalry when he had executed dozens of French knights – all of whom expected to be ransomed – after the first stage of the Battle of Agincourt.

The ransoming of prisoners was a lucrative process for everyone involved in the capture, from the king down to the lowest foot soldier. Glyndwr himself had benefitted from the ransoming of Lord Grey and Dafydd Gam. So such a massacre was not something that was ordered lightly and was certainly something that would have been against the wishes of the ordinary soldiers of the English army. Despite being totally immersed in the heat of battle, Henry would have thought seriously about his actions before ordering the massacre.

There were practical reasons for the deaths, Henry believing that the French army was reforming after being soundly beaten in the early stage of fighting. The prospect of the captives joining in to fight once more, this time attacking in the rear of the English, was very real.

Even so, executions such as those at Agincourt were a rare event, one that symbolised the ruthless nature of the young English king. And what he had done to the French he could easily replicate with Owain Glyndwr. What did one more Welsh rebel mean to him? If it suited him he could have a pardoned, free and easily accessible Glyndwr arrested and hanged, or perhaps just assassinated, in the blink of an eye. The risk was too vast.

Much better, Glyndwr might have thought, to get out while the going was still good, leaving behind a legend, some spectral wisp or phantom that had once held everyone in thrall. It fitted the Celtic ideas of mythology and the superstitious nature both of Owain Glyndwr and of the Welsh nation.

Hopefully it would be a legend that would comfort people in the cold winters to come. Not even the superstitious Owain Glyndwr could be sure about that, nobody could, but with luck and good fortune the legend would grow. With a little help from the bards and the seers, the prophets of Wales, it might evolve into a power that was able to reach out across the centuries and offer his people a dream.

It was not possible for Glyndwr to predict the future – despite what the English soldiers believed – but it would be a dream that might, one day, become reality. And, of course, the Welsh bought it. They fell hook, line and sinker for that dream, for the myth of Owain Glyndwr.

In this they were aided in no small degree by poets and writers like Iolo Morganwg and Thomas Pennant. After a few centuries of being almost forgotten, Owain Glyndwr was eventually built – perhaps rebuilt might be a better description – into a figure of some substance. By the nineteenth century he had become the Welsh nation's erstwhile and future king, a man who had almost beaten the mighty English war machine. God alone knew what he might do when he finally returned to life!

Beaten but unbroken, perhaps more glorious in defeat than in victory, that was what the sudden disappearance of Owain Glyndwr signified to the Welsh. It was a unique requiem and a magnificent gift to the nation, far better than a battered body lying helpless in the dust. You might almost think he had planned it.

The exact date of Glyndwr's death is unknown but he is now commonly thought to have died at some stage between the years 1415 and 1416. Or did he? Even after 1416 Glyndwr's fate remains uncertain. Was he alive? Was he dead? We simply do not know, not for sure but we will return to the issue later.

The place of his death, despite various claims to the contrary, is also unrecorded. Whatever you might say about Owain Glyndwr he certainly knew how to play his audience and this time he kept the part going until the absolute end.

Chapter Eleven

The End of the Race

When Henry V returned from France, perhaps inspired by his victory at Agincourt and by his political manoeuvrings that had brought him closer to the French throne than he had ever dreamed possible, he began to pick up the threads of domestic policy once more. He was still inclined to be magnanimous towards his old enemies.

Another offer of pardon was made to the Welsh rebels, the message again being carried by the ever-faithful Gilbert Talbot. This time Talbot was ordered to treat with Glyndwr's son Maredudd.

It was now 24 February 1416 and neither Henry nor Talbot had any idea if Glyndwr was alive or dead. He had not been seen for four years and none of Henry's spies had any inkling of his whereabouts. That was unusual but it did not stop the king making the gesture, and, almost inevitably, there was no response from the Welsh prince. Maredudd also refused the pardon.

That lack of response from Owain Glyndwr would not have surprised Henry. He had tried to offer terms before. He had fought the man and seen for himself how stubborn Glyndwr could be. There was, of course, always the other obvious reason for his silence.

First suggested by the bards, then advocated by the writer Thomas Pennant, the date 20 September 1415, the Eve of St Matthew, was, for many years, traditionally regarded as the moment of Glyndwr's death. It is, therefore, entirely possible that Glyndwr's lack of response to Henry's offer was down to the simple fact that he had passed away calmly and quietly, almost without anyone noticing. It would fit. But the lack of response could equally be due to the fact that his hiding place was so secure that no one could locate him, not even his son Maredudd.

Alive or dead, by 1416 the world had certainly changed from the moment Glyndwr had first unfurled his banner and Henry IV had caused havoc in Wales. During the course of Glyndwr's war England had had two monarchs, three if you include Richard's brief tenure in the period leading up to the beginning of the rebellion. Each of them brought their own brand of turmoil to the country and to the wider European scene.

Since 1400 civil conflict had raged up and down Wales, England and Scotland. On the Continent France was in the hands of a man who believed he was made of glass! The Great Schism had created total confusion in the religious communities across Europe, with the idea of two rival popes fighting over the blood and body of Christ fuelling the anti-establishment beliefs of groups like the Lollards.

The economy of Europe was beginning to recover after the depredations of the Black Death and constant war, but it was not there yet. There was still a long way to go even though everywhere you looked there was a feeling of change in the air. As far as Owain Glyndwr was concerned it was not necessarily change for the better.

The situation in France had not improved since the alliance between Charles VI and Glyndwr had been broken, or, rather, been allowed to stagnate. France was still divided by internal conflict and controlled by scheming noblemen. Charles VI's championing of the Avignon Pope had not helped – indeed it had led to even more discord.

A General Council of the Holy Catholic Church had actually been called in 1409 in an effort to sort out the confusion caused to the religious world by the Great Schism. The existence of the two popes had gone on long enough.

The members of the council – four Patriarchs, twenty-two Cardinals and eighty bishops – met at Pisa in Italy on 25 March 1409. Debate ran on and on. There was furious argument and discussion, which ended with both popes, Benedict XIII of Avignon and Gregory XII from Rome, being deposed. Their crimes were promoting the Great Schism and, far more serious, 'manifest heresy'.

Having deposed the two popes, the College of Cardinals was faced by the thorny issue of what to do next. Undaunted, the council – made up of representatives acceptable to both Avignon and Rome – set about attempting to make the situation better. It was undoubtedly a poisoned chalice.

Neither Benedict nor Gregory accepted the ruling of the council and continued to claim their positions as God's representative on earth. The new Pope, as elected by the council, was Alexander V and naturally enough he also claimed the papacy. As it happened Alexander lived for only a few months and was succeeded by Pope John XXIII. The whole affair would have been disastrous if it had not been so ludicrous. From a situation where there had been two popes in Europe there were now three.[1]

It was several more years before the schism was eventually healed and just the Roman Pope left to command the Church. The chaos and confusion in church ranks did not affect Glyndwr directly, but his support for Benedict, in an effort to keep Charles of France at his side, meant that he was no longer a free agent. He was honour bound to give his allegiance to the Avignon papacy.

It was a time of 'Monstrous Perjury', as Adam of Usk called it when describing the situation in 1415. As usual Adam was virulent in his comments: 'Our Pope John the twenty third, false to his promises of union, other two, to wit Gregory and Benedict, being popes along with him (an unnatural thing) for that he was rebellious, and was otherwise guilty of perjuries and murders, and adulteries and simonies, and heresy, and other excesses, and for that he twice fled in secret.'[2]

Ultimately the confusion, the double dealing and the lack of any credibility over the issue of the Pope took France out of the picture as far as Glyndwr was concerned. With the country toppling about their ears, the French had more to worry about than the situation in Wales. For Glyndwr, of course, it meant disaster. He needed Charles, he needed an alliance, he needed friends – and he got none of them.

*****

Owain Glyndwr had always been a 'border' man. He loved the Marches, he had grown up there, and it stands to reason that if he was given the opportunity, the Marches was where he would spend the final years of what had been a very adventurous and dangerous life.

Herefordshire, where arguably he went to ground in one or the other of the houses of his daughters, was an area of contrasts. Bordering on Wales, it was inevitable that there were Welsh enclaves where the Welsh language was spoken as easily and readily as English: 'It is certain that there were monoglot Welsh speakers among the population [...] The record of the Bishop of Hereford's visitation in 1397 testifies interestingly to the complaint of the parishioners of Garway that their priest could not properly administer to their souls as he knew no Welsh.'[3]

The county of Herefordshire was marked down as Welsh – or was intended to become Welsh – as part of the Tripartite Indenture. If Glyndwr and his compatriots had been successful in dethroning Henry IV the diocese of Herefordshire would have become subordinate to that of St David's in West Wales. Then there would have been no argument about priests not being able to speak Welsh.

It was not just in ecclesiastical matters that the influence of Wales was strong in the English border county. There was also a fair degree of support, both emotional and practical, within the lay community of Hereford for Glyndwr in his war against the English Crown. Two of the most sympathetic supporters, as sincere in their opinions of Glyndwr and his mission as any Welshman, were Lewis Byford and Walter Brut.

A career priest, Byford was a curate in the Welsh border country of Radnor but spent much of his life at the Papal Court in Rome before being appointed Bishop of Bangor in 1404. In 1406, on the orders of the Pope in Avignon, he was deprived of his long-held parish in Radnorshire and replaced as Bishop of Bangor by Gruffudd Young. That same year he was declared an outlaw because of his long-time support for Glyndwr and the Welsh rebels.

Byford was an active and enthusiastic follower of Henry Percy, the Earl of Northumberland, and co-signatory along with Glyndwr and Edmund Mortimer on the Tripartite Indenture. Despite the distances involved, he journeyed northwards to take part in Percy's final attempt at gaining the throne and was captured by royalist forces at the Battle of Bramham Moor in 1408.

Having escaped post-battle execution because he was wearing religious garments rather than armour, Byford was later reinstated as Bishop of Bangor by Pope John XXIII in Rome. He travelled to Germany and went on to participate as a court official at the trial and eventual execution of the well-known heretic Jan Hus.

Walter Brut from Hereford was renowned as a Lollard and as an extreme critic of the established Church. Whether or not this was the case, he certainly held what were, in the early fifteenth century, regarded as radical religious views. Amongst them was the belief, thought scurrilous and heretical by many, that women should be allowed to preach. They should also, Brut declared, be permitted to administer the sacraments.

When summoned before the Bishop of Hereford in 1393 to answer charges of heresy Brut was insistent that the Welsh – although he was himself predominantly English – had been blessed by God as one of the most religious of all nations. He also asserted that the Pope was the anti-Christ.

An unusual man, possibly the only known Lollard of Welsh descent, Brut was also a layman when most of those who risked their lives to push John Wycliffe's doctrines were members of the clergy. A fervent supporter of Glyndwr's rebellion, Brut had been lucky to survive the earlier accusation of heresy. Such luck could not last and it was inevitable that he would be called to account for his beliefs. In 1402 he was arrested and executed for treason.[4]

With support like that it is easy to see why Owain Glyndwr felt at home in the border county. However, there were many in Herefordshire and the other border regions who thought the opposite way. These men were radically opposed to Glyndwr and were happy to fight for their beliefs.

Gilbert Talbot from Goodrich and his brother John were two of his most notable opponents, men who spent large portions of their adult lives opposing the Welsh prince. There were others such as John Merbury and Roland Leynthale who happily served the English Crown in various capacities throughout the course of the rebellion.

Possibly the most renowned of Glyndwr's Herefordshire opponents – apart from the Talbots – was Sir John Oldcastle. He held Builth and Kidwelly castles for the king during the early stages of the rebellion and fought in the royalist victory at Pwll Melyn. He was also present during the final siege of Aberystwyth Castle.

A confirmed Lollard, Oldcastle fell from grace and was eventually declared a rebel, and therefore outside the protection of the Crown, because of his religious beliefs. He tried to ally himself with Glyndwr's son Maredudd, but, probably due to his earlier antipathy towards Owain, failed to gain his support. Hunted and arrested, he was eventually executed in 1417.

No matter how much support or opposition Glyndwr received from the people of the region or how much he enjoyed the atmosphere of the remote border country, Herefordshire was still English. It was one of the old Marcher Lordships and was strategically placed at the centre of English opposition.

If Hereford was his base for the last few years of Glyndwr's life, it leaves the interested reader more than a little confused. It is surprising, stunning even, that Glyndwr did not draw his career and his life to a conclusion in his native Wales, the country he had striven so long to protect. That would have been the logical decision, the one that the English would expect.

There is no way of knowing, but if the English county of Herefordshire really was his final resting place one cannot help thinking that Owain Glyndwr was enjoying one last laugh at the expense of his opponents. Going to ground in Herefordshire was surely a case of settling down almost under their noses. It had to be the ultimate act of rejection, Glyndwr being anti-establishment to the end. Or am I being too poetic? I rather think not.

*****

Attempting to pinpoint the marriages, the homes and even the spouses of Glyndwr's surviving children is not easy. By 1515 all his sons apart from Maredudd had died, leaving only the girls in what Iolo Goch had once described as 'a fair nestful of chieftains'.

With Maredudd still heavily involved in the final stages of the rebellion, these daughters were all that remained to offer comfort and companionship to their aged family members. Provision of such care was an expectation in the medieval world, something everyone offered and acknowledged, knowing that one day it would be their turn to receive such attention.

Girls in families like Glyndwr's were never quite as important as boys, useful in the forming of advantageous marriages and for the acquisition of dowries but otherwise of little major significance. Owain Glyndwr, like most men of the period, would have given the majority of his attention to his sons. They were the ones who would carry his line into the future – that was the theory, anyway.

Glyndwr's daughters were married off, as was customary, but it is interesting to note that three of them (four if you include Catherine who was married to Edmund Mortimer and widowed some years before Glyndwr's decline and death) were wedded to Herefordshire men. Only Mortimer, the captured and converted border nobleman, was an obvious, out-and-out supporter of the rebellion.

The early marriage, imprisonment and death of Catherine takes her out of the picture as a potential shielder of Glyndwr during his final years. The other daughters, however, were all alive and therefore all possibilities for the role. All three of them settled with their husbands in Herefordshire. With that in mind, to begin with at least, it is worth attempting to put the daughters of Glyndwr and their family situations into some sort of Hereford context.

Herefordshire is significant in the story of Owain Glyndwr mainly because of its Welshness, the solid core of Welsh and Welsh-supporting people then living in the county making it virtually an adjunct or addendum to the mother country.

The Welsh enclave did not mean that the Welsh speakers in the county automatically and immediately pledged unconditional loyalty to Glyndwr – or the non-Welsh speakers come to that. Like everything it was a matter of personal choice, opportunity and circumstances.

Repeated bandit raids on property and towns along the border had alienated many of the Hereford gentry for whom the attacks were costly in economic terms and in the time they were forced to dedicate towards protecting their property. As leaders of the various communities they would have been expected to show an example to their tenants. Many of them did just that.

The ordinary men and women of the county also had much to fear from the pillaging Welsh as much as their counterparts on the other side of Offa's Dyke in Radnor or Powys. A field of ravaged crops, a storehouse emptied of wheat or corn, farm animals stolen or run off – the people of Herefordshire suffered and endured it, regardless of their affiliations.

It is difficult to know how far and how deep the effects of something like rebellion and internal war reached in the medieval period when communication was poor and travel was notoriously difficult. In all probability for most people in Herefordshire, particularly those furthest away from the border with Wales, Glyndwr's war was something that was happening 'out there', beyond their concern or understanding. Scratching a living and trying to survive were far more important issues.

While support for Owain may not have been universal in Herefordshire it was, however, still significant. His status, his acknowledged position as a freedom fighter and his reputation as a man with mythical powers helped make him an important figure. It was an importance that was crucial, both in the defence of the nation as a whole and in the choice of Herefordshire as a possible location for Glyndwr's final years.

To begin with, Herefordshire was at the heart of the Marches. That was one of the reasons Henry V, while he was still Prince Henry, had chosen Hereford – the largest and most important town in the region – as a mustering centre or capital during his military campaigns against Glyndwr.

From Hereford most parts of north, south and central Wales were accessible. By the standards of the day the roads into and out of Wales were relatively good, something which was both a bonus and a disadvantage for people on either side of the border.

The topography and physical location of the county made it an obvious target for attack by rebels and also established it as a good supply base for the forces of the Crown. Important trade routes for cattle, foodstuffs and other essentials had long existed between the county and the Welsh market towns – more easy targets for Glyndwr's raiders.

Welsh or English, pro Glyndwr or anti, Herefordshire was where the surviving members of Owain's family chose to settle. Their husbands were Hereford men, not Welshmen as you might expect, and in this respect they were falling into the same pattern as their border-loving father. It was just that their spouses came from the 'other side' of the dividing line between England and Wales.

Scribes and chroniclers from the time were notoriously cavalier when it came to recording and reporting on things like marriages and deaths. And Glyndwr's family was no exception. On several occasions the husbands of Glyndwr's daughters were mistakenly identified by the chroniclers. On occasions they were said to have been married to his sisters or even to his aunts rather than his daughters. There was also the suggestion from one scribe that his daughter Catherine married Glyndwr's lifelong opponent Lord Grey of Ruthin. The writer had obviously confused Grey with Edmund Mortimer, both of whom had fallen into Glyndwr's clutches at about the same time.

It is now acknowledged, however, that all of his daughters made advantageous marriages to well-off English/border gentlemen. Potentially, Catherine had made the best match with her marriage to Edmund Mortimer. He was relatively rich, at least by the standards of the day, and came from a renowned border family that had a perfectly respectable claim to the throne of England. It was a claim that was certainly more valid than that of Henry IV.

Edmund Mortimer's line to the English throne is perhaps a spurious point, something of a red herring, as Catherine and Edmund would never have met had it not been for his capture by Glyndwr and his subsequent decision to change sides. That of course led to his claim to the throne being nullified. In the eyes of England's rulers he was now an outlaw and a rebel. His early death was soon followed by that of his widow.

That left three daughters: Jonet, or Janet as she is sometimes known, Margaret and Alys. All of these women settled with their husbands in Herefordshire and therefore have a distinct relevance to Glyndwr's final years.

Jonet married Sir John Croft of Croft Castle, which was located between Ludlow and Leominster, close to Mortimer's Cross, the site of a future battle in the Wars of the Roses. Croft's ancestral home was on the site of an ancient building, but by the fifteenth century was more in keeping with a grand manor house than a medieval castle.

Sir John had more than a little sympathy with the Lollards, fanatical opponents of the established Church. Many of the more extreme Lollards were accused of heresy and Sir John had spent a period in prison at Windsor because of his beliefs. He was considerably older than his wife and may well have served in the same Scottish campaign as Glyndwr many years before. That made him a man of Owain's generation rather than Jonet's – not an altogether unusual situation as older men did, at that time, tend to take young women as their wives. If nothing else it allowed the young widows to remarry.

Croft died sometime after 1410 and, as the system expected or at least predicted, Jonet remarried. This second marriage was poorly recorded so there has been confusion over the identity of the new husband, but it was possibly Sir Richard Monnington, another Herefordshire grandee.

Richard Monnington is also sometimes identified as the husband of Glyndwr's youngest daughter, Margaret. Little more is known about Margaret who, being the youngest of Glyndwr and Margaret Hanmer's family, seems to have had only peripheral involvement in the story. It is possible that she may also have died, leaving Jonet to marry her widowed husband. We simply do not know.

We do know, however, that Monnington was the owner of Lawton's Hope, a small village overhung by a low, flat hill midway between Croft Castle and Kentchurch Court, the homes of the last two remaining children. That is an important point and we will return to it later.

The one daughter about whom we have a clear view is Alys. She married Sir John Scudamore – Skydmore as the family spelled their name at the time – of Kentchurch Court near Archenfield. He was an active and prominent supporter of the Crown during the rebellion, which makes the marriage to Alys an unusual, if not somewhat mysterious, affair. Some accounts say that the marriage was actually a secret one, but secret from whom – the king or Glyndwr – is not clear. Amongst other positions, Scudamore held the post of constable of Carreg Cennen Castle in Carmarthenshire, a fortress which came under assault by Glyndwr in 1403.

An interesting letter written by Scudamore was sent that year from Carreg Cennen to John Fairford, Receiver of Brecon. The letter asked, firstly, that the king should be informed of the situation. Secondly, Scudamore's letter requested that the monarch should despatch aid to help him fight 'these false traitors,' a term that gives some indication of how he felt about the rebels. The letter also shows the ruthlessness of Owain Glyndwr: 'All of Carmarthenshire – Kidwelly, Carnwyllion and Iscennen were sworn to Owain yesterday [...] I was there (Dryslwyn Castle) and spoke with him under a truce, and asked for a safe conduct under his seal to send home my wife and her mother and their company, but he would not grant me one.'[5]

For a long while it was thought that Scudamore was here referring to his wife, Alys, and her mother – in other words Glyndwr's daughter and his wife, Margaret Hanmer. If so it was something that would have made Glyndwr's response to the request yet more brutal. It now seems, however, that Sir John was referring to his first wife and her mother, not Glyndwr's own wife and daughter.

That was relatively early in the rebellion. At some stage during the war Sir John Scudamore changed his allegiance, coming over to Glyndwr's side. Or did he? There is a school of thought that says Scudamore had always been a 'Glyndwr man' and from the beginning of the revolt was working undercover to send information and funds to his true leader. There is no proof, but his brother Philip had been an openly acknowledged rebel supporter who had been executed for treason in 1411. This might be regarded as the Scudamore family showing some propensity for support of the rebel cause.

Whatever his political allegiance, Sir John married Alys after the death of his first wife, somewhere around 1410-1412, and thereafter was a firm if surreptitious supporter of his father-in-law. It remains a chicken and egg situation – which came first, his allegiance to Glyndwr or his marriage to Alys? Either way, one would have influenced and led to the other.

Like many men in his position, Glyndwr had a number of illegitimate daughters. They were not, in the main, heavily involved in his campaigns or his war but one of them was referred to by writers as Margaret – the same Margaret who supposedly married Richard Monnington perhaps? She is better known as Gwenllian and was married to Philip ap Rhys of Cenarth, a renowned Glyndwr supporter who lived on the borders of Pembrokeshire and Cardigan.

*****

If we accept that Glyndwr's death occurred sometime in 1415 or 1416 – and the more you look at it the more the originally proposed date of 20-21 September 1415 looks likely – it leaves only the location of that death and the burial place to make the story complete.

If Margaret was indeed married to Sir Richard Monnington that would have made Monnington Court in the village of Monnington Straddle her principal home. If Margaret was not lady of the house it would have been her sister Jonet, who was also, for a while at least, resident at Croft Castle. Alys would have been living, nominally at least, at Kentchurch Court.

All of the houses are within easy travelling distance of each other and Glyndwr, no matter how old or infirm he had become, would have had little difficulty moving from one home to another.

For the reader and researcher it comes down to a simple choice – was Glyndwr's final period of life spent as a hunted bandit or as an aged family relative who was maintained in a degree of comfort by the daughters who felt it was their duty to help? The latter is a far more attractive option than that of Owain spending his final years cowering and starving in a cave or forest, as so many chronicles would have us believe.

How long Glyndwr spent in each house is, of course, unknown. He would probably have moved on a regular basis, simply to keep any inquisitive neighbour or local dignitary from learning the truth of his identity. If Glyndwr did indeed shuttle between the various houses of his daughters it would still have been a relatively pleasant existence. He would have had good food, a solid roof over his head and a warm bed at night. The only things to trouble him would have been the dread of possible capture and the dream of what might have been if all of his plans had reached fruition.

The favourite location for Glyndwr's preferred residence, perhaps because the Scudamore family have always been happy to play up the association, is Kentchurch Court. The house sits easily and elegantly on the banks of the River Monnow near Monnington Straddle and Monnington-on-Wye. It is exactly the type of place you would like to imagine for the old warrior in the twilight of his days.

Unfortunately for the accuracy of that image, the family did not spend much time at Kentchurch during the first and second decade of the century. The Scudamores also leased a substantial property called La Verne at Bodenham, to the north of the county, and were probably in residence there during most of the time the rebellion was raging. La Verne was thought safer than Kentchurch, less vulnerable to attack.

Kentchurch Court still holds the imagination, however, particularly as it is within a mile of the Welsh border. There is now a Glyndwr Tower and a Glyndwr Room at the house. That does not automatically make them genuine, and they would certainly not have borne the appellations while Owain was alive, but they do give an indication of the type and style of accommodation Glyndwr might have enjoyed in the final stages of his life.

Between La Verne, Monnington and Kentchurch lies the village of Lawton's Hope. Remote, lonely even, a low hill which is now covered with trees overlooks the village. The whole parish, village and church had been once owned by the Bishopric of Hereford. By the early fifteenth century the village and the hill behind it were in the possession of the Monnington family. Glyndwr's daughter – either Margaret or Jonet – sometimes lived there with her husband in one of the houses they owned and a local tradition states that this was the place where Owain finally died.

Lawton's Hope is barely three miles from La Verne. It is possible that Glyndwr was travelling from La Verne to Monnington and had reached Lawton's Hope when he was taken ill and died. Yet again it is conjecture.

*****

The place of Glyndwr's burial is perhaps more difficult to locate than many of the towns or areas related to him. Attempting to identify where he lived during his decline, or where he eventually died, are difficult enough, but where he was laid to rest remains a matter of utter conjecture rather than reality. Keeping that place a secret was no accident.

If, as I firmly believe, he deliberately chose anonymity to cloak his final years Glyndwr would not have wanted to spoil what he had created by revealing his final resting place to everyone. That was a mystery that would accompany him out of the world and survive him by many hundreds of years.

According to Adam of Usk – although he does not name the location – there were difficulties around the burial of Owain: 'Died Owen Glendower, after that during four years he had lain hidden from the face of the king and the realm; and in the night season he was buried by his followers. But his burial having been discovered by his adversaries, he was laid to rest in the grave a second time; and where his body was bestowed may no man know.'[6]

The idea of Glyndwr being buried at night and in secret certainly fits with his disappearance and his desire to remain hidden. The image of silent, solemn men gathered around the graveside, of lanterns and torches breaking the covering darkness, with perhaps the sobbing of women away in the distance has a romantic appeal that fits only too well into the story of Glyndwr's last days.

How much truth there is in Adam's claim about his body being exhumed and then reburied after his 'adversaries' discovered its whereabouts is a different matter altogether. It certainly seems considerably less plausible. If his enemies had in fact uncovered his body would they not proclaim their discovery and then display it to the world?

There are numerous stories and legends concerning Glyndwr's last 'home'; so many in fact that it is worth recounting one or two. Like all good mysteries there might be at least an element of truth in some of them.

In 1680 the parish church at Monnington was in the process of being rebuilt. In order to facilitate the work a sycamore tree in the churchyard was cut down. The tree was apparently 9ft in height and measured 2½ ft in diameter. The process of just getting it down caused the labourers considerable difficulty.

A foot below the surface, underneath the spot where the tree had stood, the workmen discovered a large gravestone with no inscription. Beneath this lay a stone-lined grave and the body of a tall man in almost perfect condition with no decay or disintegration of flesh or limbs. The complete lack of decomposition is an important part of the story and of what has since become legend. Like all good myths, however, there was a 'get out' – the body crumbled into ash the moment it was touched.

The remains, everyone immediately presumed, were those of Owain Glyndwr. After two days the body was covered up, earth shovelled on top and the 'grave' closed again. Quite why this should be recognised as the body of Glyndwr is not immediately obvious.

The story was taken a stage further by locals keen to embroider the legend. The body, they claimed, was buried with its legs outside the church walls, the top half within. If it was true it would have been a bizarre way to bury anybody, but the symbolism – within and without the law – would suit Glyndwr perfectly.

A similar legend concerning John or Jack of Kent, a famous character from the area who apparently sold his soul to the devil, also exists, in his case at Grosmont Church. John of Kent is often confused with Glyndwr, perhaps deliberately. He lived at Kentchurch Court, legend declares, and was a magician and poet who knew Glyndwr well.

Within the confines of the Monnington Court Farm estate sits a 12-ft mound. Now overgrown and covered in foliage, the mound is surrounded by a ditch fed by a small stream, and is often reputed to be the grave of Owain Glyndwr. The mound may well have been part of an ancient motte and bailey castle but other than that it seems to serve no other logical function.

A twenty-first century geophysical examination of the mound found no trace of a grave or body under the earth. It was reported, however, that any remains inside the mound could have been degraded over the years, to such an extent that they could not be identified as anything different from the main make-up of the surrounding soil.

It is highly unlikely that Glyndwr would have allowed himself to be buried in unconsecrated ground. Despite his brutality – which was there for a purpose, after all – he was an intensely spiritual man who saw and understood the power of religion, as well as superstition, in people's lives.

He would have stated his desire to lie in consecrated ground long before his death and perhaps reiterated it as he lay dying. His wishes would have been obeyed after he had breathed his last. Even in death Glyndwr's word would have been sacrosanct.

If we believe the explanation and the idea of interment only in consecrated ground, that eliminates places like the Monnington Court mound and the hill at Lawton's Hope as possible burial sites. It also destroys legends such as the one declaring that he died and was buried in Haywood Forest, south west of Hereford.

The stories around the matter of Glyndwr's burial are legion. Places as diverse as a lonely cave outside Beddgelert and the mighty, awe-inspiring knave of Bangor Cathedral have been put forward. Then there are Ruthin, Corwen, Llanfair Caereinion and Valle Crucis Abbey, all of which been suggested as possible burial spots. Chapel Cottage near Monnington and Dore Abbey, home of the Cistercians in Wales, have also been identified as his final resting place. And there are many more.

The truth is that nobody really knows and the reader or researcher is inevitably drawn back to Herefordshire, the county where he seems to have spent the last few years of his life.

All of the potential Herefordshire burial sites have drawbacks, but there is, of course, another possibility. To some extent this alternative theory falls in with the chronicle of Adam of Usk which promulgates a possible reburial: 'If the claim about Glyndwr's reburial is believed one can only speculate as to whether he was originally buried somewhere in Herefordshire and then reburied in another place within the county or whether his body was moved […] to another more secure and secret burial site beyond the borders of the county, most probably in Wales.'[7]

There is no proof that this actually took place but the suggestion that Glyndwr's body might have been removed, particularly the idea that it might then have been taken back to Wales, does have a certain appeal. It would certainly provide a degree of symmetry to his life.

Border lover he may have been, but for many people there is something intrinsically wrong with the idea of Owain Glyndwr being laid to rest on the English side of the frontier. A Welshman through and through, would he have wanted that, or did it not really matter to him?

One suggestion is that his remains were taken far away from the border country and carried to Llanwrda in Carmarthenshire where they were buried in the chancel of the parish church. His illegitimate daughter Gwenllian and her husband, Philip ap Rhys, a confirmed Glyndwr supporter, lived not far away in Cenarth so there might just be an element of truth in the tale.

On a personal level, probably allowing sentiment and romance to take the place of hard historical fact, I rather like the inability to pinpoint Glyndwr's grave. It is, I think, almost a tribute to a man who was above ideology, a man who would have actively disliked thousands of day trippers flocking in a never-ending flood to stand and gossip at his graveside.

The unknown burial place of Owain Glyndwr is as much a part of his legend as the other elements in his story – reversing the shoes on his horse to make pursuers think he was going the other way, having the ability to summon spirits from what Shakespeare called the 'vasty deep' and so on. They are all elements that combine to make him such an important figure to the Welsh: 'He functions both as a local hero, especially significant to the inhabitants of the areas in which he lived and fought, and as a national hero who once almost won independence for Wales [...] (He was) a leader endeavouring to redeem his nation.'[8]

A rhetorical question: what would we gain from knowing where Owain Glyndwr was buried? He does not need shrines or monuments built over his grave; he remains a spiritual presence, someone who has the power to stimulate and bring together a whole nation – if we will let him.

Unfortunately, so many people do not agree and seem to be hell-bent on finding the grave, establishing the exact date of Glyndwr's death and so on. Invariably they are forced back onto guessing and conjecture.

Speculation, speculation, speculation: there appears to be no end of it. And that is part of the mystery and majesty of Owain Glyndwr. Nobody knows how or where or when he died – just like he wanted. And arguably that is how it should remain.

Chapter Twelve

A National Figure

In the 600 years since his death Owain Glyndwr has become a national figure, an icon rather than an individual. He is now a symbol that is often invoked or called upon whenever there is danger or a perceived need. He is no longer a threat to peace and prosperity, far from it; he has become acknowledged for what he always was, a man of the people.

Revered and venerated as he had hoped – arguably as he had planned – he now remains the ultimate hero for the Welsh. But attaining the position of national hero has not always been a smooth or constant ride.

In the years after his death, while the memories of his brutal war against the English Crown remained strong in the minds of the people, Glyndwr was relegated to the position of a troublesome thug. His achievements were minimalised and virtually ignored. He was certainly not regarded as a patriotic freedom fighter.

In some quarters it went beyond that, and Owain Glyndwr, the man who had sacrificed his life to a cause, was even reviled. He had inflicted untold damage on Welsh society. He had killed hundreds, probably thousands, of his own people, and it appeared as if he had done it willingly, without concern or compassion.

More significantly, he had upset or possibly destroyed forever the delicate balance between the Welsh and the English. It had been tenuous before 1400; after the rebellion began it simply did not exist. As the war ground on, distrust changed to dislike, and, eventually, in the hearts and souls of some people at least it mutated into real hatred. The Penal Laws were part of the problem but the activities of Owain Glyndwr were integral to the dislike. Arguably he had begun it all.

It has always been easier to hang unpopular ideas and concepts onto the shoulders of one individual rather than accept group responsibility – the victim concept as it is known. Owain Glyndwr was a perfect fall guy, particularly as he was no longer there to fight back. When people looked at the carnage of his fifteen-year-long war it was easy to apportion blame and point the finger of accusation at the one man who had kept the revolt going for so long.

As ever there were shades of grey; it was not all one-way traffic. There were those who admired him and held his memory close. Henry Tudor, who fought at Bosworth Field to become Henry VII, well prodded and prompted by his uncle, Jasper Tudor, used the Glyndwr story to prop up Henry's own rather lame or limited claims to the throne of England.

Polydore Virgil, a Tudor propagandist of some skill and something of a personal scribe for the first two Tudor monarchs, took the story of Glyndwr's rebellion and used it as justification for the Acts of Union. There would have been dozens more, unknown, unheralded, who remembered Glyndwr and held him to their hearts.

It is all guesswork, and, for the majority of the Welsh people, Glyndwr's war was something they would rather forget than commemorate. It was an attitude that lasted, incredibly, for at least 300 years.

During that period the Welsh were still subservient to the English, but this time they were contained by a more subtle form of oppression than anyone had ever imagined possible. People like Henry IV and his son, inveterate enemies of Glyndwr, had believed in keeping the Welsh in their place, but even they had never dreamed the oppression would be so vast or so long lasting.

The Penal Laws of Henry IV remained in place throughout the fifteenth century and for most of the sixteenth. That was bad enough, but then Henry VIII, despite his Welsh roots and connections, took things a stage further with the Acts of Union of 1536. The Union signified many things but above all it meant that any Welsh man or woman with ambitions to succeed in life had no option other than to become a surrogate Englishman.

It was coldly and deliberately done. The Welsh language was dismissed, virtually destroyed, and courts like Star Chamber and the Council of Wales and the Marches were unashamedly used to browbeat the people. You have a choice, Henry's government was saying, stay in Wales and live a second-rate life or come to London and prosper. Many Welshmen fell for the line.

To the people of Wales, certainly the ambitious ones, Glyndwr continued to be branded as a bandit, an outlaw who had had no compunction about destroying the livelihood of his own people as long as it suited his own aims. He symbolised the old Wales, the nation and the attitudes that the Acts of Union had been created to wipe out – he was acknowledged but definitely not celebrated.

Then, finally, the nineteenth century, with its industrial-based oppression of the working classes and the growth of the British Empire and its peculiar brand of muscular Christianity, led to significant social changes in Britain. They also led to a resurgence of Glyndwr's reputation.

The immense and rapid growth of empire meant that nationalism began to resurface, not just in Wales but in any country where thinking men and women were able to see the benefits of imperialism and yet also acknowledge its drawbacks. Among other things, empire meant slavery – both literal and metaphorical – and an emotional subservience to a stronger power.

Glyndwr's name and his fame grew once more, so that by the beginning of the twentieth century he was being invoked by nationalists, by politicians and by activists – in fact, by almost anyone seeking to create exactly what Glyndwr had sought to achieve so many years before.

Glyndwr's importance as a symbol went beyond the borders of Wales. In the autumn of 1914, at a time of jingoism, of hatred of Germany and Kaiser Wilhelm, when belief in the empire as the saviour of smaller nations was considered a virtue, there was only one man to stand as a representative of freedom and independence for all: 'We had hoped to celebrate Owain Glyndwr's five hundred year anniversary in peace. But of a struggle like his struggle, and one infinitely broader, it is said today – "Owain Glyndwr and his armies/are preparing themselves for battle."'[1]

It took over a hundred years to fully redress the reputation of Owain Glyndwr, but eventually his significance as a leader – as opposed to his status as a war leader – began to be understood. Gradually it came to be seen that this was a man who had held a clear vision for Wales.

As the country's self-confidence blossomed, as pride in the nation grew and dreams of another Welsh Parliament came to fruition with the Senedd and devolution, Glyndwr became a central figure amongst a cluster of Welsh heroes.

His importance was not limited to what he did – or what he had failed to do – but was down to what he planned and intended to do for his country. His intentions were a crucial part of his vision. He dared to dream of an independent Wales and did his damndest to make those dreams come true. A role model as much as an icon, he still manages to convey what might one day come true.

*****

If there is one group of people, one element of Welsh society that was intricately bound up with the history of Owain Glyndwr it has to be the bards of Wales. Throughout Glyndwr's childhood, his adolescence and his early manhood these bards were the men who, in their verses and stories, lamented the passing of a golden age, but, more importantly, foretold the coming of a new one.

There would soon be, they declared to the world, a prince who would pull the country out of its slough of despond. That prince was, of course, Owain Glyndwr, and he responded to their words in the only way he knew how – with action.

Once the rising had begun, the bards celebrated Glyndwr's achievements, sang of his glory, and when it was over they were the men who lamented his passing. Such is their significance that you cannot really contemplate Glyndwr without some understanding of his poets – and vice-versa.

It would be overstating the point to say that without the bards there would have been no Glyndwr, but there is no doubt about the significance of these wandering poets in the rebellion, and, ultimately, in the standing of Owain as a national figure.

In ancient Welsh society there was a clear association between what can be loosely described as Bardism and Druidism. The role of the druids in pre-Roman Britain has been described and spoken about many times. Druidism provided the laws of Wales, invoked judgement and oversaw both religion and education. The three orders or divisions of Druidism, succinctly outlined by the writer and historian A.G. Bradley, were as follows: 'The three orders were known as Druids, Bards and Ovates. The first were the priests and judges, the second poets; the third were the least aristocratic, practiced the arts and sciences, and were a probationary or qualifying order through which candidates for the other two had to pass.'[2]

The Romans effectively destroyed Druidism in mainland Britain, but the bards managed to survive the great massacre on the shores of Ynys

Mon in AD78. It is easy to see why. As a group they were not perceived as presenting any great challenge to Roman rule, their main duties seeming to be to compose and recite stories and poems. The Romans had their own storytellers and writers, men like Tacitus who described the massacre of the druids on Anglesey, and so appreciated the art of poetry and versification.

It was a significant mistake on the part of the Roman conquerors as the bards, as well as preserving family genealogies, also maintained the traditions and the legends of the Welsh people – and as long as they were intact the spirit and the heart of the Welsh would never die.

Both during and after the Roman occupation the bards became valued and significant members of the royal courts of Wales, so important that they were ranked eighth amongst the officers of state in the laws of Hywel Dda. Insult a bard and it would cost you dearly – six cows and twenty silver pennies.[3]

The bards sang songs of praise with the result that every important family in Wales had its own incumbent permanently in residence at the court or hall of the leader or the chief. It was not long before such an appointment became a mark of huge significance, almost a badge of office both for the bard in question and for the family.

There were also the wandering minstrels or poets who visited not just the great courts but also the houses of the less renowned leaders in society. They were a different sort of men, younger and more dynamic, but their verses were equally as special to the men and women who sat and listened to their poetry, their songs and their playing.

Poetry and music went together. Many of the most able bards would not dream of appearing and performing in public without their harp which was used either as an accompaniment or as an instrument to strike a single chord and so emphasise a word or a phrase.

The Irish and the Scots had their bagpipes, the Welsh their harps or a crude early version of the violin called a *crwth*. The Welsh were noted for the sweetness of their music, either when performed alone or as an adjunct to their poetry.

In the post-Roman period, particularly the sixth to the ninth centuries, Bardism flourished. Poets like Aneurin and Taliesin became household names in Wales, as celebrated in their own way as the great warriors and soldiers from the past.

In beautifully crafted lines, haunting in their simplicity, they and many others, most of whose names are now forgotten, captured the tragic history of a country that was conscious of its past but was still unsure about its future:

> Cynddylan's Hall is all in gloom – tonight;
> No fire, no lighted room:
> Amid the stillness of the tomb.
> Cynddylan's hall is left alone – tonight:
> A hall with none to own.
> O Death, take me where he is flown.[4]

In the tireless struggle against the Norman and English incursions the bards of Wales kept the culture and the traditions of Wales alive and flourishing. They were not just reflective; they urged retaliation and were often quite violent in their presentations.

Edward I, in his long series of campaigns against Llewelyn, understood the power of the bardic verses, seeing them as important elements in the motivation of his opponents. It was a craft and a call to arms that he could not hope to match. And there is no doubt about the extent of Welsh hatred of the English, an emotion that came through violently and clearly in the words of the bards:

> The ravens croaked and human blood
> In ruddy streams poured o'er the land;
> There burning houses war proclaimed;
> Churches in flames and palace halls;
> While sheets of fire scale the sky
> And warriors "On to battle" cry.[5]

With the defeat of Llewelyn the Last in 1284 the bards became decidedly less warlike in their offerings. As the tyranny of the English overlords settled across the land their poems became gentler, less brutal. It was as if the poets, like the rest of the nation, had accepted their lot. For the time being at least passivity had replaced virulence.

With men like Dafydd ap Gwilym leading the way, the subjects for the bards were now love and nature. The poems that they produced, Dafydd in particular, are still regarded as some of the finest of their type.

However, when looked at more closely, there is also a hard edge to many of the bardic verses from this time. It was more subtle than many of the earlier calls to arms that the poets produced – little blood and guts but lots of dreams and plans for the future.

The verses now are not celebrating battles and the glory of individual warriors but they are often concerned with the 'second coming' of the great warrior chief who would rescue Wales from the tyranny to which it had been subjected. Poems like this became something of a preserve for men like Iolo Goch and Gruffudd Llwyd.

Owain Glyndwr saw and heard the message. It was impossible for him not to be influenced by the stories that the bards flung at him every time they visited his family home at Sycharth. The idea that he was destined to greater things than being a mere *uchelwyr* began to build and grow in his breast. It is doubtful if that would have happened without the subtle urging of Iolo Goch and his comrades. He was the man the Welsh had been waiting for, the bards urged, and it was not long before Owain Glyndwr began to believe their words.

The wars of Owain Glyndwr undoubtedly stirred the fighting spirit of the bards. After his death and defeat their product subsided into verse that was highly competent, technically correct and beautiful in its own right, rather in the style of Dafydd ap Gwilym. It was lyrical and admired but it lacked the political edge that had marked the coming of Owain Glyndwr.

For a while at least the bards contented themselves with memories of Glyndwr's glory and with dreams of his future return from the cave where he was waiting, like King Arthur and his knights. That brought comfort to many people. It was a personal, internal belief and it was certainly not treasonable.

In the years leading up to 1485 Henry Tudor, the future King Henry VII, called the bards to action once more in his campaign to dethrone King Richard III. Born in Pembroke Castle in West Wales, Henry was of Welsh blood and although he had little real affection for the country of his birth he was not above using every advantage he could lay his hands on. Glyndwr reborn, the return of the 'Son of Prophesy' – the message was relayed by every possible means in order to gain the support of the Welsh for Henry Tudor's enterprise. It was all part of the Tudor gamble.

If Henry and his Uncle Jasper, his long-time mentor and befriender, had got it right that would include the efforts of the country's bards.

A descendent of the two Tudor brothers from Anglesey, Rhys and Gwilym, who had been so valuable an asset to Glyndwr, Jasper remains something of an unsung hero in the rise of the Tudor monarchy.

Jasper was the prime mover in the subtle but highly effective propaganda process. He had been around a long time and, as both victor and vanquished in many of the battles of the Wars of the Roses, understood the value of an effective PR machine. A good helping of mythology, Jasper knew, was worth at least a couple of hundred men-at-arms. Even before he and Henry landed in Milford Haven in the summer of 1485 Uncle Jasper had been using his contacts, drip-feeding the message – the son of prophesy is coming!

There was indeed an upsurge of bardic composition before and during Henry Tudor's invasion, bardic compositions in support of the man who was actively promoted as an honest Welshman striving for the throne of England.

The ploy worked on several different levels. For many Welshmen, Henry VII was not just the last Lancastrian prince, an adventurer making a final thrust for the throne, but the mightiest Welsh hero since King Arthur, who had come back to relieve them of oppression and to claim his rightful position as monarch. Glyndwr and the bards of old would have been proud of him.

Epilogue

Not to be too blasé, this book has been about Owain Glyndwr. His deeds, his motives and his thoughts have been the main focus – and rightly so. However, in order to tell the story effectively and fully, many other peripheral characters have flitted onto and off the pages. Some of the more significant ones have been described within the main body of the text. Inevitably, others have received just mentions. In an attempt to make the story of Glyndwr more rounded I append here a few extra details of some of these 'mentioned' men and women.

An indeterminate number of characters in search of a story

Adam of Usk One of the main sources of material from the time of Owain Glyndwr, Adam of Usk was a renowned figure in medieval Wales. He was a priest and chronicler who studied and lectured in law at Oxford. He was a supporter of Henry Bolingbroke in his power grab, being highly critical of Richard II, whom he met while the former king was being briefly held in the Tower. Adam forfeited the favour of the new king, Henry IV, after an affray in Westminster with Walter Jakes over the prebend of a church in Cardiganshire. He was forced to leave the country, spent time in Rome where he met and worked with both popes before returning to Britain. He received a royal pardon in 1411, wrote his *Chronicle* and died in 1430.

Geoffrey Chaucer Born in the 1340s, Chaucer is now regarded as the greatest English poet of what we glibly call 'the Middle Ages'. He was also a highly respected 'civil servant', a career diplomat and amongst other positions held the post of comptroller of customs for the port of London. He is accepted as the primary source/proponent of the vernacular tradition of English writing with, amongst other works, his famous *Canterbury Tales*. A close friend of John of Gaunt, he was rewarded with a pension of £20 a year from Richard II (a grant that was perpetuated and continued by Henry IV) which enabled him to concentrate on literature. He died on 25 October 1400.

Dante Alighieri An Italian poet, his *Divine Comedy*, written in three parts – Purgatory, Hell and Paradise – and including his famous *Inferno*, is now regarded as the most important poem of 'the Middle Ages'. He predated Chaucer, whose work he greatly influenced, in his use of vernacular language as opposed to the traditional Latin. He led an adventurous life, at one stage being exiled for many years from his native Florence after becoming involved in the religious and political dissention of the time. He died in 1321.

Stephen de Frankton Stephen de Frankton was one of those shadowy figures who emerge briefly from the crowd then disappear forever from history's view. A low-ranking knight or man-at-arms from Ellesmere in Shropshire, de Frankton was given the rank of centenar in the English/ Border army opposing Llewelyn the Last in 1282. A centenar equates roughly with the rank of centurion in the Roman army, having 100 foot soldiers at his command. Interestingly, de Frankton does not appear to have been rewarded – a knighthood or a gift of land – for killing Llewelyn, as might have been expected. We hear no more of him after the battle of Orewin Bridge.

Giraldus Cambrensis A Norman/Welsh cleric from Pembrokeshire, Giraldus rose to the position of Archdeacon of Brecon. Born sometime in the 1140s he was offered several bishoprics but turned them all down, hoping to be made Bishop of St David's. It never happened. As clerk to the king and two archbishops he travelled widely, including two pilgrimages to Rome. Giraldus was renowned for his two books – *The Description of Wales* and *A Journey through Wales* – which were the result of a trip he made up and down Wales, a recruiting campaign for the Third Crusade, with the Archbishop of Canterbury. Arguably one of the country's first travel writers, he died in approximately 1223.

Gruffudd Llwyd A renowned Welsh language poet who travelled endlessly around Wales like many other bards, he was born circa 1380 and died in 1410. He wrote poetry on a wide variety of topics including love and religion. He is best known, however, for his virulent anti-English work which was hugely significant in the life and career of Owain Glyndwr.

Dafydd ap Gwilym Perhaps the most famous of all the bards, Dafydd was active during the first half of the fourteenth century. His dates are unclear but he seems to have died around 1350-60, possibly from the Black Death. He was renowned as a writer and performer both on the Continent and in his native Wales. His work was revolutionary in that, unlike so many other bards of the time who preferred to remain above or outside their verses, he was the first writer of real skill to fill his poems with his own feelings and emotions. His subjects were nature and love rather than any overtly political themes.

Gregory Sais A Welsh soldier from Flintshire, Gregory acquired his name because he could speak English – obviously a rare skill in the fourteenth century. He fought for the English Crown in France and in Scotland and was the leader of the military expedition when Owain Glyndwr went into Scotland as a soldier of the Crown in 1384. Little else is known about him.

Gwilym ap Gruffydd One of the 'fair weather' supporters of Glyndwr, Gwilym ap Gruffydd was related to the Tudors of Penmynydd on Anglesey. After reverting to the Crown and pledging himself to Henry he was awarded large tracts of land, including those of his relatives, the Tudor brothers. His descendants went on to serve the Tudor monarchs, notably Henry VIII, but did not manage to achieve much prominence, perhaps because of Gwilym's earlier antipathy to the family during Glyndwr's rebellion.

Hywel Dda The King of Deheubarth (modern-day West Wales) until his death in AD 948, Hywel came to rule virtually all of Wales in the ninth and tenth centuries through clever diplomacy. He is renowned for his codification of Welsh law, a series of regulations that were both just and fair. The laws were based on compassion rather than punishment and were strong on the rights of women in society. Hywel died in AD 948 whereupon his kingdom was split into three separate units, thereby losing forever the possibility of presenting a united front against any invader.

Iolo Goch Little is known about Iolo. He came from the Vale of Clwyd and was born somewhere around about 1320. Renowned as one of the finest exponents of a detailed and difficult form of poetry known as *cywydd*, he wrote three particularly powerful poems about Owain Glyndwr and his life. He died in approximately 1398, a year or two before Owain's revolt began, and thus managed to keep himself free from the dangerous area of outlawry.

Iolo Morganwg Real name Edward Williams, Iolo Morganwg was the bardic name given to this strange and unscrupulous man who lived in South Wales and London in the eighteenth and nineteenth centuries. He was a poet, an antiquarian and collector of manuscripts – and an unashamed forger and faker. Considered to be a leading expert on medieval Welsh literature, it was discovered after his death in 1826 that he had forged several manuscripts that he had claimed to be genuine. Despite this his impact was great, including the founding of the Gorsedd and many of the doctrines of the Welsh National Eisteddfod, and debate has continued about his life and work.

John of Gaunt The third son of Edward III, in the second half of the fourteenth century John of Gaunt was one of the most powerful men in England. He was also the richest. As Duke of Lancaster he effectively founded the House of Lancaster that eventually saw Henry VII ascend the throne. Like most men of his class he fought long and hard during the Hundred Years' War. Never himself king of England, he was certainly a begetter of monarchs as an ancestor of Yorkist kings like Edward IV, Edward V and Richard III. He was also father of Henry IV, grandfather of Henry V and great-grandfather of Henry VI.

John or Jack of Kent A mysterious figure known by several different names such as Sion Cent, Jacky Kent and Jack of Kent, he was a bard who resided at Kentchurch Court where he may have been a secretary to Sir John Scudamore and a tutor to his children. A painting at Kentchurch Court, possibly by Flemish artist Jan van Eyck, is sometimes said to be of him. It is also sometimes said to be Owain Glyndwr. He is often confused with Glyndwr and also with a border folklore figure of the same era. As a poet he was apparently violently opposed to the 'praise poem' concept.

Maredudd ab Owain Glyndwr The last surviving son of Glyndwr and Margaret Hanmer, Maredudd was probably too young to participate in the early stages of the revolt. However, he effectively took over the leadership of the rebellion once Owain became too old and infirm to continue in the role. He was named as a principal individual in the offer of pardon in 1417, something that predisposes the notion that Owain Glyndwr was by then already dead. The legend that he fought alongside Henry at Agincourt has no credibility – in 1415 he was still battling against the king and the English forces. Maredudd did finally accept a pardon from Henry V in 1421 and served with the king in France in 1422. After the death of Henry that year Maredudd seems to have disappeared from view.

Owain Lawgoch His name can be translated into English as Owain of the Red Hand. Leader of a Free Company fighting for the French in the Hundred Years' War, Lawgoch was the last male descendent of Llewelyn the Great and therefore a claimant of the title Prince of Gwynedd. He was a much-feared warrior and in order to remove his threat a Scottish spy/agent by the name of John Lamb was sent to kill him. Lamb stabbed Owain to death in July 1378, for which he was rewarded with a sum of £20. Owain Lawgoch is another Welsh hero who, in legend, lies asleep waiting to be called back to duty.

Rhys Ddu Rhys was one of the most constant and trustworthy of all Glyndwr's many supporters. He came from Cardigan and fought bravely at the two sieges of Aberystwyth as well as in other campaigns and battles. Eventually captured and executed in London, the description of his death is one of the most gruesome but accurate depictions of the punishment known as hanging, drawing and quartering: 'Laid on a hurdle and so drawn to Tyburn through the city and there hanged and let down again. His innards drawn, his head was smitten off and his body quartered and sent to four towns and his head set on London Bridge.'[1]

The Lord Rhys Rhys ap Gruffydd, ruler of Deheubarth, was probably not known as The Lord Rhys in his lifetime. He was, however, known as the Prince of South Wales. He fought against various Norman/English kings, notably Henry II and Richard I, but also knew when it was time to make peace and work together. Giraldus Cambrensis described him as 'a cunning and artful man'. As well as calling the first eisteddfod in Wales in 1176, he may well have been instrumental in pulling together the various texts of Welsh law that were later codified by Hywel Dda.

John Scudamore Son-in-law of Glyndwr, married to Alys, John Scudamore managed to survive the fallout from the rebellion. He was still alive in 1432 when it was discovered that his wife was the daughter of Glyndwr – the connection with the great rebel had apparently not been realised until then. When the news became public Scudamore was stripped of his honours by Henry VI and deprived of his roles as steward of Monmouth, White and Grossmont Castles. His brother Philip had been executed during Glyndwr's rebellion but John, apart from losing the stewardship of the three castles, survived. His family still live at Kentchurch Court where, legend declares, Glyndwr sheltered during the last part of his life.

Gilbert and John Talbot The two brothers were implacable opponents of Owain Glyndwr and supporters of the Crown. They were both natives of Shropshire:

John Talbot was born in1383 and served in Ireland with Richard II in 1395. He was well respected as a wrestler and archer but was a brutal and uncompromising soldier. He was present at the sieges of Aberystwyth and Harlech, served in France and Normandy on behalf of the king and evinced great admiration for 'the maid,' Joan of Arc. Made 1st Earl of Shrewsbury, he was active during the final stages of the Hundred Years' War, being killed while charging enemy artillery at the Battle of Castillon in 1453 when his horse was struck by a cannonball. It fell and pinned him to the ground where he was finished off by French foot soldiers.

Gilbert Talbot was the 5th Earl Talbot, taking the title on the death of his father. Born in 1382, the year before his brother John, Gilbert was a great friend and ally of Henry IV and later, of Henry V. A renowned warrior, he was trusted to carry the offers of pardon to Owain Glyndwr and to hold the position of major crown representative in North Wales. Like his brother, he also fought in France on behalf of the king during the final stages of the Hundred Years' War and was killed at the siege of Rouen on 19 October 1418.

Wat Tyler, Jack Straw and John Ball These men were the three great leaders of the Peasants' Revolt of 1381. They lived in and originated from different parts of the country but came together, almost on an ad hoc basis, to advance the cause of England's working classes. The Peasants' Revolt was an unplanned upsurge of popular feeling, an unofficial outpouring of anger and frustration at the situation in which working men found themselves during the late fourteenth century:-

Wat Tyler was born in 1341 and at the time of the Peasants' Revolt was living in Kent. Tyler may not be his actual name and could well be taken from his profession or trade. An able public speaker, he led a large group of working men and women, marching them from Canterbury to London to protest at the levying of a poll tax – four pence from every man and woman in the country. After joining with other similar groups Tyler met with King Richard at Blackheath on 15 June. The Lord Mayor of London, annoyed by what he saw as over-familiarity from Wat, arrested the rebel leader. Tyler fought back, was slashed across the throat and stabbed from behind. He rode away for 30yds but fell from his horse before being taken by his comrades to a local hospital for the poor. The mayor tracked him down and he was taken to Smithfield and decapitated.

Jack Straw remains the most enigmatic of the three best-known leaders of the Peasants' Revolt, and yet very little is actually known about him. He may have been a priest but there is also a school of thought that says he did not even exist! His name, some people say, was merely a pseudonym used by Wat Tyler. Several of the rebel leaders did use false names but there is no record of Tyler doing this in 1381. It does now seem, however, that Straw did exist and came from Bury St Edmunds. He was the leader of the Essex men during the Revolt. When Wat Tyler was killed Jack Straw fled but was discovered in hiding at an old house close to Smithfield. He was beheaded along with other rebel leaders in 1381.

John Ball, who trained as a priest, was associated with John Wycliffe and the Lollards although he had been expressing articles contrary to the faith almost ten years before Wycliffe appeared on the scene. He came from the Colchester area and was actually under arrest in prison because of his religious views when the Peasants' Revolt began. He was released by Tyler's Kent rebels and promptly joined them. He delivered a sermon to the assembled thousands on Blackheath, inspiring the crowd with his invective. In the aftermath of the Revolt he was again imprisoned and was finally hanged, drawn and quartered at St Albans on 15 July 1381, in the presence of King Richard II.

Gruffydd Young (or Griffin Yonge) The most able of Glyndwr's advisors, Young was illegitimate and with poor prospects when he won the favour of Anne of Bohemia, first wife of Richard II. Between 1391 and 1403 he held several church positions in Wales but in 1403 he became Glyndwr's chancellor and together with John Hanmer negotiated the Welsh-French Alliance of 1404. He became Bishop of Bangor in 1407 and then moved to St David's before becoming Bishop of Ross in Scotland. He finished his life, sometime after 1430, as titular Bishop of Hippo in Africa.

*****

When Maredudd finally accepted his pardon from Henry V in 1422 it was an indication that the war between Wales and England was officially over. In reality, of course, it had been finished for several years. There was no peace treaty; Maredudd's acceptance of the king's offer was considered enough and, besides, the English government certainly believed that hostilities had ended ten years earlier.

If we accept that Owain died sometime around 1415, Maredudd had done well to maintain the spirit of defiance in his father's people. The free pardon extended to him by Henry V gives some indication of the status in which Owain's son was held by the English Crown, but he could never be Owain Glyndwr – nor did he ever want to be.

The attempt to gain freedom and independence for Wales had failed but perhaps Owain Glyndwr had given the country and its people more in defeat than he could ever have done in victory. In defeat he became a legend, a symbol of Welsh courage and determination. Victory would only have been a temporary respite from the more powerful kings of England who came after Henry IV, the Tudors in particular. At some stage one or the other of those monarchs would have stretched out his arms and gathered in the Welsh nation once again.

Even in the more peaceful times ahead the value of Wales – its coal mines, its iron mills, its fields of corn and, in a military sense, it's position

191

as a buffer between England and the western ocean – would have been too great for England to allow it to slip out of its grasp. And that meant, in some respects, that Glyndwr's war, from beginning to end, had been little more than a pointless exercise which had brought only misery and destruction to the Welsh people.

So where does that leave Owain Glyndwr? At the risk of being regarded as too simplistic, too off-hand, he was, in many respects, both a hero and a villain to the Welsh people. His war against the English Crown undoubtedly caused great suffering for the Welsh, but he would surely have subscribed to the notion that you cannot make an omelette without breaking a few egg shells. The analogy would have been unknown to him but he would probably have appreciated its significance.

Glyndwr was determined to create an independent Wales, whatever it cost. In the years after September 1400, when his rebellion suddenly erupted and took hold, he would strive to do that for each and every remaining day of his life. If that meant some of the people for whom he was working, the very people he was attempting to guide would be hurt, well, it was sad but it could not be helped. He was making decisions and judgements on their behalf, because, in a paternalistic and protective way, he firmly believed that they were not capable of making such decisions for themselves.

Such an attitude displays a degree of ruthless autocratic thinking that was worthy of the English medieval kings – they knew best and would operate on that premise. There can be little doubt that Owain Glyndwr thought exactly the same.

Glyndwr's brutality was part of his vengeful nature. The legend of the hollow tree – and at this distance it can be little more than a legend – sums up this character trait where anyone who crossed him or did not comply with his wishes was liable to come to a very unpleasant end.

The myth begins with Owain and his cousin Howel Sele out hunting. Sele attempts to kill Glyndwr who is saved by the armour he is wearing under his clothes. The nineteenth-century writer Thomas Pennant takes up the story: 'Enraged at this treachery he (Glyndwr) seized on Sele, burnt his house and hurried him away from the place; nor could anyone ever learn how he was disposed of till forty years after when the skeleton of a large man was discovered in the hollow of a great oak.'[2]

Supposedly, Glyndwr deposited his cousin in the tree, alive, and left him there to die slowly and in excruciating agony. Other accounts say

Sele was already dead when he was placed in the tree. True or false, either way the message was clear – do not annoy Owain Glyndwr.

In hindsight it is easy to sit in judgement on the activities and attitudes of someone like Glyndwr. However you view him, there is little doubt that he rode roughshod over the lives and liberties of his people. He might have done it for their good but it was painful and not always understood by the people, or for that matter by his supporters.

Above all, Glyndwr's actions have to be taken in the context of the time. We cannot judge him by our modern-day standards. We have to look at what he did and why he did it in the context of his day. That is not always easy to do.

So, was Owain Glyndwr an autocratic, judgemental, paternalistic would-be monarch? I don't think there is any doubt about it. Add in a more than minimal share of ruthless dynamism and you have the makings of the man. A ruthless man, a driven man, a noble man and, above all, a great man, Owain Glyndwr in a nutshell.

The fifteenth century was hardly the time for democratic discussion and true equality. Dictatorship, benevolent or otherwise, was the order of the day in a society where the last remnants of feudalism were still able to provide security for most people.

To have someone to protect and defend you – in return for a degree of servility and acceptance – was quite a comforting idea at a time when most people were not really capable of doing it for themselves. It was only when feudalism came to an end that people realised its value.

Owain Glyndwr knew that only too well. He knew that most people would have neither the knowledge nor the capacity to be able to make the decisions and the judgements that he would have to make on their behalf. In 1400 Glyndwr's way was the only way. It is a point worth remembering.

Endnotes

Introduction

1. Adam of Usk, *The Chronicle*, Llanerch Enterprises, p6.

Chapter One

1. Glanmor Williams, *Owain Glyndwr*, University of Wales Press, p85.
2. Adam of Usk, *The Chronicle*, p107.
3. William Shakespeare, *Henry IV, Part One*, Act III, Scene I.
4. Ibid.
5. Gruffydd Aled Williams, *The Last Days of Owain Glyndwr*, Y Lolfa, p87 and p190.

Chapter Two

1. Glanmor Williams, p3.
2. Adam of Usk, p85.
3. Matthew Paris, 'Flores Historiarum,' quoted in David Fraser *The Defenders*, p176.
4. Adam of Usk, p93.
5. Phil Carradice, *Pembroke: For King and Parliament*, Pembroke Town Council, p.36
6. David Fraser, *The Defenders*, University of Wales Press, p182.
7. Giraldus Cambrensis, *The Description of Wales*, Penguin, p233.
8. Ibid, p231, 234.
9. Giraldus Cambrensis, *The Journey through Wales*, Penguin, p113.
10. Iolo Goch, quoted in Adrian Eliot Hodgkin, *The Archer's Craft*, Faber, p24.

11. Ibid.
12. Iolo Goch, quoted in Gruffydd Aled Williams, p24.
13. Ibid, p25.

Chapter Three

1. John Davies, *A History of Wales*, Penguin, p194.
2. Dillwyn Miles, *Portrait of Pembrokeshire*, Pembs County Council, p86.
3. Iolo Goch, 'Owain Glyndwr's Court,' translated from Welsh, c1387-1395, quoted in *A Casebook*, p33.
4. Ibid, p19.
5. Anne Curry, 'France, England and the Political Climate 1400-1415,' in *The Online Froissart*.
6. Gruffudd Llwyd 'I Know No Greater Lord,' 1386-87, translated from Welsh and quoted in *A Casebook*, p23.
7. Guto's Wales website, gutorglyn.net/gutoswales
8. Glanmor Williams, p22.
9. Gruffudd Llwyd poem, quoted in *A Casebook*, p21.
10. Ibid.

Chapter Four

1. Edward Laws, *The History of Little England Beyond Wales*, Dyfed County Council, p195.
2. 'Report from the Town of Oswestry, 1400', translated from Latin and quoted in *A Casebook*, p37.
3. Giraldus Cambrensis, *Description of Wales*, p260.
4. Quoted in *A Casebook*, pp29-30.
5. 'The Rolls of Parliament, February 1401', translated from Anglo-Norman, quoted in *A Casebook*, p45.
6. John Clarke 'Letter,' quoted in *A Casebook*, p55.
7. Adam of Usk, p107.
8. Ibid.
9. Ibid, p109.
10. Owain Glyndwr 'Letter to the King of Scotland,' translated from Latin, quoted in *A Casebook*, p65.
11. Deborah Fisher, *Princesses of Wales*, University of Wales Press, p27.

Chapter Five

1. 'The Rolls of Parliament 1402,' quoted in *A Casebook*, p69.
2. Popular Fifteenth Century Rhyme – author's collection.
3. Adam of Usk, p117.
4. Hodgkin, *The Archer's Craft*, pp21-22.
5. Adam of Usk, p118.
6. Iolo Goch, 'When His Authority was Greatest,' translated from Welsh, quoted in *A Casebook*, p71 (date of MS uncertain).
7. Letter from Jankin Harvard 'Plea for Aid' 1403, translated from Middle English, quoted in *A Casebook*, p85.

Chapter Six

1. Adam of Usk, pp122-123.
2. Ibid, p127.
3. Glanmor Williams, p53.
4. Giraldus Cambrensis, *Description of Wales*, p256.
5. Letter from Richard Kingston to Henry IV, 1403, in *A Casebook*, p87.

Chapter Seven

1. 'The Tripartite Indenture,' translated from Latin, quoted in *A Casebook*, p115.
2. Guillem Pepin 'The French Offensive of 1404-1407,' Academia Education.
3. Letter from Prince Henry to Henry IV, quoted in *A Casebook*, p117.
4. Adam of Usk, p152.
5. A G Bradley, quoted in Gruffydd Aled Williams, pp185-186.
6. Edward Laws, p 204.
7. RR Davies, *Owain Glyndwr: Prince of Wales*, Y Lolfa, p 95.

Chapter Eight

1. Adam of Usk, p168.
2. Pennal Letter Number One, in *A Casebook*, p121.

3. Pennal Letter Number Two, in *A Casebook*, p 127.
4. 'The Rolls of Parliament for 1411,' translated from Middle English in *A Casebook*, p139.
5. Pip Bickerstaffe, *The Heritage of the Longbow*, private printing, p 10.
6. RJ Macdonald, 'Medieval Artillery,' in *Journal for Army Historical Research*, Vol 1, No 3, p105.
7. Gideon John Brough, 'Medieval Diplomatic History: France and the Welsh,' PhD Cardiff, p295.

Chapter Nine

1. Gideon John Brough, p295.
2. Pip Bickerstaffe, p10.
3. Hodgkin, *The Archer's Craft*, pp30-31.
4. *A Casebook*, p133.
5. RJ Macdonal, *Medieval Artillery*, p105.
6. Iolo Goch, yLolfa.com.
7. 'The Rolls of Parliament' for 1414, quoted in *A Casebook*, p149.

Chapter Ten

1. RR Davies, p133.
2. Adam of Usk, pp178-179.
3. *The Chronicle of Owain Glyndwr* (Aberystwyth), p175.
4. Quoted in Glanmor Williams, p42.
5. Arthur Granville Bradley, *Owen Glyndwr,* Putnam & Sons, pp302-306.

Chapter Eleven

1. Gideon John Brough, p296.
2. Adam of Usk, p176.
3. Gruffydd Aled Williams, p59.
4. Maureen Jurkowski, 'Who was Walter Brut?' in *English Historical Review*, Issue 525.

5. *A Casebook*, p85.
6. Adam of Usk, p183.
7. Gruffydd Aled Williams, p135.

Chapter Twelve

1. OM Edwards, quoted in Elissa R Henken, *National Redeemer: Owain Glyndwr in Welsh Tradition*, University of Wales Press, p178.
2. Arthur Granville Bradley, p334.
3. Ibid, p336.
4. Anon 'Cynddylan's Hall,' in *Presenting Welsh Poetry*, Faber, p20.
5. Howell Gwynedd, quoted in Bradley, p341.

Epilogue

1. *Chronicle*, p377.
2. Thomas Pennant, *Tours in Wales*, Humphreys, pp310-311.

Bibliography

Primary Sources

Adam of Usk, *The Chronicle of Adam of Usk*, c1477-1421, (translated by Henry Frowde, facsimile version published by Llanerch Enterprises, 1904).

Anon, *The Chronicle of Owain Glyndwr*, c1415-20 (held in National Library of Wales, Aberystwyth).

Jean Froissart, *Chroniques*, c1326-1400, (available on *The Online Froissart* website)

Matthew Paris and other writers, 'Flores Historiarum,' written in Westminster Abbey and St Albans, c1200-1327

A large collection of documents and other primary sources have been collected together and published as *Owain Glyndwr: A Casebook*, edited by Michael Livingstone and John K Bollard, (Liverpool University Press, 2013).

The documents in *A Casebook* include selections from various chronicles, the Rolls of Parliament relating to Owain Glyndwr, poetry by Iolo Goch and other bards, letters to and from the king, Glyndwr's Pennal Letters and so on. The material is published in its original language – Welsh, Latin, Anglo-Norman, Middle English and French – as well as modern translations. There are also commentaries by several distinguished historians.

Books

Bickerstaffe, Pip, *The Heritage of the Longbow*, (privately printed, 2001).

Bradley, Arthur Granville, *Owen Glyndwr and the Last Struggle for Welsh Independence*, (Putnam and Sons, London, 1902).

Cambrensis, Giraldus, *The Journey through Wales*, (Penguin, London, 2004).

Cambrensis, Giraldus, *The Description of Wales*, (Penguin, London, 2004).

Carey, John (editor), *The Faber Book of Reportage*, (Faber, London, 1987).

Carradice, Phil, *Pembroke, for King and Parliament*, (Pembroke Town Council, Pembroke, 1992).

Carradice, Phil, *Following in the Footsteps of Henry Tudor*,(Pen and Sword, Barnsley, 2019).

Davies, John, *A History of Wales*, (Penguin, London, 1994).

Davies, RR, *Owain Glyndwr, Prince of Wales*,(y Lolfa, Talybont, 2009).

Fisher, Deborah, *Princesses of Wales*, (University of Wales Press, Cardiff, 2005).

Fraser, David, *The Defenders*, (University of Wales Press, Cardiff, 1975).

Fraser, David, *The Invaders*, (University of Wales Press, Cardiff, 1965).

Henken, Elissa, *National Redeemer: Owain Glyndwr in Welsh Tradition*, (University of Wales Press, Cardiff, 1996).

Hodgkin, Adrian Eliot, *The Archer's Craft*, (Faber, London, 1951).

Laws, Edward, *The History of Little England Beyond Wales*, (Bell & Sons, London, 1888).

Miles, Dillwyn, *Portrait of Pembrokeshire*, (Dyfed County Council, Haverfordwest, 1995).

Pennant, Thomas, *Tours in Wales*, (Humphreys, Caernarfon, 1883).

Shakespeare, William, *The Complete Works*, (Nelson Doubleday, New York, undated).

Skidmore, Chris, *Bosworth*, (Phoenix, London, 2014).

Toulson, Shirley, *The Drovers' Roads of Wales*, (Wildwood House, London, 1977).

Williams, Glanmor, *Owain Glyndwr*, (University of Wales Press, Cardiff, 1993).

Williams, Gruffyd Aled, *The Last Days of Owain Glyndwr,*'(y Lolfa, Talybont, 2017).

Williams, Gwyn, *Presenting Welsh Poetry*, (Faber, London, 1959).

Unpublished Papers/Research Documents

Gideon John Brough, 'Medieval Diplomatic History: France and the Welsh, 1163-1417,' (PhD Thesis, Cardiff University, September 2012).

Magazines/Newspapers

The English Historical Review, 19 January 2012, Vol CXXV11, Issue 525.

The Journal of Military History, 1992, Vol 57.

Journal of the Society for Army Historical Research, Vol 1, No 3, March 1922.

BBC History Magazine, various dates.

Websites

academia.edu/14169126/The_French_Offensive_of_1404-1407_against_ Anglo_Gascon-Aquitane

https://www.owain.glyndwr.wales/word_web_pages/Tripartiteindenture. htm

en.wikipedia.org/wiki/Glyndwr-Rising

en.wikisource.org/wiki/Iolo-Goch-(9DN300)

ylolfa.com/articles/new-revelations-Owain-Glyndwr

canolfanglyndwr.org/hanesglyndwr.phd

Gutorglyn.net/gutoswales

dhi.ac.uk/onlinefroissart

Index

INDEX